Marriage and Death Notices from Schuyler County, New York Newspapers

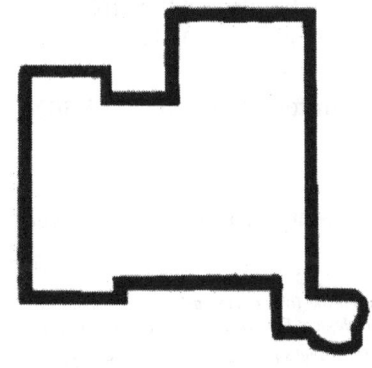

Compiled by

Mary Smith Jackson

and

Edward F. Jackson

HERITAGE BOOKS
2006

HERITAGE BOOKS
AN IMPRINT OF HERITAGE BOOKS, INC.

Books, CDs, and more—Worldwide

For our listing of thousands of titles see our website
at
www.HeritageBooks.com

Published 2006 by
HERITAGE BOOKS, INC.
Publishing Division
65 East Main Street
Westminster, Maryland 21157-5026

Copyright © 1993 Mary S. Jackson and Edward F. Jackson

Other books by the authors:

1850 Census for the Town of Howard, Steuben County, New York and Genealogical Data on the Families Who Lived There

Death Notices from Steuben County, New York Newspapers, 1797-1884

Death Notices from Washington County, New York Newspapers, 1799-1880

Marriage and Death Notices from Seneca County, New York Newspapers, 1817-1885

Marriage Notices from Steuben County, New York Newspapers, 1797-1884

Marriage Notices from Washington County, New York Newspapers, 1799-1880

Other books by Mary S. Jackson:

Marriages and Deaths from Tompkins County, New York Newspapers

All rights reserved. No part of this book may be reproduced or transmitted in any form or by any means, electronic or mechanical, including photocopying, recording or by any information storage and retrieval system without written permission from the author, except for the inclusion of brief quotations in a review.

International Standard Book Number: 978-0-7884-3173-0

Introduction

This volume contains marriage and death notices abstracted from microfilm copies available at the New York State Library up to 1900 for Schuyler County, New York. Other newspapers may be available elsewhere.

Vital records were being recorded by the Town Clerks in New York State beginning in 1885. However, not all marriage and deaths were recorded until 1906 when it became mandatory. This book contains those vital records before 1885 that are otherwise very difficult to find. Verification of the information contained in this volume should be made by using a primary source whenever possible.

Altho these newspapers were published in Schuyler County, they include many notices for people living in other nearby counties such as Seneca, Cayuga, Yates, Tompkins, Tioga, Chemung and Steuben as well as many people who have moved out of New York State.

Additional information is often given in the obituaries such as birth dates and place of birth, marriage dates, parents, children and place of residence. Only the information of genealogical interest has been abstracted for this book. There are many other articles of interest such as sale of properties, notices for probate of wills, advertising, personal items, reunions etc. They can be very entertaining as well as informative.

There are variations in the spelling of names in the newspapers. When using the surname index provided, be sure to check all possible spellings.

Part I

MARRIAGES

Havana Journal April 16, 1853 - April 4, 1857

Travis James of Torry, NY **Warner** Mrs. Eliza of Havana, NY	March 31, 1853 Havana, NY
Cogswell Gold Of Millport, NY **Cole** Azada	April 11, 1853 Elmira, NY
Robinson J. B. of Horseheads, NY **Brown** Catherine of Painted Post, NY	April 12, 1853
Wheeler Samuel of Hector, NY **Costes** M. B. of Hector, NY	May 22, 1853 Hector, NY
Babcock Perry of Havana, NY **Darling** Margaret A. dau of Andrew	June 7, 1853 Ithaca NY
Mandeville W. M. of Havana, NY **Tracy** Maria F. of Newfield, NY	July 19, 1853 Newfield, NY
Houghtaling Benjamin of La Salle, Ill. **Cleveland** Jane of Lodi, NY	July 14, 1853 Lodi, NY
Hamilton Daniel of Catherine, NY **Jacoby** Fanny of Catherine, NY	August 25, 1853 Catherine, NY
Abbott Reuben of Varick, NY **Potter** Sarah A. of Starkey, NY	August 12, 1853 Havana, NY
Nichols Richmond A. **Weeks** Helen J. of Mt. Morris, NY	September 5, 1853 Mt. Morris, NY
Hurd Orlando of Watkins, NY **Townsend** Julia A. of Genoa, NY daughter of L. G.	September 12, 1853
Decker Henry of Lima, NY **Hall** Catherine of Havana, NY	September 28, 1853 Havana, NY
Wanzer Charles of Ledyard, NY **Webley** Emeline of W. Groton, NY	September 21, 1853 W. Groton, NY

Morehouse George of Pine Valley, NY October 27, 1853
Wilbur Helen of Havana, NY Havana, NY

Beardsley Philo of Odessa, NY October 24, 1853
Campbell Margaret of Odessa, NY Odessa, NY

Wakefield Levi S. of Grass Valley, Cal. October 2, 1853
Compton Maria F. formerly of Havana, NY Havana, NY

Higgins John A. of Tyrone, NY November 28, 1853
Gleason Fanny A. of Ithaca, NY Ithaca, NY

Nye Ebenezer M. W. of Hector, NY December 7, 1853
Sharp Margaret Havana, NY

Huggins Rev. M. of Havana, NY January 3, 1854
Simpson Isabella of Geneva, NY Geneva, NY

Erway George F. January 11, 1854
Knapp Ruth Ann of Catherine, NY Catherine, NY

Mulford John E. of Oswego, NY January 25, 1854
Goodwin Frances H. dau of Col E. H. of Havana Havana, NY

Bowlby E. T. of Ripleyville, Ohio February 15, 1854
Mc Clure Mary of Havana, NY Havana, NY

Hall John H. of Catherine, NY February 23, 1854
Jessup Sarah E. of Newfield, NY Newfield, NY

Frost Eli of Catherine, NY March 2, 1854
Mc Connell Sarah of Canandaigua, NY

Ireton Edward of Millport, NY March 18, 1854
Smith Cynthia of Millport, NY Millport, NY

Sheardown Dr. S. B. of Havana, NY March 29, 1854
Winton Mary A. of Havana, NY Havana, NY

Henyon Stephen of Dix, NY February 27, 1854
Sturdevant Almira of Dix, NY Havana, NY

Catlin George of Dix, NY April 12, 1854
Gano Elizabeth of Dix, NY Dix, NY

Ingersoll Samuel E. of Burdett, NY May, 7, 1854
Ransom Margaret E. of Burdett, NY Burdett, NY

Straitor Mulford May 17, 1854

MARRIAGE NOTICES 3

Wakely Mary A. of Dix, NY   Dix, NY

Dumar R. R. R. of Elmira, NY   June 6, 1854
Davidson Henrietta of Elmira, NY   Chemung, NY

Baxter J. Jr. of Havana, NY   June 14, 1854
Hyslop Margaret A. of Havana, NY   Havana, NY

Benjamin Charles W. of Harwick, NY   June 8, 1854
Cuffman Mrs. Marcia of Dix, NY

Munson Prince of Havana, NY   June 13, 1854
Hazen Susan of Havana, NY   Havana, NY

Holton David C. of Havana, NY   June 13, 1854
Nash Rebecca of Havana, NY   Havana, NY

Adams George Q. of Nichols, NY   June 29, 1854
Beardsley Maria L. of Catherine, NY

La Fever Lewis of Dix, NY   June 28, 1854
Bates Sarah of Dix, NY

Mc Donald George H. of Canada West   July 10, 1854
Mapes Melissa of Havana, NY   Havana, NY

Johnson Dr. A. H. of Orangeville, Michigan   July 16, 1854
Leek Harriet E. formerly of Moreland, NY   Thornapple

Roe Harris of Havana, NY   August 5, 1854
Fox Eunice of Homer, NY   Havana, NY

Wood Harrison of Jacksonville, NY   August 20, 1854
Adamy Esther A. of Odessa, NY   Odessa, NY

Jackson William T. of Havana, NY   August 31, 1854
Aylworth Alma of Havana, NY   Havana, NY

Johnson William of Penn Yan, NY   August 26, 1854
Canfield Helen M. of Danby, NY   Danby, NY

Holmes Clark of Corning, NY   September 14, 1854
Barclay Grace E. of Havana, NY   Havana, NY

Doty Edward of Catherine,   September 6, 1854
Owens Phebe of Dix, NY   Dix, NY

Phelps Charles R. of Beaver Dams, NY   September 13, 1854
Crum Ann Augusta of Beaver Dams, NY   Beaver Dams, NY

  Daughter of Rev. Gardner Crum

Morgan A. B. of Prattsburg, NY   September 25, 1854
Look Sarah B. of Prattsburg, NY

Bennett George of Havana, NY   September 4, 1854
Tregilious Jane of Havana, NY   Havana, NY

Hyslop M. J. of Havana, NY   October 19, 1854
Bennett Mrs. Hannah of Havana, NY   Havana, NY

Woodruff Frederick of Candor, NY   October 24, 1854
Hamilton Harriet E. of Catherine, NY   Catherine, NY

Huston Alexander of Dix, NY   November 1, 1854
Henderson Jane of Reading, NY   Reading, NY

Coon Simeon of Alpine, NY   November 28, 1854
Dill Mahala Jane of Milo Center, NY   Havana, NY

Pierce David G. of Veteran, NY   December 12, 1854
Andrus Nancy M. of Veteran, NY   Havana, NY

Cronk Jonathan of Havana, NY   November 30, 1854
Griffith Jane of Havana, NY   Havana, NY

North Theodore of Elmira, NY   December 13, 1854
Bradley Ann of Elmira, NY

Haight Daniel   December 27, 1854
Cormack Betsey of Geneva, NY   Geneva, NY
  Daughter of Rev. William of Plainville, NY

Rockwell Henry E. of Monterey, NY   January 4, 1855
Culver Letticia M. of Dix, NY   Dix, NY

Phelps C. P. of Havana, NY   January 10, 1855
Tuthill Ethel of Kellogsville, NY   Kellogsville, NY

Bigger John Henry of Ingersoll, W. Canada   January 20, 1855
Ward Phebe of Havana, NY   Havana, NY

Cooper John of Catlin Center, NY   January 18, 1855
Frank Elizabeth of Moreland, NY   Moreland, NY

Gano Levi of Dix, NY   February, 8, 1855
Leonard Miranda T. of Dix, NY   Elmira, NY

Stone L. of Rhoadsport, NY   February, 18, 1855

MARRIAGE NOTICES

Cronk Abigail of Rhoadsport, NY   Rhoadsport, NY

Bryant J. S. of Sweden, NY   March 1, 1855
Henry Frances Marion of Havana, NY   Havana, NY

Culver W. W. of Big Flats, NY   March 21, 1855
Seelye Jannette of Catlin, NY   Catlin, NY
adopted daughter of Watson **Cole**

Personius Isaac of Havana, NY   March 11, 1855
English Helen of Ithaca, NY   Ithaca, NY

Cooper Peter of Catherine, NY   March 8, 1855
Osterhout Margaret of Catherine, NY   Catherine, NY

Howard J. W. of Millport, NY   March 27, 1855
Allen Charlotte dau of Caleb of Veteran, NY   Veteran, NY

Carpenter George of Hector, NY   March 13, 1855
Couch Esther M. of Catherine, NY   Catherine, NY

Miller R. Bruce of Jackson, Michigan   April 12, 1855
Durkee Josephine L. dau of John of Havana, NY   Havana, NY

Fletcher George of Havana, NY   April 15, 1855
Slocum Mary Ann of Havana, NY   Havana, NY

Watworth Almers of Enfield, NY   April 17, 1855
Roloson Lavina of Havana, NY   Havana, NY

Leonard Richard of Enfield, NY   April 17, 1855
Allen Deborah of Hector, NY   Havana, NY

Rogers Harrison of Albion, Michigan   April 22, 1855
Wood Lavina of Enfield, NY   Havana, NY

Shelton Phineas of Catherine, NY   May 2, 1855
Cooper Mary Jane of Montour, NY   Montour, NY

Hammond J. B. of Ithaca, NY   May 1, 1855
Cain Lavina of Ithaca, NY

Mead Edwin D. of Hector, NY   May 8, 1855
Swan Theodosia of Catherine, NY   Catherine, NY

Knapp Samuel of Havana, NY   May, 27, 1855
Jobbit Miss of Havana, NY   Havana, NY

Bronson Freegift of Beaver Dams, NY   May 23, 1855

Mc Donald Elizabeth of Catherine, NY

Franklin Benjamin of Havana, NY
Atwater Clara of Havana, NY

Wright Dr. E. S. of Syracuse, NY
Jackson Mary dau of William T. of Havana, NY

Dunn Tompson of Elmira, NY
Tuthill Mary E. dau of C. G.of Burdett, NY

Campbell Thomas B. of St. Paul, Minn.
Catlin Louisa dau of Cap. T. of Odessa, NY

Mathews Jerry of Ovid, NY
Chapman Sarah J. of Catherine, NY

Wilcox John B. of Hector, NY
Bement Lorinda of Hector, NY

Coe Loren L. son of Asa of Catherine, NY
Nevins Ellen dau of Rev. J. W. of Catherine

Tracy Daniel of Havana, NY
Watkins Louisa of Havana, NY

Hubbell Daniel of Hector, NY
Leonard Harriet M. of Enfield, NY

Scutt William of Orange, NY
Waugh Rebecca of Orange, NY

Van Vechten Charles B. of Catherine, NY
Ross Julia dau of John **Mitchell** of Catherine, NY

Fitzgerald James of Veteran, NY
Herrick Betsey

Anable Zacheus of Canton, Pa.
Lamkin Sarah A. dau of Rev. H.

Robylier James of Townsend, NY
Tracy Jane C. of Townsend, NY

Leland Hiram F. of Hamilton, Canada
Bryant Cornelia J. of Havana, NY

Palmer Martin K. of Catherine, NY
Hamilton Fanny of Catherine, NY

Catherine, NY

May 29, 1855
Havana, NY

May 30, 1855
Havana, NY

September 11, 1855
Burdett, NY

September 7, 1855
Odessa, NY

October 5, 1855
Havana, NY

October 10, 1855
Hector, NY

October 18, 1855
Catherine, NY

November 1, 1855
Havana, NY

October 30, 1855
Havana, NY

November 1, 1855
Havana, NY

November 7, 1855

December 19, 1855
Havana, NY

December 27, 1855
Johnson Settlement

January 1, 1856
Townsend, NY

January 22, 1856
Havana, NY

January 24, 1856
Catherine, NY

MARRIAGE NOTICES

Beardsley Albert of Union Springs, NY
Watkins Emma Kay of Havana, NY
February 5, 1856
Havana, NY

Hawkins Lucius of Catlin, NY
Moore Mary of Catlin, NY
February 3, 1856

Tidd Charles of Millport, NY
Kingsbury Clara L. of Millport, NY
February 20, 1856
Millport, NY

Beard Stephen of Veteran, NY
Albertson Eliza of Elmira, NY
February 21, 1856
Havana, NY

Owens Thomas of Dix, NY
Sellick Mrs. Mary of Dix, NY
March 11, 1856
Dix, NY

Shelton Ralph of Catherine, NY
Bowlby Mary M. of Catherine, NY
March 13, 1856

Lyon Jesse of Catherine, NY
Gaylord Elizabeth of Penn Yan, NY
March 26, 1856
Penn Yan, NY

Tuttle Ebenezer B. of Catherine, NY
Morgan Phebe of Dryden, NY
March 15, 1856

Dodson N. T. of Watkins, NY
Munger Kate E. of Watkins, NY
March 23, 1856
Watkins, NY

Smith Alvin of Havana, NY
Crawford Mrs. Elizabeth of Havana, NY
April 19, 1856
Havana, NY

Laman John J. of Toledo, Ohio
Rumsey Carolyn of Kanona, NY
April 9, 1856
Kanona, NY

Sloan F. D. of Havana, NY
Whippy Sarah E. of Havana, NY
April 4, 1856
Havana, NY

Wood James J. of Havana, NY
Irvin Diana Ann of Odessa, NY
May 25, 1856
Odessa, NY

Strong Asa of New York City
Jackson Helen M. of Havana, NY
June 14, 1856
Havana, NY

Shelton David L. of Odessa, NY
White Caroline of Van Etten, NY
June 10, 1856
Van Etten, NY

Benson Charles of Havana, NY
Jackson Delphine dau of William L. of Havana daughter of William L. Jackson
June 26, 1856
Havana, NY

Bronson Sylvester of Dix, NY
Collins Calista
August 14, 1856

Simmons Charles of Watkins
Ross Nancy A.
August 14, 1856
Havana, NY

Bates Charles M. Md. of Havana, NY
Hoxie Fanny C. of Albany, NY
September 1, 1856

Bailey Harvey of Dix, NY
Hunt Esther
August 31, 1856

Coe John of Veteran, NY
Bennett Margaret of Catherine, NY
September 18, 1856

Hall Edward of Catherine, NY
Mallet Lucy Ann of Catherine, NY
September 4, 1856

Sherwood Davis H. of Southport, Conn.
Beardsley Antoinette of Catherine, NY
October 7, 1856

Johnson Daniel of Catlin, NY
Owen Maryette of Catherine, NY
October 7, 1856
Catherine, NY

Bush George W. of Erin, NY
Harrington Lina M. of Horseheads, NY
October 20, 1856
Horseheads, NY

Vernon William N. of Veteran, NY
Bates Lavina of Veteran, NY
November 5, 1856
Havana, NY

Ryon John of Enfield, NY
Hanes Catherine of Enfield, NY
November 5, 1856
Veteran, NY

Robyen Simeon C. of Hector, NY
Douglas Polina of Newfield, NY
November 6, 1856
Hornby, NY

Hill Frederick A. of Catherine, NY
Lee Toressa of Catherine NY
(date of newspaper)
November 22, 1856

Baldwin L. Jr. of Elmira, NY
Tillotson Hellen of Elmira, NY
November 16, 1856
Elmira, NY

Winton Nelson of Shaw's Flat, Cal.
Crane C. Augusta of Alemeda, Cal.
October 18, 1856

Kryser Alpheus of Havana, NY
Maxwell Maria of Havana, NY
November 20, 1856
Havana, NY

Turner David Jr. of Veteran, NY
December 17, 1856

MARRIAGE NOTICES

Lyon Mary C. of Catherine, NY

Force David of Jennings Co. Ind.   December 15, 1856
Day Sarah of Tyrone, NY   Tyrone, NY

Stewart D. B. formerly of Havana, NY   December 18, 1856
Crowell Louisa dau of Moses of Newfield, NY   Newfield, NY

Maynard John   December 4, 1856
Johnson Anna B. dau of T. A. of Corning, NY   Corning, NY

Risdon Frank of Penn Yan, NY   December 18, 1856
Walter Minerva A. of Havana, NY   Havana, NY

Cooper Ezra of Kanona, NY   December 15, 1856
Rumsey Jennie of Kanona, NY   Kanona, NY

Jones Samuel T.   December 8, 1856
Brainard Miss formerly of Elmira, NY   Stephen's Pt. Wis.

Barton Willard of Watkins, NY   January 1, 1857
Carmer Mary E. of Dix, NY   Havana, NY

Clauharty O. M. of Havana, NY   January 15, 1857
Quigley Kate M.

Benham Jackson of Orange, NY   January 11, 1857
Hayes Mary Ann of Orange, NY   Orange, NY

Henderson Freeman of Catherine, NY   January 11, 1857
Brown Mary of Catherine, NY

Stone E. of Dix, NY   February 4, 1857
Deavenworth Philena S. of Catherine, NY   Catherine, NY

Rumsey David of Dix, NY   February 10, 1857
Crout Ann Elizabeth of Dix, NY

Baily Lorenzo Wilson of Millport, NY   February 17, 1857
Sleeper Mary Lock of Millport, NY

Morrison Harvey C. of Eddytown, NY   January 1, 1857
Tuttle Margaret Elizabeth of Eddytown, NY

Brown Renscellar of Catherine, NY   November 20, 1856
Ennis Adeline of Catherine, NY

Kline John of Horseheads, NY   March 3, 1857
Squire Lydia A. of Havana, NY   Havana, NY

Fish Asa P. of Barrington, NY
Haviland Charlotte of Havana, NY

March 18, 1857
Havana, NY

Mc Stay Edward of Dix, NY
Dickenson Mary Jane of Burdett, NY

March 18, 1857
Dix, NY

Howell John V. of Rochester, NY
Griffith Mary R. of Havana, NY

March 31, 1857

Cady John W. of Havana, NY
Granger Mary A. of Havana, NY

April 2, 1857
Havana, NY

Eaker David of Big Flats, NY
Jackson Elizabeth A. of Catherine, NY

March 9, 1859

Purple Jasper of Elmira, NY
Wakely Louise of Havana, NY

September 10, 1860
Havana, NY

Bond James H. of Logan, NY
Couse Lottie of Logan, NY

November 4, 1863
Milo Center, NY

Miller Barnabas of Catherine, NY
Mitchell Caroline of Odessa, NY

November 5, 1863

Bement Otis B. of Hector, NY
Allbright Araminta C. of Hector, NY

November 12, 1863

Titchener John of Jacksonville, NY
Ameigh Larah L.

November 12, 1863
Mechlinburgh, NY

Peck Joel S. of Tyrone, NY
Culver Lola

November 19, 1863
Altay, NY

Benham Marvin of Reading, NY
Kress Elizabeth of Reading, NY

November 22, 1863

Mc Vamara James of Hammond
Houghtaling Mrs. B. of Tyrone, NY

November 24, 1863

Dolph William V. of Schuyler Co. NY
Reed Eliza D.

December 3, 1863
Elmira, NY

Blount William of Hector, NY
Lane Hester of Hector, NY

December 7, 1863

Swick Hiram of Hector, NY
Low Eliza Ann of Hector, NY

December 9, 1863

Ellis George F. of Lodi, NY

November 17, 1863

MARRIAGE NOTICES

Skinner Eliza Jane of Covert, NY

Bush John L.	December 11, 1863
Delameter Adeline	Burdett, NY
Jones Tartulas of Ulyssis, NY	December 3, 1863
Thompson Marcia C. dau of William of Ulysses	Ulysses, NY
Van Gorder George E. of Horseheads, NY	February 16, 1880
Morgan Frances dau of J. of Oregon	
Ogden George H. of Elmira, NY	February 21, 1880
Wescott Emma	N. Hector, NY
Thompson Zeband	April 10, 1887
Woodruff Mrs. Eliza	Elmira, NY

Watkins Express January 5, 1871 - May 3, 1900

Gregory Frank E.	January 29, 1870
Nichols Jennie	Elmira, NY
Goltry Judson of Reading, NY	January 8, 1871
Broderick Emma M. of Reading, NY	Reading, NY
Duvall John M. of Beaver Dams, NY	December 30, 1870
Colegrove Sarah of Catlin, NY	Havana, NY
King Albert of Big Flats, NY	January 5, 1871
Tenbroek Urania V. of Dix, NY	Dix, NY
Darling Homer C.	January 4, 1871
Woodward Fidele of Hector, NY	Elmira, NY
Weller Leroy of Elmira, NY	January 5, 1871
Jones Flora H. of Trumnasburg, NY	
Symonds Alonzo of Elmira, NY	January 4, 1871
Mosher Rebecca of Horseheads, NY	Elmira, NY
Shapper T. B. of Big Flats, NY	January 8, 1871
Campbell Mrs. Sarah of Pine Valley, NY	Veteran, NY
Finlan James of Bolona, NY	January 11, 1871
Lott Emma of Reading, NY	Reading, NY
Hutchins Charles J. of Hector, NY	January 25, 1871

Alexander Addie of Breesport, NY

Houston Leroy of Logan, NY
Bunn Mary J. of Logan, NY
              January 24, 1871
              Burdett, NY

Baldwin Andrew of Watkins, NY
Holmes Emily S. of Watkins, NY
              January 26, 1871
              Havana, NY

Wilmot James H. of Starkey, NY
Nickerson Loie of Starkey, NY
              January 26, 1871
              Starkey, NY

Gullick Elisha D. of Eddytown, NY
Bailey Emma E. dau of George of Eddytown, NY
              January 26, 1871

Eldridge Col. S. of Lawrence, Kansas
Torey Caroline of Dundee, NY
              January 26, 1871

Barber Cyrus of Searsburg, NY
Woodworth Mrs. Adeline E. of Searsburg
 daughter of David F. Sears
              February 5, 1871
              Hector, NY

Comstock Edward F. of Rome, NY
Hulett Mary Frances dau of Charles
              January 25, 1871
              Horseheads, NY

Wilson Herman of Ovid, NY
Clawson Jennie of Lodi, NY
              January 18, 1871

Dunlap Clement J. of Ovid, NY
Post Lelia J. of Romulus, NY
              January 25, 1871

Dart Hinckley J. of Ovid, NY
Griffin Mary of Ovid, NY
              February 2, 1871
              Ovid, NY

Post Lilburne P. of Romulus, NY
Van Doren Anna of Ovid, NY
              January 18, 1871

Yarington George of Watkins, NY
Coon Jennie of Watkins, NY
              February 5, 1871
              Elmira, NY

Banker John D. of Ovid, NY
Losey Libbie B. of Reynoldsville, NY daughter of William
              February 1, 1871

King Cornelius of Hector, NY
Chapman Josephine of Catlin, NY
              February 18, 1871
              Watkins, NY

Dubois Daniel of Elmira, NY
Dubois Esther E. of Monterey, NY
              February 15, 1871
              Horseheads, NY

Welsh James M. of California
              March 15, 1871

MARRIAGE NOTICES

Wheeler Mary E. daughter of Thomas

Margeson Alvin C. of Starkey, NY April 4, 1871
Beckworth Delia of Starkey, NY

Pope H. G. Md. of Lathrop, Missouri April 12, 1871
Catlin Mary G. daughter of late Leman

Wasson Andrew of Hornby, NY April 6, 1871
Jack Susanna of Watkins, NY

Frost Edwin S. of Watkins, NY April 13, 1871
Andrews Sarah of Watkins, NY Watkins, NY

Robson David of Watkins, NY April 16, 1871
Ross Louisa of Watkins, NY Watkins, NY

Wentz John of Watkins, NY April 15, 1871
Smith Mate of Watkins, NY Havana, NY

Buchanan John C. of Watkins, NY May 4, 1871
Badgely Emma of Watkins, NY Watkins, NY

Protts William of Newfield, NY May 14, 1871
Rumsey Dellie of Newfield, NY Watkins, NY

Jones Hiram of Varick, NY May 30, 1871
Guinnip Carrie A. of Romulus, NY Watkins, NY

Ferguson Isaac R. of Athens, Pa. June 5, 1871
Williams Frank R. of Athens, Pa. Watkins, NY

Reisinger Roe of Meadville, Pa. June 1, 1871
Barnes Mary A. dau of H. R. of Rock Stream Rock Stream, NY

Johnston John W. of Barryville, NY June 7, 1871
Love Sarah H. of Watkins, NY Watkins, NY

Stevens Reuben G. of Watkins, NY June 10, 1871
Adams Dollie of Watkins, NY Watkins, NY

Fanton Hall of Havana, NY June 10, 1871
Skellenger Mrs. Mary Thomas of Havana, NY Havana, NY

Henry Rev. W. M. of NY City (formerly Havana) June 15, 1871
Ferris Nellie daughter of Rev. W. H.

Seaman H. W. of Millport, NY June 7, 1871
Rhodes Frankie of Millport, NY Millport, NY

SCHUYLER COUNTY NEWSPAPERS

Everts Alanson G. of Havana NY
Baker Sarah A. of Jersey City, NJ

June 10, 1871
Havana, NY

Moonan James of Elmira, NY
Fitzpatrick Kate of Havana, NY

June 4, 1871

Beardsley Watson of Catherine, NY
Coryell Helen of Bridgeport Conn.

June 23, 1871
Watkins, NY

Hodges Ward W. of Watkins, NY
Catlin Lela of Watkins, NY

June 25, 1871
Watkins, NY

Mc Intyre William G.
Sproul Mary E. of Tyrone, NY

June 24, 1871
Watkins, NY

Compton Lewis P. of Flushing, Michigan
Tolbert Eliza J. of Orange, NY

June 8, 1871

Slawson George W.
Jefferson Ida E.

July 12, 1871
Watkins, NY

Lamoreaux A. of Watkins, NY   (newspaper date)
Curry Ida A. of Watkins, NY

September 7, 1871
Watkins, NY

Barry Charles M. of Watkins, NY
Wentz Rose B. of Watkins, NY

September 7, 1871
Watkins, NY

Gillis Andrew of Reading, NY
Gould Susan of Reading, NY

September 3, 1871
Havana, NY

Fero John D. of Watkins, NY
Backer Hattie M. of Dix, NY

September 23, 1871
Bennettsburg, NY

Warner Rev. J. K. of Jacksonville, Florida
Brown Mary Louisa dauof Dr. E. of Burdett, NY

September 26, 1871
Burdett, NY

Case Joseph B. of Hector, NY
Dutcher Caroline B. of Ithaca, NY

September 13, 1871
Ovid, NY

Green William M. of Reading, NY   (newspaper date)
Whitehead Louisa L. of Altay, NY

October 5, 1871
Altay, NY

Amsden Albert E. of Watkins, NY
White Marietta C. of Watkins, NY

October 7, 1871
Watkins, NY

Sebring George W. of Newport, NY
Lanning Louisa of Newport NY

October 11, 1871
Watkins, NY

Payne Emmett C.

October 4, 1871

MARRIAGE NOTICES

Hillerman Cordelia Adelia	Watkins, NY
Cronk Dewitt of Dix, NY **Austin** Anna of Dix, NY	October 5, 1871 Havana, NY
Lanning Warren L. of Enfield, NY **Cronk** Nettie of Dix, NY	October 5, 1871 Havana, NY
Knapp Lucius E. of Downsville, NY **Coats** Ella F. of Watkins, NY	October 4, 1871 Watkins, NY
Scott Ahira of Buffalo, NY **Parker** Belle of Rochester, NY	October 1, 1871 Watkins, NY
Owen Marion K. of Dix, NY **Kimber** Addie M. of Dix, NY	November 1, 1871 Watkins, NY
Pangbourn Norman L. of Beaver Dams, NY **Baker** Sarah of Havana, NY	October 26, 1871 Watkins, NY
Decker Clarence Alonzo of Havana, NY **Viele** Lauretta of Corning, NY	October 31, 1871 Havana, NY
Roberts Morris of Reading, NY **Swarthout** Alice of Reading, NY	November 9, 1871 Penn Yan, NY
Charles Horton L. of Odessa, NY **Shelton** Frank L. of Odessa, NY	November 15, 1871 Watkins, NY
Hayes Freeman of Dresden, NY **Hunter** Leah of Watkins, NY	November 14, 1871 Watkins, NY
Williams James D. of Newfield, NY **Rumsey** Frank M. of Newfield, NY	November 23, 1871 Watkins, NY
Sloan James R. of Reynoldsville, NY **Hill** Anna M. of Trumansburg, NY	November 26, 1871 Watkins, NY
Hughson William of Watkins, NY **Hunter** Cora of Watkins, NY	November 21, 1871 Watkins, NY
Wager Joshua of Burdett, NY **Miles** Mary E. of Reading, NY	November 30, 1871 Watkins, NY
Dickenson Edgar of Mecklenburg, NY **Ellis** Laura of Mecklenburg, NY	November 29, 1871 Havana, NY
Fitzgerald William **Frost** Nellie M. of Watkins, NY	December 21, 1871 Watkins, NY

Wells Elisha D. of Weston, NY
Roosa Mary Of Bethel, NY

December 21, 1871
Bethel, NY

West George of Hector, NY
Mathews Mary of Hector, NY

December 26, 1871
Havana, NY

Poyner Lawrence J. of Penn Yan, NY
Sellen Eva V. of Watkins, NY

December 27, 1871
Watkins, NY

Doolittle Alva E. of Tompkins Co. NY
Rumsey Mary E. of Tompkins Co. NY

December 27, 1871
Watkins, NY

Betteridge Edward of Elmira, NY
Harris Nancy of Watkins, NY

April 27, 1872
Watkins, NY

Hall Rev. U. S. of Watkins, NY
Briggs Sophia

April 30, 1872
Southport, NY

Frost John E. of Watkins, NY
Robinson Eva daughter of Dyer

May 2, 1872
Watkins, NY

Goodyear Hiram of Big Flats, NY
Bowers Mary of Horseheads, NY

June 5, 1872
Watkins, NY

Terry Charles F. of Veteran, NY
Weeks Lovina of Veteran, NY

June 8, 1872
Watkins, NY

Taber Charles E. M.
Chester Julia A.

June 11, 1872
Watkins, NY

Brown Menzo of Horseheads, NY
Harsh Ida L.

June 13, 1872
Watkins, NY

Norris Gilbert of Weston, NY
Buggis Adeline of Bradford, NY

June 13, 1872
Weston, NY

Russell E. B.
Lockwood Libbie of Watkins, NY

June 14, 1872
Watkins, NY

Randall J. T.
Wasson Sarah J. of Orange, NY

June 15, 1872
Orange, NY

Stillwell David P.
Jeffers Nancy

June 19, 1872
Watkins, NY

Gray Alexander H. of Watkins, NY
Prince Mary Josephine of Catherine, NY

June 20, 1872
Catherine, NY

Price Harvey E. of Altay, NY

June 25, 1872

MARRIAGE NOTICES

Sebring Hannah | Tyrone, NY

Bond Freling of Bennettsburg, NY | July 2, 1872
Dean Eva of Bennettsburg, NY | Bennettsburg, NY

Otto Charles of Merilla, NY | July 5, 1872
Arnold Harriet of Merilla, NY | Weston, NY

North Orrin L. of Ithaca, NY | July 11, 1872
Bennett Amelia E. of Millport, NY | Watkins, NY

Moore Charles A. of Lodi, NY | July 20, 1872
Terryberry Rachel A. of Lodi, NY | Bennettsburg, NY

Smith Albert of Hector, NY | July 21, 1872
Mickel Viola of Hector, NY

Locke W. W. of Millport, NY | August 9, 1872
Teneyck Mary L. of Bradford, NY | Havana, NY

Ferris Ellis S. | August 8, 1872
Agins Rosa C. formerly of Rochester, NY | Watkins, NY

Pease Daniel of Elmira, NY | August 29, 1872
Perry Addie of Elmira, NY | Watkins, NY

Harrison Charles of Columbia, Pa. | August 29, 1872
Hackett Hulda | Watkins, NY

Goodwin Alfred of N. Hector, NY | September 9. 1872
Smith Minnie O. of Peach Orchard, NY | Peach Orchard, NY

Arnold William of Tyrone, NY | September 18, 1872
Mc Kinney Mrs. S. Maria of Mecklenburg, NY | Mecklenburg, NY

Gorton James P. | September 18, 1872
Berry Olive L. | Watkins, NY

Young Mathias of Ithaca, NY | September 18, 1872
Bird Ella of Ithaca, NY | Watkins, NY

Gabriel E. R. C. of Reading, NY | September 11, 1872
Price Julia H. of Hamptonburg, NY | Hamptonburg, NY

Higgins James E. of Castile, NY | September 26, 1872
Tompkins Maggie A. of Mecklenburg, NY | Mecklenburg, NY

Bolt Daniel age 77 of Orange, NY | October, 9, 1872
Dean Mrs. Polly age 72 of Dix, NY | Watkins, NY

Bailey John of Hector, NY
Lewis Alida of Hector, NY

October 15, 1872
Bennettsburg, NY

Clawson George W. of Rock Stream, NY
Wilson Amelia of Woodhull, NY

October 9, 1872
Reading, NY

Slaght George of Spencer, NY (newspaper date)
Johnson Christine M. of Hector, NY

November 7, 1872
Hector, NY

Shattuck Henry C. of Altay, NY
Monroe Lydia A. of Rock Stream. NY

November 5, 1872
Reading Center, NY

Drake G. Emmet
West Ella J. of Watkins, NY

November 6, 1872
Watkins, NY

Drake Charles of Elmira, NY
Bell Mary A. of Dundee, NY

November 20, 1872
Dundee, NY

Harvey Fred of Watkins, NY
Wager Nellie of Watkins, NY

November 15, 1872
Watkins, NY

Wedgewood John
Tracy Fanny H.

November 7, 1872
Dix, NY

Bement Jackson of Hector, NY
Bodle Phebe B. of Hector, NY

November 19, 1872
Burdett, NY

Wallenbeck Marshall of Hector, NY
Murphy Roxie S. of Hector, NY

December 10, 1872
Watkins, NY

Byron Joseph N. of Glens Falls, NY
Kilborn Lizzie of Pike, Pa.

December 17, 1872
Watkins, NY

Aber J. D. of Wilkesbarre, Pa.
Bishop Isabel B. of Watkins, NY

December 24, 1872
Watkins, NY

Wilson Charles M.
Swarthout Emma A.

January 1, 1873
Watkins, NY

Lott John S. of Reading, NY
Green Mary J. of Starkey, NY

December 31, 1872
Starkey, NY

Ellis Sidney of Hector, NY
Williams Jennie of Montour, NY

January 8, 1873
Montour, NY

Corbin John M. of Eaton Rapids, Michigan
Scott Hettie of Scott's Corners, NY

December 25, 1872
Scott's Corners, NY

Mc Swain Horace D. of Starkey, NY

December 25, 1872

MARRIAGE NOTICES

De Long Melissa of Starkey, NY | Watkins, NY

Foster James F. of Williamsport, Pa. | January 8, 1873
Wright Nellie R. of Watkins, NY | Watkins, NY

Caldwell William of Orange, NY | January 15, 1873
Buck Ellen J. of Orange, NY | Orange, NY

Ladow Orlando of Watkins, NY | January 15, 1873
Baldwin Frank J. of Watkins, NY | Watkins, NY

Johnson James of Reading, NY | February 5, 1873
Vosburgh Mary | Reading, NY

Campbell Miles D. of Dundee, NY | February 22, 1873
Lanphere Morilla of Monterey, NY | Weston, NY

Stevens Burnett of Beaver Dams, NY | April 5, 1873
Pangborn Kate of Reading, NY | Watkins, NY

Skuse Daniel of Reading, NY | April 2, 1873
Drake Fanny of Reading, NY | Watkins, NY

Bennett Charles H. of Lemars, Iowa | March 29, 1873
Wilcox Emma A. of Watkins, NY | Watkins, NY

Hobbee John A. of Elmira, NY | April 17, 1873
Hayes Susan H. dau of Dr. P. H. of Watkins | Watkins, NY

Caldwell Robert of Sugar Hill, NY | April 24, 1873
Lafor Eliza of Townsend, NY | Weston, NY

Sherman Jerry of Hector, NY | May 10, 1873
Joiner Julia A. of Hector, NY | Watkins, NY

Carpenter William of Scranton, Pa. | May 3, 1873
Hall Ida L. of Elmira, NY | Watkins, NY

Skinner Leroy W. of Veteran, NY | May 7, 1873
Nichols Julia A. of Breesport, NY | Watkins, NY

Easterbrook Henry O. of Owego, NY | June 6, 1873
Chapman Ruth E. dau of Porter of Watkins, NY | Watkins, NY

French Norman B. of Elmira, NY | June 2, 1873
Sanford Anna of Urbana, NY | Urbana, NY

Gunderman Monroe of Elmira, NY | July 3, 1873
Ovitt Mary of Reading, NY | Watkins, NY

Bozzard Jervis L. of Dix, NY　　　　　　　　　July 3, 1873
Richardson Hattie O. of Dix, NY　　　　　　　Watkins, NY

Fuller Frank of Meridan, Illinois　　　　　　　July 6, 1873
Howard Minnie daughter of Roswell H.　　　　Mendots, Illinois

Reynolds G. P. Md. of Burdett, NY　　　　　　August 8, 1873
Blackwood Clemma E. of Haywood, California　New York City

Bishop John of Havana, NY　　　　　　　　　August 27, 1873
Wade Carrie of Dundee, NY　　　　　　　　　Watkins, NY

Lawton J. D. of Watkins, NY　　　　　　　　　September 17, 1873
Shewman Della S. of Watkins, NY　　　　　　　Watkins, NY

Hall Dr. James A. of Watkins, NY　　　　　　　October 2, 1873
James Candice I. of Bloomingdale, Michigan　　Bloomindale, Mich.

Vescelius F. M. of Reading, NY　　　　　　　　October 1, 1873
Johnson Sarah of Wayne, NY　　　　　　　　　Wayne, NY

Huggins William of Erwin, NY　　　　　　　　October 13, 1873
Fulford Olive of Painted Post, NY

Stackhouse John of Havana, NY　　　　　　　　October 21, 1873
Olmstead Kittie of Tyrone, NY　　　　　　　　Tyrone, NY

Wixon Sanford of Dix, NY　　　　　　　　　　October 22, 1873
Buck Libbie E. of Orange, NY　　　　　　　　Sugar Hill, NY

Carpenter Sanford L. of Andover, NY　　　　　November 12, 1873
Slaght Mary A. of Lodi, NY　　　　　　　　　Watkins, NY

Wheeler John A. of Watkins, NY　　　　　　　November 18, 1873
Freer Elvira daughter of Mrs. Morgan Freer　　Watkins, NY

Comstock John C. of Urbana, NY　　　　　　　October 12, 1873
Crawford Elouisa of Urbana, NY　　　　　　　Weston, NY

Andrews Henry C. of Hector, NY　　　　　　　November 15, 1873
Oltz Lydia L. of Danby, NY　　　　　　　　　Danby, NY

Howard George O. of Watkins　　　　　　　　November 20. 1873
Scofield Carrie E.　　　　　　　　　　　　　Bristol, Illinois

Howard Frank of Watkins, NY　　　　　　　　October 26, 1873
Dennis Delia A. of Clinton, Iowa　　　　　　　Horseheads, NY

Swick Charles L. of Watkins, NY　　　　　　　October 26. 1873

MARRIAGE NOTICES

Burritt Helen   Horseheads, NY

Smith Francis M. of Dix, NY   December 11, 1873
Owens Ella J. of Dix, NY   Dix, NY

Abbey Frank C. of Rock Stream, NY   December 11, 1873
Thompson Austin of Watkins, NY   Watkins, NY

Sterling Warren of Watkins, NY   December 23, 1873
Kendall Mary of Watkins, NY   Watkins, NY

Cook Col E. B. of Havana, NY   December 24, 1873
Batterson Mrs. Lucretia M. of Havana, NY Havana, NY

Beyea Frank of Wayne, NY   December 24, 1873
Wood Jennie of Weston, NY   Weston, NY

Witter George of Geneva, NY   January 5, 1874
Waters Belle of Geneva, NY   Watkins, NY

Halsey William   January 14, 1874
Day E. Augusta   Watkins, NY

Kishpaugh D. J. of S. Bradford, NY   January 29, 1874
Bremer C. of Townsend, NY   Townsend, NY

Holden Theodore of Dundee, NY   February 11, 1874
Hatch Allie of Millport, NY   Millport, NY

Drake James T. of Reading, NY   February 19, 1874
Hutchins Adelle A. of Townsend, NY   Watkins, NY

Starkey Dr. J. C. of Owego, NY   February 25, 1874
Andrews Emma R. of N. Reading, NY   N. Reading, NY

Swift Loren D. of Branchport, NY   February 24, 1874
Huey Margaret J. of Tyrone, NY   Watkins, NY

Batey John of Himrods, NY   February 25, 1874
Frank Mary of Starkey, NY   Starkey, NY

Mitchell William Jr. of Postville, Iowa   March 10, 1874
Love Jennie E. dau of William of Pine Grove   Pine Grove, NY

Huey Joseph O. of Orange, NY   March 12, 1874
Henderson Jennie of Orange, NY   Reading Center, NY

Fish J. Corey of Trumansburg, NY   March 11, 1874
Weidman Loretta A. of Watkins, NY   Watkins, NY

Hall Henry of Watkins, NY
Hannon Emma J. of Watkins, NY

March 14, 1874
Watkins, NY

Sutton Monroe M. of Reading, NY
Clark Satie M. dau of Benjamin of Altay, NY

March 11, 1874
Altay, NY

Nichols A. B. of Orange, NY son of Harvey
Coon Hannah M. of Plainfield, NJ

March 11, 1874

Dodd William of Tyrone, NY
Hughey Celia of Sugar Hill, NY

March 25, 1874
Sugar Hill, NY

Owen Frank of Big Flats, NY
Esley Helen of Post Creek, NY

March 29, 1874
Townsend, NY

Kellogg Charles F. of Palo, Michigan
Fausett Mary E. of Smith Valley, NY

March 31, 1874
Smith Valley, NY

Silvernale Egbert of Wayne, NY
Van Amburg Elizabeth of Orange, NY

March 31, 1874
Smith Valley, NY

Robinson Lyman
Robbins Mattie of Watkins, NY

April 7, 1874
Watkins, NY

Wilson David of Hector, NY
Newcomb Emmeline of Hector, NY

April 16, 1874
Watkins, NY

Webber Henry D. of Watkins, NY
Smith Marion E. of Watkins, NY

April 16, 1874
Watkins, NY

Simpson Henry W. of Lodi, NY
Townsend Nellie M. of N. Hector, NY

April 22, 1874
N. Hector, NY

Hughey Emmett of Sugar Hill, NY
Dodd Libbie of Tyrone, NY

April 23, 1874
Tyrone, NY

Seaman Charles W. of Watkins, NY
Kress Maggie of Watkins, NY

April 23, 1874
Watkins, NY

Berry Henry of Watkins, NY
Everts Maggie of Watkins, NY

May 6, 1874
Watkins, NY

Fenwick Sylvester of Watkins, NY
Simmons Frankie

May 4, 1874
Watkins, NY

Pierce Henry N. of Towanda, Pa.
Hunter Frances of Watkins, NY

May 9, 1874
Watkins, NY

Edwards Albert of New York City

May 12, 1874

MARRIAGE NOTICES

Stewart Arabella daughter of late Duncan S. — Paris, France

Skiff Myron of Tyrone, NY
Sage Lizzie of Dundee, NY
May 20, 1874
Middleville, Mich.

Maugham James Jr. of Buffalo, NY
Simonson Nellie G. dau of J. C. of Watkins
June 10, 1874
Watkins, NY

Chapman Willie
Jones Libbie
June 25, 1874

Langdon Andrew J of Elmira, NY
Featherly Emma of Watkins, NY
June 8, 1874
Watkins, NY

Compton Gaylord A. of Grass Valley, NY
Whippy Mary E. of Havana, NY
July 30, 1874
Grass Valley, NY

Hurman E. D. of Watkins, NY
Hibbard Sarah L. of Watkins, NY
June 30, 1874
Watkins, NY

Knight Elmer F. of Utica, NY
Miller Ida J. of Watkins, NY
July 28, 1874
Watkins, NY

Armstrong Arnold of Havana, NY
Plumstead Lavina of Havana, NY
August 9, 1874
Havana, NY

Hamilton John H. of Watkins, NY
Ogden Clarissa of Mecklenburg, NY
August 12, 1874
Mecklenburg, NY

Wagner Samuel of Elmira, NY
Long Louisa of Corning, NY
August 13, 1874
Watkins, NY

Wells David C. of Pemberton, NJ
Reid Mary E. of Pemberton, NJ
August 14, 1874
Watkins, NY

Mc Nemer George of Reading, NY
Sutton Lilly of Reading, NY
September 9, 1874
Reading, NY

Ogden Elbert of Monterey, NY
Hollingsworth Mary R. of Chicago, Illinois
September 30, 1874
Chicago, Illinois

Buck J. L. of Orange, NY
Congdon Emma E. of Nelson, Pa.
September 30, 1874
Nelson, Pa.

Andrews Perry of Watkins, NY
Smith Annie B. of Watkins, NY
October 15, 1874
Watkins, NY

Thompson R. N. of Rooeville, Illinois
Harris Mary of Obington, Illinois
October 5, 1874
Watkins, NY

Bennett Martin P. of Havana, NY
Lewis Fannie M. of Watkins, NY
    September 27, 1874
    Watkins, NY

Wilson Perry L. of Hornby, NY
Mc Elwell Maggie M. of Hornby, NY
    October 14, 1874
    Watkins, NY

Harris Abraham W. of Lodi, NY
Brooks Minnie J. of Lodi, NY
    October 15, 1874
    Watkins, NY

Swarthout James P. of Torrey, NY
Hultz Flora A. of Starkey, NY
    October 28, 1874
    Starkey, NY

Hunt William of Pulteney, NY
Hultz Eva J. of Starkey, NY
    October 28, 1874
    Starkey, NY

Hoag George of Montour, NY
Dingman Margaret of Montour, NY
    October 31, 1874
    Montour, NY

Wilbur Samuel of Dix, NY
Blodgett Anna of Dix, NY
    November 1, 1874
    Havana, NY

Smith Sherman of Watkins, NY
Miller Estella of Reading, NY
    November 4, 1874
    Beaver Dams, NY

Overhiser Charles of Monterey, NY
Beckwith Estella of Watkins, NY
    November 7, 1874
    Havana, NY

Haight George of Starkey, NY
Pettingill Fanny dau of William of Starkey
    November 6, 1874
    Dundee, NY

Cook Harman of Dundee, NY
Bigelow Zadie E. of Altay, NY
    November 18, 1874
    Altay, NY

Smith F. Duane of Catherine, NY
Ervay Minnie A. on Montour, NY
    November 12, 1874
    Montour, NY

Brush James H. of Bennettsburg, NY
Archer Hattie of Hector, NY
    November 21, 1874
    Watkins, NY

La Fever Philander S. of Starkey, NY
Phinney Clara of Reading, NY
    November 24, 1874
    Reading, NY

Catlin Willis B. of Bay City, Michigan
Vaughn Minnie
    November 19, 1874
    Watkins, NY

Sutherland W. J. of Bennettsburg, NY
Smith Eliza of Bennettsburg, NY
    November 26, 1874
    Bennettsburg, NY

Slaght A. P. of N. Hector, NY
    December 24, 1874

MARRIAGE NOTICES

Parish Mary L. of Ovid, NY   Ovid, NY

Rumsey Edward M. of Seneca Falls, NY   December 22, 1874
Osborne Anna K. of Seneca Falls, NY   Seneca Falls, NY

Small Jesse B. of Watkins, NY   December 24, 1874
Travis Orcelia B. of Watkins, NY   Watkins, NY

Neate H. Irvin of Mecklenburgh, NY   December 24, 1874
Gee Eola of Mecklenburgh, NY   Watkins, NY

Sullivan T. M. of Pulaski, NY   December 21, 1874
Thompson Hattie L. of Dix, NY   Dix, NY

Baldwin David L. of Watkins, NY   January 10, 1875
Morse Louisa of Watkins, NY   Watkins, NY

Spear Frederick   January 27, 1875
Ellis Hattie E. of Townsend, NY   Townsend, NY

Kendall Alba of Altay, NY   January 24, 1875
Comb Carrie dau of Lewis & Hannah of Ovid, NY   Ovid, NY

Goldsmith Frank H. of Mecklenburg, NY   January 20, 1875
Woodruff Laura of Romulus, NY   Romulus, NY

Lewis John L. of Starkey, NY   January, 20, 1875
Townsend Belle of Starkey, NY   Starkey, NY

Van Allen John J. of Watkins, NY   February 24, 1875
Bennett A. Augusta of Norwich, NY   Norwich, NY

Henderson James of Starkey, NY   February 13, 1875
Bost Mary C. of Starkey, NY   Altay, NY

Burd L. T.   February 21, 1875
Proper Nancy M.   Mecklenburg, NY

Doolittle L. H. of Havana, NY   February 17, 1875
Dohs Lena K. dau of Daniel of Newark Valley   Newark Valley, NY

German Lemuel H. of Lodi, NY   March 17, 1875
Crisfield Nellie of Hector, NY   Hector, NY

Sloan Humphrey of Hector, NY   March 24, 1875
Murphy Mary of Hector, NY   Watkins, NY

Ketcham George of Watkins, NY   October 28, 1874
Ellas Clara of Watkins, NY   Watkins, NY

SCHUYLER COUNTY NEWSPAPERS

De Witt George of Monterey, NY
Gardner Mary of Hornby, NY

April 29, 1875
Havana, NY

Carroll John of Ovid, NY
Mc Caw Mary A. of Ovid, NY

August 8, 1875
Ovid, NY

Porter George G. of Seneca, Falls, NY
Taylor Eliza of Lodi, NY

August 4, 1875

Brigham Johnson of Watkins, NY
Gano Nettie of Watkins, NY

September 1, 1875
Watkins, NY

Williams Alywn of Corning, NY
Owens Emma G. of Painted Post, NY

September 2, 1875
Havana, NY

Grimes Daniel of Wayne, NY
Crans Louisa of Wayne, NY

September 4, 1875
Wayne, NY

Goble George of Starkey, NY
Hopkins Miss of Beaver Dams, Wis.

September 21, 1875
Starkey, NY

Queal O. H. of Pensecola, Florida
Gillespie Elma A. of Havana, NY

September 28, 1875
Havana, NY

Tracy Edmond Thompson of Havana, NY
Platt Hattie Cecelia of Havana, NY

September 28, 1875
Havana, NY

Smith Dr. G. O. of Odessa, NY
Mallory Lottie dau of A. E. of Hector, NY

October 7, 1875

Mc Nair Richard F. of Fall Brook, Pa.
Newman Mary Alice dau of John H. of Watkins

October 12, 1875
Watkins, NY

Smith Willie E. of Hector, NY
Ameigh Franc D. of Montour, NY

September 29, 1875
Mecklenburgh, NY

Chapman George M. of Catherine, NY
Hall Delphine of Catherine, NY

September 20, 1875

Seaman William D. of Starkey, NY
Mariner Mrs. Eliza of Dresden, NY

October 3, 1875

Gibbs Charles B. of Waverly, NY
Barrows Maggie of Havana, NY

October 13, 1875
Havana, NY

Sunderlin Daniel of Wayne, NY
Lazear Emma of Barrington, NY

October 6, 1875
Barrington, NY

Sayre Edward A. of Starkey

November 11, 1875

MARRIAGE NOTICES

Longcore Mary of Himrods, NY   Himrods, NY

Hanmer J. W. of Pine Grove, NY   November 11, 1875
Raplee Carrie L. of Himrods, NY   Himrods, NY

Erwin Samuel S. of Corning, NY   November 11, 1875
Williams Susan daughter of Alonzo   Tyrone, NY

Parshall Francis A. of Penn Yan, NY   November 10, 1875
Bank Ella of Millport, NY   Millport, NY

Catlin Phineas of Odessa, NY   November 17, 1875
Kimble Deborah of Odessa, NY   Odessa, NY

Chandler Daniel F. of Trumansburg, NY   Trumansburg, NY
Robertson Cecelia (newspaper date)   November 25, 1875

Todd Horace of W. Danby, NY   November 3, 1875
Smith Myrta of Cayuta, NY   Cayuta, NY

Beardsley David of Hector, NY   November 21, 1875
Phelps Mira R. of Beaver Dams, NY   Watkins, NY

Barber Guy of Watkins, NY   November 22, 1875
Banker Julia H. of Watkins, NY   Watkins, NY

Rappleyee John of Waterloo, NY   January 21, 1876
Marshall Emma of Waterloo, NY   Elmira, NY

Charles Truman L. of Dix, NY   January 14, 1876
Mallory Libbie of Catherine, NY   Dix, NY

Hazleton William C. of Ovid, NY   January 1, 1876
Pitcher Sarah E. of Ovid, NY   Ovid, NY

Spaulding Elmer C. of Mecklenburgh NY   December 29, 1875
Owen Mrs. A. E. of Mecklenburgh NY

Plumstead Ralph D. of Watkins, NY   January 26, 1876
Burrell Delilah C. of Watkins, NY   Watkins, NY

Mallory Judson of Hector, NY   January 26, 1876
Ely Flora E. dau of William B. of Hector, NY

Brush R. B. of Ithaca, NY   January 26, 1876
Shannon Mrs. Jane of Lodi, NY   York, Pa.

Purdy Charles of Newfield, NY   January 26, 1876
Smith Cornelia of Watkins, NY   Watkins, NY

Jayne Benjamin F. of Townsend, NY January 30, 1876
Roor Frances S. of Corning, NY Townsend, NY

Teeter Andrew of Enfield, NY February 3, 1876
Leonard Mrs. Statira Watkins, NY

Overshire George of Starkey, NY February 11, 1876
Smith Josie of Starkey, NY

Sample Lloyd of Starkey, NY February 1, 1876
Carroll Emma of Milo, NY

Barnes Charles Md. of Rochester, NY February 28, 1876
Smith Mrs. S. M. of Corning, NY

Brown Johnie of Havana, NY (newspaper date) March 2, 1876
Burke Jennie of Odessa, NY Starkey, NY

Wright William R. of Seneca Falls, NY March 1, 1876
Boardman Alma J. dau of D. B. of Seneca Falls Seneca Falls, NY

Stevens Theron of N. Hector, NY February 26, 1876
Drake Libbie dau of F. M. of N. Hector, NY

Hicks Samuel of Sugar Hill, NY February 29. 1876
Wood Mrs. Catherine of Sugar Hill, NY Sugar Hill, NY

Newfield James of Newfield, NY February 29, 1876
Woodward Matilda dau of Gilbert of Odessa, NY Odessa, NY

Graham James D. of Orange, NY March 7, 1876
Hughey Diantha of Pine Grove, NY Pine Grove, NY

Armstrong D. D. of Wayne, NY March 12, 1876
Washburn Katie H. of Wayne, NY Dundee, NY

Sackett Samuel W. of Watkins, NY March 22, 1876
Thurston Mrs. Anna R. of Watkins, NY Watkins, NY

Rich Charles B. of Reading, NY April 10, 1876
Lockwood Estella of Townsend, NY Reading Center, NY

Brown Joseph of Montour, NY May 17, 1876
Leffler Mrs. Phebe of Ovid, NY widow of Christopher

Coolbaugh Emmett of Watkins, NY May 4, 1876
Huey Agnes of Watkins, NY Watkins, NY

Stilwell John Wesley of Hector, NY June 20, 1876

MARRIAGE NOTICES

Crisfield Celia of Lodi, NY — Lodi, NY

Ash J. Wesley of Ohio, NY — June 19, 1876
Austin Phebe dau of Asa of Dix, NY

Patterson George B. of Burdett, NY — June 14, 1876
Thompson Nettie of Burdett, NY

Fletcher Floyd of Havana, NY — July 15, 1876
Kendall Marilla of Odessa, NY — Millport, NY

Elwell Samuel A. of Tyrone, NY — July 3, 1876
Lewis Permelia of Watkins, NY — Watkins, NY

Harvey George W. of Alpine, NY — July 4, 1876
Dean Olive of Hector, NY — Hector, NY

Rawson J. G. of Watkins, NY — August 24, 1876
Murdock Maggie of Adrian, Michigan — Adrian, Michigan

Chrysler K. M. of N. Hector, NY — August 30, 1876
Brokaw Crissy of Lodi, NY — Lodi, NY

Totten John J. of Dix, NY — September 18, 1876
Thompson Ella M. of Dix, NY — Orange, NY

Dalyrimple Thomas H. of Havana, NY — September 16, 1876
Corwin Carrie E. of Havana, NY — Havana, NY

Jansen Dewitt C. of Ithaca, NY — September 28, 1876
Howard Alice dau of Daniel of Watkins, NY — Watkins, NY

Gardiner Abram S. of Weston, NY — September 27, 1876
Griffith Susan of Wayne, NY — Wayne, NY

Kels George of Weston, NY — October 7, 1876
Carbear Polly of Orange, NY — Weston, NY

Howard Henry S. of Reading, NY — October 25, 1876
Sackett Delia M. dau of S. W. of Watkins, NY — Watkins, NY

Smith Francis Marion — October 25, 1876
Mekeel Carrie of N. Hector, NY — N. Hector, NY

Marshall E. J. of Townsend, NY — August 5, 1876
French Zelma of Millport, NY — Havana, NY

Johson Dempster A. of Reading Center, NY — October 26, 1876
Simmons Laurie E. of Reading Center, NY — Reading Center, NY

SCHUYLER COUNTY NEWSPAPERS

Van Vleet Samuel G. of Ovid, NY
Smeltzer Addie dau of Phillip of Lodi, NY

October 18, 1876
Lodi, NY

Rappleye Wirt W. of Lodi, NY
Rogers Adeline of Hector, NY

November 8, 1876
Hector, NY

Porter William H. of Barrington, NY
Stanton Minnie of Starkey, NY

November 1, 1876

Halsey W. D. of Chicago, Illinois
Seymour Louise M. of Trumansburg, NY

November 1, 1876
Trumansburg, NY

King William M. of Mecklenburg, NY
Hendershot Mary of Mecklenburg, NY

November 15, 1876
Ithaca, NY

Crookston Frank of Wayne, NY
Ellis Ida of Dundee, NY

November 5, 1876
Dundee, NY

Ely Myron H. of Hector, NY
Reynolds Ida May dau of Samuel of Hector, NY

November 15, 1876
Penn Yan, NY

Gano William of Ovid, NY
Conover Mrs. Mary of Clinton, NJ

November 18, 1876
Clinton, NJ

Tyrrell H. H. of Burdett, NY
Mathews Altia of Burdett, NY

September 30, 1876

Gunderman Albert M. of N. Hector, NY
Curtis Mrs. Stella J. of N. Hector, NY

November 29, 1876
N. Hector, NY

Sprague Nathan of Hector, NY
Hinckley Sarah Jane of Ulyssis, NY

November 19, 1876
Mecklenburg, NY

Broas James H. of Enfield, NY
Updike Viann of Enfield, NY

November 29, 1876
Enfield, NY

Hubbell E. B. of Mecklenburgh, NY
Johnson Josephine S. of Mecklenburgh, NY

November 29, 1876
Mecklenburgh, NY

Sharp Charles F. of Mecklenburgh, NY
Hazelitt Anna B. of Mecklenburgh, NY

December 3, 1876
Mecklenburgh, NY

Smelzer Baxter T. of Havana, NY
Tracy Lucy A. of Havana, NY

December 4, 1876
Havana, NY

Arnold James W.
Skiff Ella formerly of Starkey, NY

November 21, 1876
Tyrone, NY

Drummond William of Hector, NY

November 19, 1876

MARRIAGE NOTICES 31

Smith Ann E. of Ulyssis, NY

Daugherty John of Watkins, NY (newspaper date) **Brown** Alma of Waverly, NY	December 7, 1876 Waverly, NY
Robbins John H. of Wayne, NY **Case** Lydia of Owosso, Michigan	December 4, 1876 Wayne, NY
Sebring W. H. of Tyrone, NY **Cole** Jennie of Tyrone, NY	December 7, 1876 Tyrone, NY
Caywood John of Cayuta, NY **Sidney** Sarah H. of Cayuta, NY	December 17, 1876 Mecklenburgh, NY
Sturdevant Allen J. of Mecklenburgh, NY **Peck** Emma J. of Cayuta, NY	December 20, 1876 Cayuta, NY
Henderson Daniel of Orange, NY **Hughey** Libbie of Orange, NY	December 20, 1876 Monterey, NY
Thompson Davie E. of Perry City, NY **Smith** Jennie M. of Perry City, NY	December 21, 1876 Ulyssis, NY
Stoughton Manning F. of Hector, NY **Pease** Flora A. of Hector, NY	December 26, 1876 Burdett, NY
Thompson George W. Jr. of Watkins, NY **Vaneps** Mattie Bell of New York City	June 26, 1876 New York City
Bates E. S. of Hornellsville, NY **Whippy** Estella of Havana, NY	December 25, 1876 Hornellsville, NY
Wygant William of Rock Stream, NY **Green** Olive of Dix, NY	December 27, 1876 Dix, NY
Lamphier Simeon of Jefferson Co. NY **Ellis** Helen dau of William S. of Barrington, NY	December 20, 1876 Barrington, NY
Cronk Abram C. of Hector, NY (newspaper date) **Broderick** Sarah Jane of Hector, NY	January 18, 1877 Bennettsburg, NY
Yost J. H. of Tyrone, NY **Van Vleet** Carmicia of Bradford, NY	December 21, 1876 Bradford, NY
Wager Charles E. of Philadelphia, Pa. **Potter** Mary E. of Watkins, NY	December 26, 1876 Watkins, NY
Frost Alvin Jr. of N. Hector, NY **Slater** Martha E. dau of Abram of Lodi, NY	December 27, 1876 Lodi, NY

Ellison Jackson of Reading, NY
Simpson Sarah E. of Dix, NY
January 18, 1877
Watkins, NY

Angel Benjamin F. (newspaper date)
Magee Mrs. D. S. (formerly of Watkins, NY)
January 25, 1877
Hudson, NY

Soule L. Lawrence of Mecklenburgh, NY
Sherwood Hattie A. of Cayuta, NY
January 10, 1877
Havana, NY

Huntley Isaiah B. of Dix, NY
Rhinehart Mrs. Phebe H. of Dix, NY
January 7, 1877
Dix, NY

Walter Henry F. of Himrods, NY
Eddy Laura H. of Dix, NY
December 27, 1876
Dix, NY

Sawyer B. Z. of Cayutaville, NY
Sherwood Florence M. of Cayutaville, NY
January 10, 1877
Havana, NY

Ennis Lowell of Cayuta, NY
Bandfield Hattie of Cayuta, NY
January 10, 1877
Cayuta, NY

Stanton Martin son of George of Barrington, NY
Howard Emma A. of Starkey, NY
January 10, 1877
Starkey, NY

Hill Dr. Alonzo D. son of Caleb of Havana, NY
Montgomery Emma of Dexter, Missouri
January 6, 1877
Dexter, Missouri

Carpenter Albert C. of Ithaca, NY
Horn Carrie E. of Dundee, NY
January 18, 1877
Dundee, NY

Mapes Cornelius V. of Townsend, NY
Miller Minerva of Townsend, NY
January 24, 1877
Monterey, NY

Sturdevant Edwin of Dix, NY
Sherman Mrs. Charity C. of Dix, NY
November 25, 1876
Dix, NY

Horton Frank of Ovid, NY
Holden Josephine of Dix, NY
January 20, 1877
Dix, NY

Kelsey Duane of Durhamsville, NY
Savory Anna of Dix, NY
February 1, 1877
Dix, NY

Gray Stephen youngest son of Hiram
Webber Adell youngest daughter of Lorenzo
January 31, 1877
Elmira, NY

Dunham Jay T.
Aldrich Eva L. of Burdett, NY
January 2, 1877
Burdett, NY

Simpson Sherman of Perry City, NY
January 25, 1877

MARRIAGE NOTICES

Swarthout Susan of Perry City, NY Burdett, NY

Soule J. G. B. of Reynoldsville, NY February 1, 1877
Grant Addie E. of Reynoldsville, NY Reynoldsville, NY

Berry Gorton H. of Watkins, NY February 14, 1877
Tracy Bina E. of Dix, NY Watkins, NY

Lewis Guy A. of Dix, NY Janauary 28, 1877
Miller Clara E. dau of Nathan of Orange, NY Orange, NY

Hetherington Robert of Newfield, NY February 5, 1877
Ackley Alice E. of Cayuta, NY

Rising Delmer C. of Thurston, NY February 14, 1877
Masters Mary D. of N. Reading, NY N. Reading, NY

Williams Adelbert D. of Cayuta, NY February 5, 1877
Robinson Alice M. of Cortland, NY Groton, NY

Crane David B. of Catherine, NY February 14, 1877
Milspaugh Jane S. of Catherine, NY Catherine, NY

Gibbs Eaton A. of Catherine, NY February 21, 1877
Thompson Minnie S. of Elizabeth, N. C. formerly of Montour, NY

Swick James H. of Searsburg, NY February 15, 1877
Hatt Mary A. of Searsburg, NY Mecklenburg, NY

Mc Intyre Samuel of Pine Grove, NY March 1, 1877
Hobson Hattie A. of Barrington, NY Monterey, NY

Green Franklin of Clarkston, Michigan March 1, 1877
Tompkins Sarah J. of Hector, NY Hector, NY

Tolbert Isaac L. of Weston, NY March 14, 1877
Vanderhoof Celia E. of Weston, NY Weston, NY

Wheaton Lyman B. of Bradford, NY March 15, 1877
Thompson Malitta J. of Bradford, NY Tyrone, NY

Turner Clark S. of Hector, NY March 14, 1877
Mathews Cynthia of Hector, NY Lodi, NY

Sebring Henry B. of Tyrone, NY March 10, 1877
Rolfe Susan of Tyrone, NY Monterey, NY

Brodrick Theodore F. of Altay, NY March 25, 1877
Price Mrs. Kate of Altay, NY Altay, NY

Thompson George H. of Havana, NY   March 23, 1877
Smith Mattie M. of Havana, NY   Altay, NY

Manning John T. of Hector, NY   March 20, 1877
Jaquish Lillie L. dau of Jonathan of Hector   Hector, NY

Sharp Ambrose of Rock Stream, NY   March 22, 1877
Marrow Mary E. dau of John of Tyrone, NY Tyrone, NY

Kress Anthony of Watkins, NY   January 30, 1877
Conley Ida of Watkins, NY   Burdett, NY

German Calvin D. of Painesville, Ohio   March 31, 1877
Swarthout Helen of Reading, NY   Reading, NY

Shannon S. W.   March 29, 1877
Finger Mary C.   Pine Creek, NY

Briggs Smith F. of Havana, NY   March 19, 1877
Hallett Sarah of Beaver Dams, NY

Smith O. D. of Cayuta, NY   March 25, 1877
Nichols Esther of Catherine, NY   Catherine, NY

Deming Ben E. of Watkins, NY   March 31, 1877
Bedient Sarah E.   Millport, NY

Starkey William B. of Watkins, NY   April 5, 1877
Cantine Julia of Brooklyn, NY   Slaterville, NY

Van Loan John R. of Catherine, NY   April 6, 1877
Angle Mary A. of Watkins, NY   Hector, NY

Lawton John P. of Watkins, NY   April 18, 1877
Ladow Della of Watkins, NY   Watkins, NY

Edwards Lewis of New York City   April 19, 1877
Magee Helen Gansvoort daughter of late Duncan

Jacobson Neil of Corning, NY   May 3, 1877
Brewer Emeline M. of Fall Brook, NY   Fall Brook, NY

Overton Clayton H. of Tyrone, NY   May 13, 1877
Humiston Helen C. of Tyrone, NY

Harvey E. B. of Enfield, NY   April 29, 1877
Dickens Edith E. of Catherine, NY

Conklin Smith K. of Reading, NY   May 16, 1877

MARRIAGE NOTICES 35

Smith Phoebe A. of Reading, NY — Reading Center, NY

Beardslee Seely A. of E. Canton, Pa.
Miller Maryetta of Catherine, NY
May 8, 1877
Catherine, NY

Close Orson
Bainbridge Helen, daughter of John
May 24, 1877
Farmer Village, NY

Foote Avery L. of N. Parma, NY
Spaulding Minnie L. of Montour, NY
June 13, 1877
Montour, NY

Tuttle Volney C. of Clinton, Wisonsin
Chamberlain Carrie M. of Havana, NY
June 27, 1877
Havana, NY

Williams George of Enfield, NY
Freeman Mary of Smith Valley, NY
June 25, 1877
Havana, NY

Smith William R. of Lodi, NY
Miller Sarah M. of Lodi, NY
July 3, 1877
Watkins, NY

Bailey William of Lodi, NY
Brown Laura A. of Lodi, NY
July 3, 1877
N. Hector, NY

Sterling Daniel of Millport, NY
Sleeper Sarah of Millport, NY
July 9, 1877
Millport, NY

Messenger Isaac O. of Park Station, NY
North Etta C. of Cayuta, NY
June 30, 1877
Cayuta, NY

Coe Asa of Monterey, NY
Westlake Arminda of Horseheads, NY
July 11, 1877
Horseheads, NY

Bronson W. W. of Veteran, NY
Briscoe R. E. of Montour, NY
July 4, 1877
Catherine, NY

Stamp John A. of Dix, NY
King Nancy A. of Dix, NY
June 19, 1877
Havana, NY

Wells Stephen D. of Milford, Pa.
Craft Alice B.
July 12, 1877

Fountain Byron H. of Havana, NY
Berring Emma of Hector, NY
August 22, 1877
Havana, NY

Brimmer Rant of N. Hector, NY
Low Cynthia A. of N. Hector, NY
September 1, 1877
Watkins, NY

French Edmond of Dundee, NY
Leslie Mrs. Henrietta of Crystal Springs NY
September 9, 1877
Altay, NY

Smith Charles D. of Scott Charge, NY
Kellogg Sarah of Hector, NY

September 12, 1877
Steamburg, NY

Crum Walter G. of Bath, NY
Fogarty Catherine of Bath, NY

September 19, 1877
Watkins, NY

Howell Dewitt C. of Hector, NY
Strader Emma J. of Hector, NY

September 19, 1877
Watkins, NY

La Fever Charles A. of Reading, NY
Townsend Emma of Reading, NY
   at bride's sister's Mrs. Lyman Skiff

October 3, 1877
Blossburg, Pa.

Woodward Charles M. of Watkins, NY
Woodward Sarah E. of Watkins, NY

October 10, 1877
Watkins, NY

Noyes Newman H. of Geneva, NY
Baker Lucy of Watkins, NY

October 10, 1877
Watkins, NY

Coy Alva of Hornby, NY
Kress Sarah E. of Monterey, NY

October 9, 1877
Monterey, NY

Palmer Nelson D. of Reading, NY
La Fever Anna L. of Reading, NY

October 16, 1877
Irelandville, NY

Prentiss Millard F.
Clark Ettie S. of Tyrone, NY

October 17, 1877
Tyrone, NY

Rutherford Robert of Rochester, NY
Forshee Catherine R. of Watkins, NY

October 29, 1877
Watkins, NY

Ovenshire William A. of Warsaw, NY
Roleson Emma of Altay, NY

October 24. 1877
Altay, NY

Van Vleet Herman M. of Hector, NY
Snyder Edna K. of Hector, NY

October 23, 1877
Hector, NY

Abbey Rev. E. W. son of T. H. of Watkins, NY
Hamill Gussie of Watkins, NY

October 31, 1877
Terre Haute, Ind.

Chapman Adelbert of Wayne, NY
Woodhouse Martha of Urbana, NY

November 1, 1877
Urbana, NY

Murphy Henry J. of Waddington, NY
Cooper Adelia S. of Watkins, NY

October 29, 1877
Catherine, NY

Wiggins John of Kelly's Corners, NY
   (newspaper date December 13, 1877)
Slater Minerva of Lodi Center, NY

No date

Lodi Center, NY

MARRIAGE NOTICES

Hicks Albert A. of Bradford, NY
Hughey Emma of Sugar Hill, NY
December 5, 1877
Monterey, NY

Harrington G. Dimock of Dundee, NY
Abbey Flora J. of Rock Stream, NY
December 13, 1877
Rock Stream, NY

Howell S. Monroe of Hector, NY
Purdy A. Endora of Burdett, NY
December 18, 1877

Coon George S. of Watkins, NY
Vanderhoof Mary of Weston, NY
November 29, 1877
Weston, NY

Backer George of Dix, NY
Thompson Eva F. of Dix, NY
at residence of Samuel Thompson
November 29, 1877
Dix, NY

Morrow John C.
Bigelow Jennie F. of Altay, NY
December 18, 1877
Altay, NY

Elwood Fred of Dundee, NY
Van Kuren Hattie of Glenora, NY
December 16, 1877
Reading Center, NY

Dean Orrin B. of Altay, NY
Gilbert Jessie of Altay, NY
December 20, 1877
Altay, NY

Insco David Martin of Reading, NY
Wilkes Osie Elizabeth dau of James of Reading
December 24, 1877
Reading, NY

Swarthout Scott of Lodi, NY
Brokaw Mary of Lodi, NY
January 2, 1878
Lodi, NY

Canfield Robert of Bath, NY (newspaper date)
Barnes Sarah A. of Watkins, NY
January 3, 1878

Putnam Ebenezer B. of Altay, NY
Clark Miriam of Altay, NY
January 7, 1878
Altay, NY

Davenport A. P. of Watkins, NY
Hanmer Melissa of Townsend, NY
January 3, 1878
Watkins, NY

Cushion Mr. of Hornby, NY
Merrills Franc of Monterey, NY
January 1, 1878

Waugh John of Monterey, NY
Jack Catherine A. of Hornby, NY
January 1, 1878

Ellison Byron of Pine Grove, NY
Hughey Matilda of Sugar Hill, NY
January 10, 1878
Sugar Hill, NY

Wiggins John D. of Bennettsburg, NY January 14, 1878
Hopkins Ophelia of Bennettsburg, NY

Giles G. L. of Waterman, Illinois January 24, 1878
Frost Emma J. of Watkins, NY Watkins, NY

Harvey Joel of Enfield, NY February 5, 1878
Wallenbeck Abbie of Enfield, NY Watkins, NY

Loney George of Hornby, NY February 7, 1878
Travis Hanna Mary of Hornby, NY Monterey, NY

Wilson James H. of Dundee, NY February 21, 1878
Muckey Ann M. of N. Hector, NY N. Hector, NY

Pierson Warren A. of Hector, NY February 20, 1878
Campbell Marion of Hector, NY Hector, NY

Robertson Washington of Dix, NY No date
Bailey Cannie of Dix, NY (newspaper date) March 7, 1878

Corbett John of Reading, NY March 13, 1878
Jefferson Dora Reading, NY

Cass Charles H. of Watkins, NY March 13, 1878
Decker Ettie of Watkins, NY Watkins, NY

Love Andrew of Watkins, NY March 20, 1878
Wasson Jane of Tyrone, NY Tyrone, NY

Vosburgh Aaron P. of Beaver Dams, NY March 20, 1878
David Hattie M. Watkins, NY

Butler W. J. of Hornellsville, NY April 3, 1878
Brown Ann A. of Moreland, NY Watkins, NY

Chapman R. L. of Altay, NY March 13, 1878
Watson Mrs. C. R. of Dundee, NY Barrington, NY

Kelly Warren V. of Mecklenburgh, NY April 3, 1878
Johnson Julia A. of Hector, NY Hector, NY

Goodier A. J. of Mecklenburgh, NY April 4, 1878
Robinson Ida Belle of Sheridan, Illinois Sheridan, Ill.

Comstock S. L. of Norwich, NY April 24, 1878
Van Allen Lottie L. dau of John of Watkins Watkins, NY

Gillette Albert O. of Italy Hollow, NY April 19, 1878

MARRIAGE NOTICES

Robson Belle of Italy Hollow, NY
Italy Hollow, NY

Griswold George L. of Watkins, NY
Taber Minnie M. dau of Henry of Watkins, NY
April 30, 1878
Watkins, NY

Pierce Fred W. of Corning, NY
Rood Mary J. of Painted Post, NY
May 14, 1878
Watkins, NY

Olmstead Ichabod of Pine Grove, NY
Griffith Mary C. of Wayne, NY
May 15, 1878
Wayne, NY

Lewis Irving of Seneca Falls, NY
Sherman Fannie recently of Palmyra, NY
May 30, 1878
Watkins, NY

Baker James W. of Orange, NY
Ellison Mary of Tyrone, NY
June 12, 1878
Monterey, NY

Baskin Lyman J. recently of Jackson, Mi.
Ingalls Ella of Watkins, NY
June 18, 1878
Watkins, NY

Farrington John R. of Searsburg, NY
Allen Libbie
June 20, 1878
Trumbulls Corn. NY

Golden Frank of Tonawanda, NY
Kies Gussie of Watkins, NY
June 25, 1878
Watkins, NY

Mills Charles R. of Watkins, NY
Phillips Mary R. of Watkins, NY
June 27, 1878
Watkins, NY

Saylor William H. of Chicago, Illinois
Coats Mary of Hector, NY
June 27, 1878
Burdett, NY

Hope J. D. of Watkins, NY
Kester Emma J. of Roxham, Quebec
July 11, 1878
Troy, NY

Nicholai W. F. of Baltimore, Md.
Cookes Susannah
August 2, 1878
Watkins, NY

Kenyon Samuel of Monterey, NY (newspaper date)
Hudson Ellen of Middletown, NY
August 8, 1878
Middletown, NY

Cowen Willis of Warren, Pa.
Davis Maria of Watkins, NY
September 24, 1878
Watkins, NY

Jordan Arthur of Richburg, NY
Brodrick Anna of Altay, NY
September 21, 1878
Altay, NY

Cooper Levi
Ward Miss
September 27, 1878
Montour, NY

Walling Frank of Tyrone, NY
Baskin Desta M. of Weston, NY

September 29, 1878
Altay, NY

Silsbee Henry B. of Watkins, NY
Diven Amanda of Elmira, NY

October 7, 1878
Elmira, NY

Pike Ambrose C. of Watkins, NY
Barnes Emma L. of Watkins, NY

October 9, 1878
Trumansburg, NY

Dunham William of Hector, NY (newspaper date)
Sterling Ella of Hector, NY

October 24, 1878
Bennettsburg, NY

Wright T. R. of Bennettsburg, NY
Benson M. S. of Bennettsburg, NY

October 16, 1878
E. Lansing, NY

Lanning B. M. of Utica, NY
Tyrell Frances of Millport, NY

October 15, 1878
Millport, NY

Loomis George H. of Mecklenburgh, NY
Gardner Mary L. of Bennettsburg, NY

October 9, 1878
Watkins, NY

Coats Lyman F.
Jaquish F. Phidelia

October 26, 1878
Burdett, NY

Bodle Elmer P.
Kempton Catherine

October 20, 1878
Burdett, NY

Smith Charles R. of N. Hector, NY
Townsend Minnie B. of N. Hector, NY

November 6, 1878
N. Hector, NY

Vining Phillip of Covert, NY
Wixom Louise E. of Covert, NY

November 12, 1878
Mecklenburg, NY

Grant Emmet C. of Mecklenburgh, NY
Lambert Grace E. of Mecklenburgh, NY

November 12, 1878
Mecklenburgh, NY

Hardenburg William H.
Brush Marena

November 6, 1878
Dix, NY

Terrell Tims J. of Starkey, NY
Roberts Minerva H. of Reading, NY

November 19, 1878
Coal Point, NY

Caywood Joseph of Altay, NY
Purdy Sarah J. of Reading, NY

November 20, 1878
Reading, NY

Moore George son of Martin of Monterey, NY
Shafer Miss

November 27, 1878
Campbell, NY

Lockwood Seeley of Monterey, NY

December 8, 1878

MARRIAGE NOTICES

Carson Sarah
Monterey, NY

Carlisle Charles B. of Rochester, NY
Watson Eva E. dau of Rev. G. S.
November 30, 1878
Bristol Ctr. NY

Travis Eli
Duvall Marietta dau of Daniel of Hornby, NY
December 18, 1878
Monterey, NY

Bailey George of Dix, NY
Thompson Libbie H. of Dix, NY
December 25, 1878
Dix, NY

Wightman Elihu B. of Odessa, NY
Leffler May C. of Bennettsburg, NY
December 25, 1878
Bennettsburg, NY

Letts Deforest of Trumansburg, NY
Brown Ella R. of N. Hector, NY
December 28, 1878
Penn Yan, NY

Adriance Dr. Frank W.
Beach Libbie dau of late George
January 8, 1879
Watkins, NY

Personius Myron of Millport, NY
Bossard Clara E. of Dix, NY
January 15, 1879
Dix, NY

Dikeman Hubert C. of Reading Center, NY
Grimes Julia A. of Campbell, NY
January 18, 1879
N. Reading, NY

Millard L. Stacy
Cook Lizzie M. dau of J. P.
January 14, 1879
Dundee, NY

Ringer Clarence A. of Watkins, NY
Davidson Lizzie of Odessa, NY
January 29, 1879
Odessa, NY

Ely William of Hector, NY
Bradner Dell C. of Orange, NY
January 29, 1879
Orange, NY

Kelly James M. of Hector, NY
Treman Ann E. of Hector, NY
January 22, 1879
Mecklenburgh, NY

Myers Alvah D. of Bennettsburg, NY
Carr Elvina S. of Bennettsburg, NY
January 12, 1879
Bennettsburg, NY

Sherman Elias D. of Watkins, NY
Thompson Minerva dau of George of Rock Stream
February 6, 1879
Rock Stream, NY

Sutton Russell of Reading Center, NY
Wood Amanda M. of Reading Center, NY
February 12, 1879
Reading Center, NY

Olin Benjamin P. of Dundee, NY
Jackson Alice A. of N. Hector, NY
February 13, 1879
N. Hector, NY

Decker James of Watkins, NY
Edwards Helen E. of Watkins, NY

February 18, 1879
Watkins, NY

Norman George D. of Watkins, NY
Clark Alice of Watkins, NY

February 25, 1879
Watkins, NY

Nelson James C. of Detroit, Michigan
Gould Emma L. of Watkins, NY

February 18, 1879
Detroit, Michigan

Royce Adelbert of Campbell, NY
Miller Eveline of Campbell, NY

February 18, 1879
Monterey, NY

Tunison Edgar of Covert, NY
Eldred Flora dau of Joseph of Hector, NY

February 25, 1879
Covert, NY

Dexter Miles of Campbell, NY
Fuller Frances of Campbell, NY

March 2, 1879

Smith Frank A. of Watkins, NY
Cross Maria A. of Reading Center, NY

February 26, 1879
Reading, NY

Folsom Otis F. of N. Urbana, NY
Benson Louise of Tyrone, NY

March 5, 1879
Tyrone, NY

Sebring Phillip of Tyrone, NY
Smith Ella

March 5, 1879
Tyrone, NY

Duryea James of Osage, Iowa
Tweedie Jane of Mecklenburgh, NY

March 4, 1879
Mecklenburgh, NY

Batty William W. of Enfield, NY
Churchill Ida M. of Watkins, NY

March 3, 1879
Havana, NY

Hoyt Charles of Dundee, NY
Howard Mary E. of Watkins, NY
    eldest daughter of Lewis Hoyt

March 12, 1879
Watkins, NY

Erway Benjamin J. of Hector, NY
Shoemaker Mrs. H. Amelia

March 12, 1879
Hector, NY

Bates John of Cayuta, NY
Markell Rosa of Alpine, NY

March 24, 1879
Horseheads, NY

Robbins Charles S. of Reading, NY
Burchfield Elizabeth E. of Watkins, NY

March 20, 1879
Watkins, NY

Van Loon Chauncey of Alpine, NY
Dean Frances of Bennettsburg, NY

March 26, 1879
Bennettsburg, NY

MARRIAGE NOTICES 43

Smith Frank M. of San Francisco (newspaper date) — April 3, 1879
Edgecomb Addie C. of Waverly, NY — Waverly, NY

Wager Frank of Wisconsin — March 26, 1879
Carr Hester of Bennettsburg, NY — Bennettsburg, NY

Dewitt Emmett of Montour, NY — February 22, 1879
Longwell Alice — Monterey, NY

Dunham Frank of Reynoldsville, NY — April 24, 1879
Grant Belle of Reynoldsville, NY — Burdett, NY

Bement Charles H. — May 1, 1879
Harrington Mrs. Susan A. — Burdett, NY

Fuller John R. of Cobleskill, NY — May 15, 1879
Gulick Anna of Watkins, NY — Watkins, NY

Jessup John W. of Dundee, NY — May 22, 1879
Simpson Augusta M. of Ovid, NY — N. Hector, NY

Robson David of Reading Center, NY — June 25, 1879
Webb Nancy L. of Reading, NY — Reading, NY

Morris David E. of Lodi, NY — June 25, 1879
Bates Emma L. of Havana, NY — Havana, NY

Gates Frank A. of Watkins, NY — June 25, 1879
Gulick Eva of Watkins, NY — Watkins, NY

Van Vleet George S. of Tyrone, NY — July 9, 1879
Van Liew Mary A. of Tyrone, NY — Tyrone, NY

Bradley Lewis H. of Watkins, NY — June 21, 1879
Smith Anna A. of Watkins, NY — Havana, NY

Voak Olin S. of Watkins, NY — July 30, 1879
Ellis Ida M. of Watkins, NY — Watkins, NY
    adopted daughter of Mr. & Mrs. Albert Ellis

Gould W. H. of Woodhull, NY — August 17, 1879
Brong Ella — Bradford, NY

Bowers Abner of Bennettsburg, NY — August 31, 1879
Smith Hannah M. of Bennettsburg, NY — Odessa, NY

Blanchard Albert E. of Wellsville, NY — September 3, 1879
Tompkins Florence E. of Wellsville, NY — Watkins, NY

Howell William Jr. of Antrim, Pa.
Mulford Mary of Burdett, NY
   daughter of late John H. Stothoff

September 4, 1879
Burdett, NY

Edgerton Erastus D. of New York City
Durland Katie G. of Watkins, NY

September 9, 1879
Watkins, NY

Beardsley Stephen R. of Montour, NY
Creeth Mary late of Philadelphia, Pa.

September 3, 1879
Catherine, NY

Kellogg Julius of Hector, NY
Wixom Edla of Hector, NY

September 14, 1879
Hector, NY

Raymond Isaac B. of Reading, NY
Smith Minnie of Reading, NY

September 10, 1879
Reading, NY

Nye Orrin of Dix, NY
Drake Carrie M. dau of George of Reading, NY

September 17, 1879
Reading, NY

Everts J. Alfred of Watkins, NY
Bowers Mary E. of Troy, NY

September 17, 1879
Troy, NY

Morgan Alexander of Hector, NY
Carmichael Mrs. Samantha E. of Enfield, NY

September 16, 1879
Mecklenburgh, NY

Chase Obadiah of Searsburg, NY
Burlew Deborah of Enfield, NY

September 27, 1879
Enfield, NY

Chapman Ezra of Monterey, NY
Darling Mary A. of Geneva, NY

October 1, 1879
Monterey, NY

Labar John K. of Bennettsburg, NY
Bush Sarah E. of Bennettsburg, NY

October 2, 1879
Mecklenburgh, NY

Stevens Lester
Marshall Ritter dau of Jefferson of Townsend

September 30, 1879
Jackson, Mi.

Crum Fred F. of Watkins, NY
Deming Sadie B. of Elmira, NY

October 9, 1879
Millport, NY

Malona Daniel Moulton of Hector, NY
Barber Susan M. of Hector, NY

October 5, 1879
Mecklenburgh, NY

Sherwood Goodwin of Hector, NY
Blauvelt Estelle of Lodi, NY

October 29, 1879
N. Hector, NY

Goltry James W. of Reading, NY (newspaper date)
Beers Ada A. of Breesport, NY

November 27, 1879
Breesport, NY

MARRIAGE NOTICES 45

Bennett Charles of Perry City, NY
Rallings Lizettie of Searsburg, NY

November 25, 1879
Searsburg, NY

Woodward Arthur C. of Watkins, NY
Everts Mary F. dau of late Alfred of Hector

December 1, 1879
Hector, NY

Ault Charles F. of Odessa, NY
Shelton Anna

September 10, 1881
Taughannock, NY

Shadrick Charles of Spencer, NY
Whiteman Minnie A. W.

September 18, 1881
Catherine, NY

Bassett Charles G. of Hector, NY
Watson Alice of Hector, NY

September 11, 1881
Hector, NY

Overton Charles W.
Overton Ella

January 4, 1882
N. Reading, NY

Meeker Lewis M. of Lodi, NY
Esterbrook Louisa of N. Hector, NY

January 11, 1882
N. Hector, NY

Booram Albert H.
Kendall Erva

January 11, 1882
Tyrone, NY

Morgan Seneca of Mecklenburgh, NY
Clock Adeline of Mecklenburgh, NY

January 19, 1882
Trumansburg, NY

Ellis Byron F. of Altay, NY
Gilbert Emma K. of Altay, NY

February 2, 1882
Altay, NY

Withiam Charles B. of Burdett, NY
Lamoreaux Clara J. of Lodi, NY

February 1, 1882
Lodi, NY

Woodford Alson of Hector, NY
Williams Nellie of Hector, NY

February 14, 1882
Bennettsburg, NY

Barto Thomas F. of Perry City, NY
Strowbridge Norma of Perry City, NY

February 28, 1882
Burdett, NY

Saxton Alvah of Newfield, NY
Roleson Anna of Mecklenburgh, NY

March 31, 1882
Mecklenburgh, NY

Vorhees Charles L. of Knapps Corners, NY
Swick Ida of Reynoldsville, NY

March 4, 1882
Farmer Village, NY

Hendricks Erie V. of Hector, NY
Koon Mary E. of Enfield, NY

March 11, 1882
Bennettsburg, NY

Kendall Chauncey of Altay, NY

March 22, 1882

Edson Mrs. Jane M. of Penn Yan, NY   Penn, Yan, NY

Bliss George of Wayne, NY   March 23, 1882
Yauger Nancy of Orange, NY   Reading, NY

Hunt George M. of Cortland, NY   April 12, 1882
Hunt Emma of Watkins, NY   Watkins, NY

Stevens James of Tyrone, NY   November 24, 1882
Hoover Rebecca of Tyrone, NY   Tyrone, NY

Coykendall Charles E. of Reading Ctr. NY   February 28, 1882
Ellison Ella of Reading Ctr., NY   Reading Ctr., NY

Orr Ira D. of Tyrone, NY   April 3, 1882
Perry Adell S. of Tyrone, NY   Tyrone, NY

Campbell A. E. of Nelson, Pa.   April 3, 1882
Sebring Carrie F. of Tyrone, NY   Tyrone, NY

Robertson Thadeus of Elmira, NY   April 8, 1882
Bedner Capitola of Elmira, NY   Watkins, NY

Switzer Almond D. of Bradford, NY   May 11, 1882
Mapes Lillie E. of Monterey, NY   Reading, NY

Kent R. G. of Reading, NY   June 21, 1882
Gabriel Libbie dau of J. P. of Reading, NY   Reading, NY

Drake Charles E. son of George of Reading, NY   June 11, 1882
Pope Alta dau of Horatio of Hornellsville, NY

Phillip Walter P. of Starkey, NY   June 17, 1882
Rarrick Ella of Painted Post, NY   Painted Post, NY

Tucker William J. of Monterey, NY   June 22, 1882
Moore Dorothy A.   Monterey, NY

Roe Fred C. of Watkins, NY   June 24, 1882
Crawford A. B. of Montour, NY

Beck Charles H. of Fayette, NY   June 27, 1882
Sullivan Mrs. Hattie of Dix, NY   Watkins, NY

Jones Willis S. of Watkins, NY   July 19, 1882
Ellsworth Lydia L. of Reading Ctr. NY   Reading Ctr., NY

Booram Eugene of N. Hector, NY   July 19, 1882
Stark Mary E. dau of Isreal of Brockport, NY   Brockport, NY

MARRIAGE NOTICES

Mottram George A. Md. of Tyrone, NY
Chapman Ida M. of Monterey, NY
July 30, 1882
Monterey, NY

Kels Fred of Monterey, NY
Casbeer Flora of Elkland, Pa.
July 26, 1882
E. Corning, NY

Sheldon Charles S. of Oswego, NY
Buck Helen A. of Watkins, NY
August 24, 1882
Watkins, NY

Hicks G. L. of Wetona, Pa.
Mathews Hannah A. of Hector, NY
August 30, 1882
Hector, NY

Mathews Kortwright of Hector, NY
Mathews Mary S. of Hector, NY
September 6, 1882
Hector, NY

Burt Leroy A. of Corning, NY
O'Neil Nellie A. of Watkins, NY
September 4, 1882
Watkins, NY

Sutton Harry E.
Phinney Hattie G. dau of L. G. of Reading, NY
September 20, 1882
Reading, NY

Rich William A. of Hector, NY
Moore Cora A. of Hector, NY
September 20. 1882
Hector, NY

Thompson Dewitt C. G. of Binghamton, NY
Walker Frances of Elmira, NY
September 25, 1882
Watkins, NY

Eddy William H. of Townsend, NY
Ressing Jennie of Hornby, NY
October 10, 1882
Hornby, NY

Brightman William C. of Aurora, NY
Hurley Minerva of Watkins, NY
October 25, 1882
Watkins, NY

Randall William of Painted Post, NY
Allen Ella M. of Painted Post, NY
October 22, 1882
Beaver Dams, NY

Hunter S. L. of Hector, NY
Mallory Ella K. of Hector, NY
November 1, 1882
Hector, NY

Drake A. J. of Townsend, NY
Kniffen Phebe of Townsend, NY
November 2, 1882
Townsend, NY

White Charles W. of Watkins, NY
Wood Lillie G. of Sodus Point, NY
November 1, 1882
Sodus Point, NY

Raynor John of Onondaga, NY
Brown Mrs. Juliet B. of Rock Stream, NY
November 16, 1882
Rock Stream, NY

Degraw John of Lodi, NY
November 22, 1882

Horton Sarah of Lodi, NY

Wright Herbert of Bennettsburg, NY
Kellogg Clara of Bennettsburg, NY

Cole Charles A. of Watkins, NY
Laraby Hattie A. of Watkins, NY

Goldsmith Schuyler of Clark, Nebraska
Norris Carrie of Hector, NY

Allen Marshall V. of Hector, NY
Sackett Grace L. of Hector, NY

Schuyler Daily
Eli Maggie

Phelps Arthur
Howell Hattie

Smith Lyman F. of Hector, NY
Kelly Myrtie E. of Hector, NY

Densen Warren of Havana, NY
Ackley Martha M. of Reading, NY

Rice William B., of Portland, Michigan
Caldwell Louisa of Sugar Hill, NY

Giles John W. of Pine Grove, NY
Huey May of Sugar Hill, NY

Ellison Horatio S. of Pine Grove, NY
Huey Helen of Sugar Hill, NY

Barnes Lewis of Monterey, NY
Mc Cain Rose of Bennettsburg, NY

Booram Homer of Farmer Village, NY
Lamoreaux Carrie dau of William of Lodi, NY

Wilcox J. of Lansing, NY
Wright Flora of Ithaca, NY

Hurd George E. of Watkins, NY
Clark Zenara Victoria of Watkins, NY

Baker Samuel W. of Bath, NY
Mead Elvira of Tyrone, NY

Mecklenburgh, NY

November 22, 1882
Mecklenburgh, NY

December 6, 1882
Watkins, NY

November 30, 1882
Hector, NY

December 6, 1882
Hector, NY

December 6, 1882
Peach Orchard, NY

December 6, 1882
Peach Orchard, NY

December 13, 1882
Reynoldsville, NY

December 20, 1882
Reading, NY

December 19, 1882
Sugar Hill, NY

December 20, 1882
Sugar Hill, NY

December 20, 1882
Monterey, NY

December 20, 1882
Bennettsburg, NY

December 20, 1882
Lodi, NY

December 23, 1882
Mecklenburgh, NY

December 24, 1882
Watkins, NY

December 24, 1882
Tyrone, NY

MARRIAGE NOTICES

Beecher Mark A. of Beaver Dams, NY
Terwilleger Loretta of Beaver Dams, NY

December 2, 1882
Beaver Dams, NY

Miller Leroy of Glenora, NY
Templar Ella of Weston, NY

December 11, 1882
Weston, NY

Beecher Elmer L. of Beaver Dams, NY
Russell Libbie of Moreland, NY

December 12, 1882
Moreland, NY

Hurley Edwin T. of Watkins, NY
Hopson Della G. of Castile, NY

December 20, 1882
Castile, NY

Tompkins Floyd of Townsend, NY
Waugh Sadie of Watkins, NY

December 27, 1882
Tyrone, NY

Price Allen of Altay, NY
Shea Libbie of Tyrone, NY

December 30, 1882
Weston, NY

Van Dyke Dr. C. M. son of Jacob of Reading
Clark Mate dau of Charles of Monterey, NY

December 27, 1882
Monterey, NY

Hurd George W. of Hornellsville, NY
Cole Edith dau of Harlem of Watkins, NY

January 10, 1883
Watkins, NY

Baldwin Z. E. of Watkins, NY
Burnet Ida B. of Logan, NY

January 7, 1883
Peach Orchard, NY

Black Joseph S. of Ulyssis, NY
Thompson Anna M. dau of P. G. of Hector, NY

January 11, 1883
Hector, NY

Secor Charles A. of Reading, NY
Carpenter Carrie A. of Hector, NY

January 31, 1883
Hector, NY

Hunter Edgar L. of Hornellsville, NY
Reynolds Carrie E. of Watkins, NY

February 7, 1883
Watkins, NY

Moore Irvin of Hector, NY
Menzie Sarah E. of Hector, NY

February 9, 1883
Peach Orchard, NY

Williams Charles B. of Montour, NY
Coon Eary M. of Montour, NY

February 14, 1883
Montour, NY

Jeffers Webster of Mecklenburgh, NY
Saylor Laura of Mecklenburgh, NY

February 25, 1883
Mecklenburgh, NY

Marshall Charles H. of Altay, NY
Gregory Louisa

February 22, 1883
Romulus, NY

Titchner Frank C. of Buffalo, NY

February 21, 1883

Smith Ella F. dau of P. B. of Logan, NY — Logan, NY

Robinson Romain of Reading, NY — February 28, 1883
Andrews Ella A. of Reading, NY — Reading, NY

Budd Burt J. of Hector, NY — April 18, 1883
Peck Minnie M. of Hector, NY — Elmira, NY

Osgood Charles H. of Lodi, NY — April 26, 1883
Bramble Ida M. of Lodi, NY — Lodi, NY

States Myron M. of Elmira, NY — April 9, 1883
Wayland Mary A. of Watkins, NY — Watkins, NY

Lamoreaux A. Wirt Md. — March 14, 1883
Rawling Hattie E. of Sheboygan, Wisconsin — Ovid, NY

Roberts Timothy of Watkins, NY — May 19, 1883
Moss Mrs. Josephine of Watkins, NY — Watkins, NY

Love Charles E. of Watkins, NY — May 26, 1883
Roberts Alice of Watkins, NY — Dundee, NY

Rogers W. F. of Watkins, NY — June 7, 1883
Rowland Emma S. dau of Luke of Watkins, NY — Watkins, NY

Hovey Hyatt S. of Rock Stream, NY — June 21, 1883
Beery Celia of Glenora, NY — Glenora, NY

Munson Edward Md. of Medina, NY — August 21, 1883
Smith Lillian dau of David H. of Watkins, NY — Watkins, NY

Mathews John D. of Dakota — September 5, 1883
Crevelling Jennie of Reading Center, NY

Newman Edgar W. of Ithaca, NY — September 5, 1883
Townsend Libbie of Burdett, NY — Watkins, NY

Hager Charles H. of N. Hector, NY — September 19, 1883
Close Ida M. of Spencer, NY — Spencer, NY

Wood Charles Julian of Jersey City, NJ — October 17, 1883
Lewis Jennie of Watkins, NY — Watkins, NY

Carpenter Charles E. of Dundee, NY — November 7, 1883
Horn Jennie E. dau of Enos of Monterey, NY — Monterey, NY

Miller Willis L. of Orange, NY — November 21, 1883
Wallace Libbie J. of Orange, NY — Bradford, NY

MARRIAGE NOTICES

Stuart Sevellon A. of Millport, NY
Pruden Susie A. of Watkins, NY
November 17, 1883
Watkins, NY

Miller Orson
Goundry Mary of Montour, NY
Thankgiving Day
Montour, NY

Youngs Isaac of Monterey, NY
Ogden Jennie of Monterey, NY
December 12, 1883
Monterey, NY

Probasco William N. of Watkins, NY
Ryan Catherine of Watkins, NY
December 6, 1883
Watkins, NY

Cobb Francis Eugene of New York City
Mann Katherine B. of Watkins, NY
January 3, 1884
Watkins, NY

States Randall W. of Mecklenburgh, NY
Walker Matie F. of Watkins, NY
January 17, 1884
Watkins, NY

Gates William H. of Monterey, NY
Miller Lizzie of Lodi, NY
February 7, 1884

Long Frank J. of Odebolt, Iowa
Deming Carrie formerly of Watkins, NY
September 16, 1884

Webster Judson J. of Addison, NY
Kent Effie E. of Watkins, NY
October 1, 1884
Watkins, NY

Johnson Alfred D. of N. Hector, NY
Coon Mary L. of Lodi, NY
February 22, 1885
N. Hector, NY

Mathews George C. of Bennettsburg, NY
Bowers Sarah O. of Bennettsburg, NY
March 21, 1885
Burdett, NY

Cornish Johnson of Washington, NJ
Banker Maggie dau of Jacob of Hector, NY
June 24, 1885
Mecklenburgh, NY

Bodle Loeser of Mecklenburg, NY
Bowers Frank of Bennettsburg, NY
June 17, 1885
Bennettsburg, NY

Smith Elmer P. of Liberty, Pa.
West Lissa J. of Havana, NY
June 28, 1885
Bennettsburg, NY

Ring Samuel C. of Hammondsport, NY
Forbes Jennie E. of Hammondsport, NY
July 22, 1885
Hammondsport, NY

Butler George of Dundee, NY
Seals Minnie of Watkins, NY
July 27, 1885
Watkins, NY

Clark Thomas R. of Watkins, NY
September 4, 1885

SCHUYLER COUNTY NEWSPAPERS

Maloney Ella of Watkins, NY
    Watkins, NY

Wait Nelson of N. Elmira, NY
Dewey Sarah E. of Pine Valley, NY
    September 5, 1885
    N. Elmira, NY

Hughey Albert of Auburn, NY
Nichols Grace M. dau of Harvey of Sugar Hill
    September 9, 1885
    Sugar Hill, NY

Powers E. W. of Canajoharie, NY
Burchfield Zelinda of Watkins, NY
    November 19, 1885
    Lyons, NY

Seaman Frank of Elmira, NY
Beckwith Mary of Watkins, NY
    November 18, 1885
    Watkins, NY

James Olin F. of Havana, NY
Featherly Mary F. of Watkins, NY
    December 24, 1885
    Watkins, NY

Gleason Dallas of Wayne, NY
Ames Celia of Sonora, NY
    December 25, 1885
    Tyrone, NY

Fordham D. C. of Dundee, NY
Tutman Mary W. of Reading, NY
    December 23, 1885

Van Loon Marion L. of Hector, NY
Mc Coy Mrs. Cora J. of Hector, NY
    December 24, 1885
    Watkins, NY

Gaylord Perry of Moreland, NY
Ganung Effie of Moreland, NY
    December 23, 1885

Spencer Alvin T. of Reading, NY
Lott Hattie P. of Van Etten, NY
    December 30, 1885
    Van Etten, NY

Howell Martin J. of Tyrone, NY
Webb Eva L. dau of David of Sugar Hill, NY
    December 21, 1885
    Sugar Hill, NY

Coleman Charles of Auburn, NY
Shulman Ella dau of Henry of Watkins, NY
    January 19, 1886
    Watkins, NY

Horton Joseph 70 of Dundee (newspaper date)
Dickens Jemima 66 of Trumansburg, NY
    January 28, 1886

Tompkins Joseph of Weston, NY
Vaughn Adelia of Weston, NY
    January 27, 1886
    Weston, NY

Harrington Mason age 73 of Waverly, NY
Whiting Mrs. Maria age 71 of Watkins, NY
    February 6, 1886
    Watkins, NY

Crawford Frank of Urbana, NY
Kleckler Mary of Urbana, NY
    February __, 1886
    Hammondsport, NY

MARRIAGE NOTICES

Dunham Irvin of Burdett, NY Erway Lydia B. of Burdett, NY	January 18, 1886 Havana, NY
Henyon Charles of Burdett, NY Carrigan Orpha J. of Burdett, NY	February 24, 1886 Burdett, NY
Grant J. Clarence Carpenter Emma M. of Odessa, NY	March 3, 1886 Odessa, NY
Bailey Irvin of N. Hector, NY Holford Ella F. of Logan, NY	March 4, 1886 Logan, NY
Tuthill E. D. Sherman Susie of Buffalo, NY	March 3, 1886
Osborn Allen G. of Ovid, NY Williams Anna M. of Lodi, NY	March 14, 1886 N. Hector, NY
Van Doren Charles F. of Burdett, NY Dusenberry Emma E. of Burdett, NY	March 17, 1886 Burdett, NY
Strader Avill J. of Burdett, NY Bement Catherine of Reynoldsville, NY	March 20, 1886 Bennettsburg, NY
Sherman Orra of Watkins, NY Van Etten Emeline of Van Etten, NY	April 13, 1886 Van Etten, NY
Coughlin John of Reading Ctr., NY Lillis Ella of Watkins, NY	April 26, 1886
Cassidy Edward Taylor Harriet of Reynoldsville, NY	April 26, 1886
Brooks John of Cortland, NY Allen Della of Cortland, NY	April 28, 1886 Watkins, NY
Thompson George A. of Watkins, NY Squire Ettie L. of Watkins, NY	April 28, 1886 Watkins, NY
Moore James M. of Westchester, NY Read Emmarean daughter of David Branson	May 19, 1886
Howell I. Newton of Reading, NY Sebring Minnie E. of Tyrone, NY	June 9, 1886 Tyrone, NY
Conroy John of Watkins, NY Ryan Anna of Corning, NY	June 29, 1886
Roe Cary A. of Williamsport, Pa.	June 30, 1886

Coats Mamie L. dau of J. B. of Watkins, NY Watkins, NY

Harris Alonzo B. of Fairfield, NY July 13, 1886
Doty Rose of Waterburg, NY Mecklenburgh, NY

Darling Will H. of Hector, NY August 3, 1886
Milspaugh Augusta of Hector, NY Mecklenburgh, NY

Sherman Urban formerly of Watkins, NY August 6, 1886
Wood Josephine of Elmira, NY Elmira, NY

Johnston Irving L. of Watkins, NY August 26, 1886
Canfield Maggie of Watkins, NY Burdett, NY

Russell Rev. Benjamin of Watkins, NY August 30, 1886
Close Elsie E. dau of Peter of Farmington, Pa Elmira, NY

Churchill Leroy of Dundee, NY August 25, 1886
Preston Julia of Monterey, NY Monterey, NY

Rood George B. of Dix, NY September 1, 1886
Wedgewood Alice I. of Dix, NY Dix, NY
 at residence of William C. Wedgewood

Kellogg A. A. of Bennettsburg, NY September 15, 1886
Hollingsworth Mrs. H. M. of Bennettsburg, NY Watkins, NY
 at her brother's, Mr. C. D. Grant

Van Horn Will of Swartwood, NY September 15, 1886
Richards Alma dau of John S. of Cayuta, NY Cayuta, NY

Mead Silas M. son of G. J. of Burdett, NY September 22, 1886
Rolfe Cora A. dau of E. M. of Corning, NY Corning, NY

Love John W. of Reading, NY October 12, 1886
Harvey Kate of Reading, NY

Shriner Myron of Searsburg, NY October 13, 1886
Chapman Marinda of Montour, NY Watkins, NY

Halpin Robert October 14, 1886
Mathews Althea B. Watkins, NY

Davenport John M. of Etna, NY November 6, 1886
Corwin Myra of Hector, NY Watkins, NY

Mc Lafferty Alonzo of Watkins, NY November 3, 1886
Harding Minnie C. of Havana, NY Havana, NY
 daughter of Captain E. C.

MARRIAGE NOTICES

Bell John G. of Burdett, NY
Rudy Emily I. of Reynoldsville, NY
October 27, 1886
Watkins, NY

Miller Mark of Moreland, NY
Clark Shirley of Moreland, NY
December 4, 1886
Watkins, NY

Castner Seymour of Elmira, NY
Cranmer Eva S. of Troy, Pa.
December 15, 1886
Watkins, NY

Hall Walton of Lodi, NY (newspaper date)
Bramble Nancy C. of Lodi, NY
December 23, 1886
Lodi, NY

La Fever Wilmer of Beaver Dams, NY
Wickham Mary E. of Hector, NY
December 15, 1886
Hector, NY

Henry William J. of Ithaca, NY
Kingsley Luella G. dau of Monroe of Ithaca
January 1, 1887
Havana, NY

Parsels Orson M. of Nelson, Pa.
Wolcott Sarah of Bennettsburg, NY
December 29, 1886

Ferris John C. of Horseheads, NY
Havens Mary L. of Corning, NY
December 23, 1886
Corning, NY

Ferris George R. of Corning, NY
Tifft Myrtie S. of Corning, NY
December 25, 1886

Corwin George M. of Hector, NY
Strang Mary E. of Catherine, NY
January 4, 1887
Odessa, NY

Race Charles W. of Watkins, NY
Collins Nettie M. of Watkins, NY
January 1, 1887
Watkins, NY

Catlin Theodore of Elmira, NY
Mosher Libbie of Catlin, NY
December 25, 1886
Watkins, NY

Campbell Clarence of Lodi, NY
Blaine Amy of N. Hector, NY
December 30, 1886
N. Hector, NY

Robinson George of Lodi, NY
Swick Louisa E. of Hector, NY
January 12, 1887
Hector, NY

Vorhees A. of Hector, NY
Fairchilds Ada of Hector, NY
January 20, 1887
Hector, NY

Cahill James of Elmira, NY
Brady Kate of Watkins, NY
January 25, 1887
Watkins, NY

Littell David of Altay, NY
January 26, 1887

Faucett Anna dau of John of Altay, NY — Altay, NY

Gibbs Manly H. of Odessa, NY
Hall M. Ella of Odessa, NY
February 15, 1887
Odessa, NY

Price J. Britain of Watkins, NY
Owen Clara H. dau of Charles of Cayuta, NY
February 17, 1887
Watkins, NY

Snyder Ellsworth of N. Hector, NY
Doolittle Franc J. of N. Hector, NY
March 2, 1887
N. Hector, NY

Stilwell Arthur (newspaper date)
Stilwell Libbie
March 24, 1887
Searsburg, NY

Peck Martin of Altay, NY
Osborn Mary of Altay, NY
April 13, 1887
Keuka, NY

Davenport Ira of Bath, NY
Sharp K. L.
April 27, 1887
Kingston, NY

Cullen Michael of Reading Center, NY
Coughlin Mary of Reading Center, NY
April 19, 1887
Watkins, NY

Stanton Eugene of Cedar Rapids, Iowa
Hillerman Libbie of Reading Center, NY
April 27, 1887
Chicago, Illinois

Bailey George of Berkshire, NY
Hovey Maggie of Rock Stream, NY
April 3, 1887
Watkins, NY

West John E. of Watkins, NY
Hager Fanny of Watkins, NY
May 4, 1887
Dix, NY

Rusco Homer of Monterey, NY
Sharp Myrtle of Monterey, NY
May 22, 1887
Monterey, NY

Swarthout Charles B. of Watkins, NY
Purdy Edna M. of E. Waverly, NY
May 25, 1887
E. Waverly, NY

Swarthout Fred R. of Watkins, NY
Purdy Carrie E. of E. Waverly, NY
May 25, 1887
E. Waverly, NY

Morris Wallace H. son of Andrew
Heald Delle A. dau of R. B. of Belleville, NY
June 23, 1887
Bennettsburg, NY

Price Floyd L. of Altay, NY
Horton Lida of Tyrone, NY
July 2, 1887
Tyrone, NY

Soper I. M. of Elmira, NY
Purdy Mattie of Watkins, NY
July 14, 1887
Watkins, NY

MARRIAGE NOTICES

Coleman H. A. of Elmira, NY
Kellie Bessie of Watkins, NY

July 14, 1887
Watkins, NY

Hamilton Joseph of Watkins, NY
Conroy Mary dau of John of Watkins, NY

July 25, 1887
Watkins, NY

Clayton John F. of Philadelphia, Pa.
Wells Ella of Elmira, NY

August 1, 1887
Watkins, NY

Ellis Albert of Watkins, NY
Gould Mrs. Matilda

August 25, 1887
Reading, NY

Beardsley Lewis of Watkins, NY
Bartlett Mary Louisa dau of George of Watkins

September 1, 1887
Watkins, NY

Quin Edward R. of Junius, NY
Lundy Lezette M. of Junius, NY

September 21, 1887
Junius, NY

Sears Frank A. of Weston, NY
Heald Matie E. of Weston, NY

November 10, 1887
Weston, NY

Everts Wilbur W. of Hector, NY
House Matie E. of Hector, NY

November 23, 1887
Farmer Village, NY

Peck William J. of Dix, NY
Heist Hebe E. of Dix, NY

November 30, 1887
Townsend, NY

Edmister Romaine of Lisle, NY
Brooks Amanda of Watkins, NY

December 21, 1887
Watkins, NY

Jeffers H. C. of Mecklenburg, NY
Van Sickle Nellie of Havana, NY

January 6, 1888
Havana, NY

Davis Charles L.
Gilbert Delia daughter of George C.

January 18, 1888
Reading, NY

Decker Burr of Monterey, NY
Doane Laura B. dau of Samson of Monterey, NY

January 29, 1888
Monterey, NY

Taylor Jacob B. of N. Hector, NY
Brush Minnie of Susquehanna, Pa.

January 25, 1888

Thompson David of N. Branch, Michigan
Wasson Ella E. dau of James F. of Dix, NY

January 25, 1888
Dix, NY

Tracy B. A. of Logan, NY
Cogswell Grace of Cogswell, Michigan

January 17, 1888
Michigan

Tower Will J. of Watkins, NY

February 12, 1888

Slaght Maude of N. Hector, NY   N. Hector, NY

Houck George of Wellsboro, Pa.   February 29, 1888
Corey Mary   Wayne, NY

Stratton Edwin   February 29, 1888
Steel Eva   Wayne, NY

Daggett Seth O. of Wellsboro, Pa.   March 14, 1888
Brown Jessie E. dau of Simeon of Watkins, NY   Watkins, NY

Ball D. P.   March 8, 1888
Lamoreaux S.   Lodi, NY

Macreery William of Dix, NY   March 15, 1888
Maine Susie T. of Orange, NY   Monterey, NY

Hasen George N. of Danby, NY   March 14, 1888
Dunham Annis E. of Bennettsburg, NY   Bennettsburg, NY

Lott H. C. of Reading Center, NY   March 21, 1888
Edsall Emma J. of Havana, NY   Havana, NY

Gilmore William S. of N. Hector, NY   March 20, 1888
Budd Winifred dau of D. Purdy   N. Hector, NY

Strader Peter of Burdett, NY   March 25, 1888
Tabor Julia M. of Burdett, NY

Tompkins Joseph   March 25, 1888
Crawford Samantha   Weston, NY

Nye David S.   April 20, 1888
Baskin Fannie E. dau of C. J.   New York City

Kelly T.   April 20, 1888
Scott Julia Ann of Burdett, NY   Burdett, NY

Watkins Democrat December 4, 1878 - May 3, 1900

Ely William of Peach Orchard, NY   January 29, 1878
Bradner Della of Orange, NY   Hector, NY

Kelly Madison of Mecklenburgh, NY   January 22, 1878
Treman Ann of Mecklenburgh, NY   Mecklenburgh, NY

Starks Almiron   January 22, 1878

MARRIAGE NOTICES

Rumsey Phebe Jane   Cayuta, NY

Hendrick Jacob   January 22, 1878
Rumsey Adeline   Cayuta, NY

Phillips Walter P. of Starkey, NY   January 24, 1882
Rarrick Ella of Painted Post, NY   Painted Post, NY

Cratsley Howard of Monterey, NY   March 11, 1886
Thompson Ida of Monterey, NY   Monterey, NY

Carman John P. of Bradford, NY   February 14, 1889
Bailey Matie E. dau of John J. of Tyrone, NY   Tyrone, NY

Wager Benjamin   February 27, 1889
Turner Grace   Havana, NY

Wickham Burt of Watkins, NY   April 6, 1889
Brown Maud of Watkins, NY   Elmira, NY

Quick John of Geneseo, NY   July 3, 1889
Clawson Athelia of Havana, NY   Havana, NY

Smith Prof. Clinton Dewitt of Minnesota   June 16, 1892
Smith Anna Cora of Trumansburg, NY

Bennett M. L. Md.   January 4, 1894
Mc Carthy Minnie   Watkins, NY

Hamill Daniel Larose of Albany, NY   June 14, 1894
Pike Minnie H. dau of H. E.   Watkins, NY

Brady John of Watkins, NY   July 2, 1894
Downes Mrs. Bridget of Watkins, NY   Watkins, NY

Sullivan James S. of Watkins, NY   July 2, 1894
Sullivan Margaret of Corning, NY   Corning, NY

Mallerson Marcus of Rock Stream, NY   last week
Bump Mrs. Mary of Monterey, NY (newspaper date)   August 2, 1894
    both aged about 80 years

Bird Lark C. of Watkins, NY   July 24, 1894
Whalen Ella F. of Penn Yan, NY   Penn Yan, NY

De Camp Albert of S. Bradford, NY   November 10, 1894
Kelly Ettie of Monterey, NY

Bishop Waldo F. of Watkins, NY   November 21, 1894

Perry Emma B. of Watkins, NY   Watkins, NY

Tenny Oscar M. of Pulteney, NY
Barrett Josie of Wayne, NY   October 14, 1896

Owen Mark H. of Wedgewood, NY   January 10, 1900
Seymour Clara M. of Big Flats, NY

Barrett Albert C. of Hector, NY   January 24, 1900
Smith Bernice of Mecklenburgh, NY

Ector Walter of Sugar Hill, NY   April 25, 1900
Love Carrie dau of Robert of Sugar Hill, NY

Watkins Review March 28, 1869 - December 19, 1900

Mc Intyre W. H. of Pennsylvania   June 24, 1896
Hazard Minnie   Reading, NY

Smith William Wallbridge   June 17, 1896
Ellsworth Elinor E. daughter of Edwin   Montour Falls, NY

Harding Charles H.   June 22, 1896
Hulett Isabelle   Altay, NY

Mc Carthy Daniel   June 24, 1896
Fitzsimmons Lizzie   Watkins, NY

Merrill Hubert Minier   July 1, 1896
Ellas Fanny Luretta

Willis Ansel M. son of Charles T.   July 9, 1896
Darren Lydia daughter of J. M.   Weston, NY

Ashley Henry Delancy of Kansas City   August 1, 1896
Mann Caroline Schuyler of Watkins, NY   Watkins, NY

Swift Edward P. of Keuka College   August 26, 1896
Owens Tedie D.   Watkins, NY

Brooks Leon O. of Rochester, NY   August 27, 1896
Nelson Lelia C. of Eddytown, NY   Rochester, NY

Smith Floyd R. of Corning, NY   August 28, 1896
Abbott Grace A. of Lyons, NY   Watkins, NY

Taylor Robert of Union City, Indianna   September 17, 1896

MARRIAGE NOTICES 61

Berry Mrs. Rosanna of Watkins, NY | Watkins, NY

Benson Charles H. of Burdett, NY | September 30, 1896
Beardsley Margaret L. of Watkins, NY | Himrods, NY
(at her sister's Mrs. Elzy Jones)

Winslow Alfred F. of Roxbury, Mass. | October 14, 1896
Wright Margaret Adelle of Watkins, NY | Watkins, NY

Smith Fred R. son of Eugene of Reading, NY | November 18, 1896
Barrett Lizzie of Reading, NY | Reading, NY

Leffler William of Monterey, NY | November 26, 1896
Johnson Edna of Monterey, NY | Bradford, NY

Kent John of Post Creek, NY | November 27, 1896
Decker Miss | Orange, NY

Jessup E. Willis | December 24, 1896
Cook Cecile E. daughter of H. C. | Dundee, NY

Earing William of Altay, NY | December 23, 1896
Fenno Mina daughter of Camillus

Tuttle E. | December 24, 1896
Hamilton Maggie of Weston, NY | Weston, NY

Covert William A. of Ogdensburg, NY | December 24, 1896
Beebe Nellie dau of William of Watkins, NY | Watkins, NY

Comstock Frederick S. of New York City | December 23, 1896
Elliot Emily Ada dau of S. D. of Eddytown, NY | Eddytown, NY

Spicer William H. son of W. J. of Detroit, Mi | December 30, 1896
Hurd Hebe Louise dau of O. P. of Watkins, NY | Watkins, NY

Barrett Wellington R. | December 31, 1896
Goltry Cora A. daughter of Judson | Reading, NY

Searles Edward of Reynoldsville, NY | December 31, 1896
Stoughton Martha of Reynoldsville, NY | Reynoldsville, NY

Stoll Andrew of Watkins, NY | January 13, 1897
Miller Mrs. Ora of Hector, NY

Bomberage Fred of Watkins, NY | January 12, 1897
Casey Mary of Watkins, NY | Watkins, NY

Goltry Arthur N. of Reading, NY | January 27, 1897

Totman Anna May of Reading, NY

Dunn Frank A. of Penn Yan, NY
Storrs Cora dau of L. H. of Tyrone, NY

White Fred S. of Watkins, NY son of George
Coe Hattie of Elmira, NY

Huston W. Bunn
Eli Anna Helen

Manning Judson
Roat Inez

Perry Thomas of Tyrone, NY
Rolfe Emma of Dundee, NY

Ralston James of Monterey, NY
Henry Jessie of Monterey, NY

Leonard Ezra of Trumbulls Corners, NY
Palmer Sarah of Mecklenburgh, NY

Bramble Sanford of Hector, NY
Gould Emma of Lodi, NY

Woodward Alfred
Baldwin Marion P.

Foot Lester of Mecklenburgh, NY
Allwood Loretta of Waterburg, NY

Carley Jerome M. of N. Hector, NY
Kirtland Marie of Trumansburg, NY

Longwell Arnnah of Bradford, NY
Perry Cora K. dau of Thomas of Tyrone, NY

Underhill Charles B. of New York City
Cronk Edith of Montour Falls, NY

Mc Lachlin Archibald of Seneca Falls, NY
Pope Sarah Catlin

Philp Francis Roswell of Reading, NY
Sutton Laura Estelle of Reading, NY

Harris George
Losey Mrs. Mary

Reading, NY

February 11, 1897
Tyrone, NY

February 14, 1897
Elmira, NY

February 24, 1897
Peach Orchard, NY

March 29, 1897
Watkins, NY

March 25, 1897
Tyrone, NY

March 31, 1897
Monterey, NY

April 12, 1897
Mecklenburgh, NY

April 10, 1897
Trumansburg, NY

April 21, 1897
Watkins, NY

April 12, 1897
Lodi Center, NY

April 21, 1897

May 27, 1897
Tyrone, NY

June 2, 1897

June 17, 1897
New Haven, Conn.

June 16, 1897

June 16, 1897
Altay, NY

MARRIAGE NOTICES 63

Foster Rev. L. R. of Scranton, Pa.
Budd Clementine of Peach Orchard, NY

June 16, 1897
Peach Orchard, NY

Stocum Charles V.
Slater Mary E.

June 23, 1897
N. Hector, NY

Mc Clure Frank Henry of Lowville, NY
Henderson Madeline F.

June 30, 1897

Reynolds Daniel M. of Watkins, NY
Eggleston Mary A. of Watkins, NY

July 1, 1897
Watkins, NY

Littell C. D.
Shannahan Mame

June 3, 1897
Watkins, NY

Thompson William C.
King Grace D.

July 22, 1897
Willover Creek, NY

Hillerman William Newman of Reading, NY
Haring Lida Maria of Reading, NY

July 28, 1897
Reading, NY

Rogers William of Odessa, NY
Butters Grace of Cayuta, NY

August 4, 1897

Overhiser Clarence of Tyrone, NY
Cullen Mary of Rock Stream, NY

August 18, 1897

Jones Grant L. of Breesport, NY
Allen Bessie dau of d. L. of Beaver Dams, NY

August 31, 1897
Beaver Dams, NY

Holley Lev S. of Reading, NY
Smith Bessie L. dau of De Clerck of Reading

September 15, 1897
Reading, NY

Tucker Frank B. of Odessa, NY
Nobles Nellie M. of Trumbulls Corners, NY

September 29, 1897

Gulick Charles of Lodi, NY
Grant Maud of Mecklenburgh, NY

October 13, 1897
Mecklenburgh, NY

Littell Edwin C.
Kendall Edna dau of F. W.

October 13, 1897
Altay, NY

Norris Mr. of Barrington, NY
Clark Emma of Altay, NY

October 10, 1897
Altay, NY

Grimes Floyd of Reading, NY
Kaywood Williet of Reading, NY

October 6, 1897
Keuka, NY

Brown Prof. A. L.

October 9, 1897

Osborn Metta of Altay, NY   Keuka, NY

Scott James A. age 78 of Sugar Hill, NY   October 20, 1897
Wallace Mrs. Mary age 55 of Sugar Hill, NY   Sugar Hill, NY
    (widow of Henry)

Spriggs Charles of Willard, NY   November 17, 1897
Huff Luella Brokaw of N. Hector, NY

Smith Olin of Bennetsburg, NY   February 16, 1898
Bush Lizzie of Bennettsburg, NY   Bennettsburg, NY

Simmons Peter age 82 of Wayne, NY
Baker Mrs. Ardella age 39 (newspaper date)   February 23, 1898

Dutton James E. of Campbell, NY   March 5, 1898
Diven Ida B. of Moreland, NY   Campbell, NY

Grant Willard H. eldest son of Crandall   March 23, 1898
Canfield Alice youngest daughter of Mathew   Watkins, NY

Granger Edson of Farmer Village, NY   March 23, 1898
Lamoreaux Lina May dau of Henry of N. Hector   N. Hector, NY

Wood Christopher of Starkey, NY   March 30, 1898
Knapp Lena A. of Starkey, NY

Thomas Evan H. of Bradford, NY   April 2, 1898
Reed Daisy May of Wayne, NY   Dundee, NY

Archer Frank G. formerly of Burdett, NY   April 3, 1898
Mathews Addie Anna dau of G. W.
    (will reside in St. Joseph, Missouri)

Wallen Byron   May 8, 1898
Weidman Mrs. Georgia   Townsend, NY

Kinner George   June 1, 1898
Fenno Sarah E.   Altay, NY

Cramer John W. of Williamsport, Pa.   June 16, 1898
Smith Augusta M. of Watkins, NY   Watkins, NY

Auble Greely of Burdett, NY   October 12, 1898
Smith Ella of Burdett, NY   Bennettsburg, NY

Dickens Fred L. of Mecklenburg, NY   September 28, 1898
Kennedy Harriet of Cayuta, NY   Cayuta, NY

Sebring Frank of Tyrone, NY
Auble Norma E. P. of Tyrone, NY

November 23, 1898
Dundee, NY

Sharp Daniel S. of Rock Stream, NY
Huey Theresa W. of Rock Stream, NY

December 14, 1898
Rock Stream, NY

Bowers Seeley
Brown Bertha

November 30, 1898
Burdett, NY

Stevens Charles N. of Knoxville, Pa.
Shewman Cynthia of Beaver Dams, NY

December 14, 1898
Beaver Dams, NY

Waugh William S. of Watkins, NY
Stone Clara of Romulus, NY

December 28, 1898
Romulus, NY

Sharpe Clark M.
Fordham Harriet

December 28, 1898
Rock Stream, NY

Benjamin Howard
Ellison Mrs. Sarah

December 21, 1898
Tyrone, NY

Mathews Samuel
Wickham Martha of Burdett, NY

December 21, 1898
Mecklenburgh, NY

Teetsel Samuel on Montour, NY
Beardsley Emma of Montour, NY

December 26, 1898
Montour, NY

Horton Wilbur Asbury
Todd Mary

March 16, 1899
Mecklenburgh, NY

Personius George Austin of Elmira, NY
Roloson Mary of Dix, NY

March 8, 1899
Millport, NY

Palmer Simeon C. of Mecklenburg, NY
Parker Sara B. of Burdett, NY

March 22, 1899
Montour Falls, NY

Niven Albert
Carlson Maggie

March 23, 1899
Wayne, NY

Smith William of Altay, NY
Love Sarah of Altay, NY

May 24, 1899
Altay, NY

Castner George of Altay, NY
Jones Lottie of Altay, NY

May 24, 1899
Altay, NY

Pierce Robert M. of Ithaca, NY
Berthoff Jessie E. of Watkins, NY

May 12, 1899
Montour Falls, NY

Decker Louis

May 14, 1899

Mc kinley Lizzie — Odessa, NY

Mulligan George
Usher Abbie daughter of Bela
May 17, 1899
Reynoldsville, NY

Spence Theodore of Starkey, NY
Penny Dortha D. dau of Jerome of Reading, NY
June 14, 1899
Reading, NY

Inscho Cleveland of Elmira, NY
Hall Bertha of Watkins, NY
June 15, 1899
Watkins, NY

Fero Emmett C. of Wedgewood, NY
Pangborn Claudia
August 9, 1899
Montour Falls, NY

Orr Guy
Knight Ann S.
September 11, 1899
Watkins, NY

Twiss Hiram V. of Watkins, NY
Wilbur Lucy E. of Trumansburg, NY
September 19, 1899
Trumansburg, NY

Gilbert Morris of Watkins, NY
Auble Jessie May of Burdett, NY
October 11, 1899
Burdett, NY

Love Ira B.
Van Duzer Mary E.
November 1, 1899
Pine Grove, NY

Berry George
Fordham Mary
January 10, 1900
Watkins, NY

Predmore Waldiee
Wilcox Libbie daughter of William D.
January 3, 1900
Logan, NY

Goodrich Charles of Ithaca, NY
Miller Alice of N. Hector, NY
January 18, 1900
N. Hector, NY

Price Randall
Peck Nina
January 17, 1900
Altay, NY

Barrett Albert C.
Smith Bernice daughter of Mrs. Mary E.
January 24, 1900
Mecklenburgh, NY

Wakley George
Duvall Jennie
January 30, 1900
Beaver Dams, NY

Miller Charles of Bradford, NY
Smith Rena of Ferenbaugh
January 27, 1900
Beaver Dams, NY

West Edd of Crosby, NY
Waugh Minnie
January 24, 1900
Monterey, NY

MARRIAGE NOTICES

Wickham M. L. of Hector, NY
Hopkins Mrs. Anna of Cortland, NY
February 7, 1900
Watkins, NY

Hurley Fred W. of Watkins, NY
Dart Lottie dau of A. B. of Mecklenburgh, NY
June 6, 1900
Mecklenburgh, NY

Maloney John H. of Watkins, NY
Boothroyd Mildred A. of Mumford, NY
June 6, 1900
Caledonia, NY

Davidson George W. of Addison, NY
Hendricks Hattie Bell of Crystal Springs, NY
June 6, 1900
Crystal Springs, NY

Carr Claude L. of Knoxville, Pa.
Wickham Harriet A. of Hector, NY
June 6, 1900
Hector, NY

Chase Orville G. of Geneva, NY
Stothoff Helen Bulkely of Burdett, NY
June 7, 1900
Watkins, NY

Stilwell Mervin J. of Reynoldsville, NY
Labar Myrtle D. of Bennettsburg, NY
June 6, 1900
Bennettsburg, NY

Miles Darwin of Barrington, NY
Foster Mrs. Lola of Wheeler, NY
July 29, 1900
Wayne, NY

Lindsey Judd
Quance Jennie
August 1, 1900
Watkins, NY

Collins Patrick of Elmira, NY
Nagle Elizabeth dau of John of Montour, NY
August 29, 1900
Watkins, NY

Austin Samuel
Yauger Lottie of Bradford, NY
November 7, 1900
Bradford, NY

Steiner John J. of Elmira, NY
Cronkite Jennie of Millport, NY
November 11, 1900
Millport, NY

Miller James R.
Merchant Martha
November 7, 1900
Beaver Dams, NY

Washburn Leon of Alpine, NY
Charles Addie M. of Odessa, NY
December 5, 1900
Odessa, NY

Koch George of Glenora, NY
Nivison Edna of Hector, NY
December 1, 1900
Burdett, NY

Wood Jerome of Penn Yan, NY
Davenport Lena of Monterey, NY
November 28, 1900
Avoca, NY

Nichols Roswell of New York City
December 20, 1900

Pellett Margaret dau of William of Watkins   Watkins, NY

Stevenson Dr. George of Buffalo, NY   December 26, 1900
Sunderlin Louise of Dundee, NY   Dundee, NY

Baldwin David of Washington D. C.   December 12, 1900
Morris Florence M. dau of A. J. of Hector   Hector, NY

Mewkill Henry of Poughkeepsie, NY   December 26, 1900
Van Deusen Lena of Poughkeepsie, NY   Poughkeepsie, NY
    daughter of Mrs. George Parker of Watkins, NY

Price Marvin J.   December 19, 1900
Gleason Eva J. of Grove Springs, NY   Grove Springs, NY

Part II

Death Notices

Havana Journal April 6, 1853 - April 4, 1857

Leonard Henry C. formerly of Havana, NY in Elmira, NY April 14, 1853

Maxwell William 21 of Havana, NY May 26, 1853

Mackenzie John shot by Sarah Flood in Savannah, NY June 4, 1853

Wood John Milton 30 suicide of Lima, NY June 5, 1853

Varey Nathan and son Charles 22 drowned at Veteran, NY June 15, 1853

Phelps John 78 of Canandaigua, NY no date (date of newspaper June 18, 1853)

Hulett Sophia 4y in Horseheads, NY (date of Newspaper June 18, 1853)

Ransom Maria Adelaide, daughter of J. L. and Rebecca Ransom June 19, 1853

Jackson Eliza 48 wife of George W. June 25, 1853

Merrill John C. (date of Newspaper July 9, 1853) Leaves wife and 2 children

Mallory Eliza Vinton in 39th year wife of Peter August 1, 1853

Hibbard Warren 5m son of George D. and Sarah Jane of Havana, NY August 3, 1853

Miller Emily Isabella 2y daughter of Dr. C. and Mary August 3, 1853

Winton Asa I. in NY State Asylum August 25, 1853

Stout Caroline in 20th year wife of Joseph August 25, 1853

Hyatt Abram August 25, 1853. Married 1829 in Covert, NY Mary **Smith**, daughter of General Isaiah Smith

Ayers Mary 3y 4m 14d daughter of Andrus September 3, 1853

Beebe Delia 7y 9m 5d daughter of Edward and Lucinda in Moreland, NY September 1, 1853

Jackson George W. near 3y son of H. W. September 16, 1853

Stevens Helen V. near 2y daughter of Samuel September 20, 1853

Smith Mary J. in 61st year wife of Caleb in Hector, NY (newspaper date October 15, 1853)

Wheeler Ephraim in 7th year, October 12, 1853

Frost Malinda 42 wife of Col E. C. Frost in Catherine, NY October 15, 1853

Whippy George 58 of Havana, NY November 8, 1853

Prince Rebecca 73y 7m relict of late William H. at Johnson Settlement, NY November 16, 1853

Prince Ruth Charlotte 36y 7m at same place.

Tyler Amelia M. 13y 12d daughter of Hiram and Ruth Ann (**Goff**) Tyler at Dresden, NY January 24, 1854

Clawson Garret suicide at Peach Orchard, NY February 27, 1854. Accused of forgery. Leaves wife and 6 children.

Lawrence Elizabeth in 74th year widow of Samuel March 8, 1854

Jackson Mary D. in 40th year, wife of William T. March 12, 1854

Clark Sarah 4y 9m 18d daughter of John and Laura J. of Moreland, NY March 23, 1854

Sherwood Elizabeth in 99th year at son-in-law's Jonathan **Frost** of Catherine, NY March 29, 1854

Fanton Sherman Sterling in 15th year son of Thomas and Betsey (**Sherman**) Fanton of Catherine, NY April 7, 1854

Brewer Arabella C. age 12y 1m 20d daughter of S. T. and Clarissa April 10, 1854

Hamblin Frederick 10m 10d son of A. B. and Mary J. formerly of Havana, NY in Auburn, NY May 10, 1854

Dibble Sedate age 14 crushed by timbers in lock, May 28, 1854

Finch John age 46 June 10, 1854

Baxter William age 42 in Milo, NY June 17, 1854

Crawford Harriet 30, wife of Marcus and daughter of George **Jackson** June 8, 1854

DEATH NOTICES

Curtis Charles 57 in Catherine, NY June 22, 1854

Gibbs Charles A. at La Porte, Indianna June 11, 1854 followed by the death of his wife, Elizabeth R. Gibbs, daughter of Upton **Dorsey** of Havana, NY

Wood Caroline wife of A. Wood at Herman, Missouri, formerly of Havana, NY and daughter of James **Pine** on July 15, 1854

Danihu Patrick 27 at Havana, NY August 7, 1854

Miller Cyrus 8m son of Cyrus at Havana, NY August 8, 1854

Durkee Wilmina 14 daughter of John T. in Dix, NY August 18, 1854

Quigly John in 44th year at Havana, NY August 21, 1854

Noble Maria 36 wife of Chauncey H. August 27, 1854

Hibbard Alice in 75th year at Havana, NY September 11, 1854

Baxter Jessie in 67th year in Mentz, NY September 10, 1854

Tracy Sarah A. in 30th year wife of Daniel September 17, 1854

Tracy Polly in 75th year widow of Daniel at Oxford, NY September 22, 1854

Smith John N. in 56th year of Hector, NY September 28, 1854

Lovell Ann 3y dau of William at Millport, NY October 17, 1854

Teats Lawrence abt 35 at Havana, NY October 28, 1854. Leaves wife and 2 children

Hyatt Ira T. 17 son of A. in Catlin, NY December 4, 1854

Hallett Mrs. Almira 20 in Havana, NY January 7, 1855

Minard Joel 22 on January 20, 1855, William 26 on January 25, 1855 and Michael 17 on January 31, 1855 sons of Joseph near Monterey, NY

Goodrich Mrs. Amelia Jones wife of Rev. Charles formerly of Havana, NY at residence of son-in-law Charles G. **Judd** January 11, 1855

Bussey Harriet Ann 15 at Beaver Damsn NY February 22, 1855

Crickmore John 78 at Barrington, NY March 27, 1855

Look Romeo 2y son of John B. drowned June 14, 1855

Hamilton Daniel 25 at Havana, NY June 21, 1855

Merchant Arlo in 52nd year formerly of Catherine, NY in Winnebago, Ill. June 28, 1855

Ganung John son of J. G. of Dix, NY in Elmira, NY June 17, 1855

Owen Lucy Ann 17 daughter of Judge A. in Catlin, NY July 25, 1855

Barnes John 31 in Havana, NY July 30, 1855

Sanford Susan Sophia 29 in Ashland, Michigan July 18, 1855, sister of Rev. M. **Huggins** of Schuyler Co.

Backman Mrs. Euphemia 70 in Havana, NY August 9, 1855

Holton Enock 7y only son of D. C. in Havana, NY August 10, 1855

Barrows Margaret Anna 10m daughter of John in Havana, NY August 6, 1855

Massiker John formerly of Havana, NY in Colony, Iowa February 27, 1855

Chapin Susan in 23rd year in Havana, NY September 7, 1855

Huston James M. in 60th year at Dix, NY September 9, 1855

Bailey Frank O. 1y 16d son of Lewis and Levina of Dix, NY September 25, 1855

Beebe John in 27th year at Havana, NY September 9, 1855

Tracy Lorenzo L. 44 in Dix, NY October 23, 1855

Mills Thomas 65 formerly of Havana, NY in Leavenworth, Kansas October 18, 1855

German Mrs. Annis 75 at Havana, NY October 30, 1855

Bennett Atilda Geraldine in 23rd year October 27, 1855

Holton David C. 35 in Havana, NY December 23, 1855

Kingwell Elizabeth 3y daughter of Mr. & Mrs. J. M. in Havana, NY January 19, 1856

Cass Moses 67 in Watkins, NY February 19, 1856

Catlin Cornelia 26 daughter of Captain P. of Odessa, NY March 13, 1856

Hastings Horace L. 3m 24d son of Lyman H. and Mary F. in Havana, NY March 13, 1856

Fraser Anna M. 21 wife of J. in Elmira, NY April 3, 1856

Wakeman William W. 23 in Millport, NY April 5, 1856

Bryant William H. H. 21 in Havana, NY April 22, 1856

Williams Harriet 64 in Hanava, NY April 30, 1856

Davis Justis D. 67 in Catherine, NY April 5, 1856

Hoffman Ogden 63 in New York City May 8, 1856

Wolverton Erva Lorraine 2y in Dix, NY April 29, 1856

Mapes Catherine 62 in Havana, NY April 17, 1856

Brodrick Anthony 56 in Havana, NY April 26, 1856

Mason George W. of Elmira, NY at sister's in E. Troy, Wis. June 3, 1856

Campbell Mary Louisa 7y 10m 11d daughter of Adam G. and Ursala in Havana, NY June 6, 1856

Owens Caroline daughter of Alanson and Martha in Dix, NY July 9, 1856

Lee Carrie Ann 3y 9m 15d daughter of M. L. in Fulton, NY July 27, 1856

Noble Silas 62 in Moreland, NY July 30, 1856

Beebe Lydia 72 in Catherine, NY September 23, 1856

Fleming Mary 39 daughter of Samuel and Phebe in Adrian, NY September 4, 1856

Hastings Mary F. 28y 9m wife of Lyman H. in Havana, NY September 24, 1856

Wisner Alfred 4y 1m 28d son of Alfred and Susan Jane (**Lee**) Wisner in Havana, NY November 16, 1856

Mapes William about 63 in Havana, NY November 29, 1856

Dunn Captain William 54 in Elmira, NY December 8, 1856

Olmstead Catherine wife of Mathew D. in Shabbins Grove, Illinois January 8, 1857. Leaves 5 children

Gregory Josiah 85 in Altay, NY February 2, 1857

Harris Charles Herbert 4m son of Charles and Elvenah in Havana, NY February 14, 1857

Tracy Albert H. 17y 9m 13d in Havana, NY February 16, 1857

Beardsley Clarina in 72nd year at Catherine, NY February 11, 1857

Hitchcock Joseph age 87 formerly of Dix, NY near Cooper's Plain, NY March 24, 1857

Corwin Lucy Ann 27d daughter of George and Louisa M. in Havana, NY March 31, 1857

Lord Sarah Marie wife of Joseph W. in Orange, NY November 14, 1863

Corwin Isaac 27 at brother's George in Havana, NY November 12, 1863

Peck James an early settler in Reading, NY November 28, 1863

Brown Cornelia M. wife of Frank B. in Corning, NY December 2, 1863

Noble Clara Bell 3y daughter of Chauncey and Jane in Moreland, NY November 24, 1863

Chamberlain Curtis J. 27y 2m at Hospital in Nashville, Tenn. Co. A 141 Reg. NY Vol. (date of nespaper December 19, 1863)

Royce Harvey 19 son of Amos in Townsend, NY December 7, 1863

Beardsley Betsey 95y 15d in Havana, NY April 11, 1887

Watkins Express January 5, 1871 - April 30, 1900

Hager Mary Heath 30 wife of Orlando December 30, 1870

Brown Fred 21 in Catlin, NY January 17, 1871

Skellenger Nathan 39 in Havana, NY January 18, 1871

Greeno Elizabeth 56 in Millport, NY January 17, 1871

Welding James E. 64 in N. Hector, NY January 15, 1871

Hurley Cynthia C. 3y 6m dau of Daniel B. and Hannah in Dresden, NY February 16, 1871

Wood Susan E. 52 widow of Gen. W. B. of Auburn, NY in Burdett, NY February 28, 1871

Hurd Bertie 3 in Branchport, NY March 28, 1871 and Freddie Hurd age 5, April 16, 1871 only children of William T. and Phebe A.

DEATH NOTICES

Saylor Libbie in 31st year wife of Henry C. in Moreland, NY April 16, 1871

Gates Ida Lahala 9y 8m daughter of G. F. and E. L. in Watkins, NY June 4, 1871

Skiff Lottie in 35th year wife of Myron at Tyrone, NY July 2, 1871

Price Ida 2y 11m daughter of William H. and Sarah in Altay, NY September 14, 1871

Wickham Martha 72 widow of late George C. in Hector, NY September 21, 1871

Hager Carrie Maud 7m daughter of Peter and Hattie E. in Watkins, NY August 31, 1871

Marvin Rev. Ezra 65y 8m 12d in Olean, NY October 1, 1871

Hunt William R. 47y 2m formerly of Starkey, NY in Warren, Illinois August 27, 1871

Swezey John W. 67 formerly of Watkins, NY at Mt. Hope, NY October 12, 1871

Bliss Angeline M. 72 in Watkins, NY October 27, 1871

King E. H. 36 in Watkins, NY November 22, 1871

Crouch Silas Dewitt 23 at Altay, NY October 28, 1871

Forrester Joel R. 33 at Reading, NY December 11, 1871

Loder Frances 34 wife of Phillip R. in Watkins, NY December 12, 1871

Hurd Abigail B. 68 in Rock Stream, NY November 1, 1871

Tomar Sarah 84 in Pulteney, NY April 5, 1872

Mills Olive 80 wife of Teal in Barrington, NY April 2, 1872

Eddy Esther in 28th year wife of Croel in Townsend, NY at Father's, John W. **Buck** April 14, 1872

Seneare John 96 in Ellicottville, NY April 17, 1872

Pratt Mrs. Daniel 31 daughter of late Rev. **Murdock** of Elmira, NY in Elmira April 21, 1872

La Fever Chester L. 3m son of H. L. and Libbie of Reading, NY April 18, 1872

Underwood Euphemia 72 in Groton, NY April 30, 1872

Haight Ambrose 87 fomerly of Jerusalem, NY at son Lewis's in Prattsburg, NY May 20, 1872

Stevens Millie wife of Theron AND daughter of George **Adriance** at Peach Orchard, NY June 5, 1872

Russell Leroy 22 at Moreland, NY June 17, 1872

Perham Charles 21 drowned at Wellsburg, NY June 25, 1872

Bodle daughter of Charles 11y of Mecklenburgh, NY June 29, 1872

Baldwin Vine 91 at Baldwin, NY June 21, 1872. Born 1782 in Sheshequin, Pa. Family from Conn.

Millspaugh Samuel Seward in 60th year of Townsend, NY at Corning, NY July 22, 1872

Woodward Florence Eugenia 2y 6m daughter of William E. and Sarah E. of Big Flats, NY July 20, 1872

Scobey George 11m 2d son of Benjamin W. and Mary H. of Watkins, NY July 22, 1872

Hunyan Emma 19 wife of Albert at Bennettsburg, NY August 4, 1872

Crandall William 19 of Watkins, NY August 9, 1872

Mc Carthy Laura wife of John of Candor, NY and daughter of Joseph **Frost** August 14, 1872. Born Catherine, NY 1804. Leaves husband, 1 son J. W. and son-in-law Jerome **Thompson**.

Gifford William suicide at Varick, NY August 24, 1872

Woodward Charles 10m son of William E. and Sarah of Watkins, NY August 30, 1872

Payne C. Adella 23y and 24d wife of Emmett C. and daughter of Henry M. and Mary F. **Hillerman** at Watkins, NY August 24, 1872

Sproul Thomas 50y 4m 5d in Tyrone, NY September 6, 1872. Leaves widow and 2 children.

Arnold Clarence 2y 2m son of James H. and Harriet E. in Mecklenburgh, NY August 17, 1872

Minier Will H. 20y 4m son of Hon. T. L. at Havana, NY August 16, 1872

Haring Lewis H. 5w 4d son of J. I. and Carrie in Watkins, NY September 19, 1872

Stanton Webster J. 26 in Watkins, NY September 20, 1872

DEATH NOTICES

Sproul Frank 18y 11m 11d in Tyrone, NY September 27, 1872

Hager Freegift 66 in Logan, NY October 15, 1872

Sebring Emily R. 18y 11m 16d at Tyrone, NY October 21, 1872

Marshall Jefferson 49 at Townsend, NY October 7, 1872

Evans Elizabeth Doty 87 at Binghamton, NY November 10, 1872

Love Mrs. Jane 75y 1m 7d at Pine Grove, NY November 5, 1872

Cook Thankful P. 59 wife of Ebert W. at Havana, NY November 21, 1872. Buried Springville, NY

Smith William E. 35y 5m 23d son of late Hiram, brother of David L. Smith at Watkins, NY November 26, 1872. Married 2 years.

Carmichael James at Mecklenburgh, NY November 29, 1872

Moore Elizabeth 78 at Jerusalem, NY December 15, 1872 widow of William who died 1867. Sister of Dr. William **Cornwell**. Born and married in Delaware Co.

Williams Esther 64y 9m 2d at Tyrone, NY December 25, 1872

Heald Fletcher 51 at Tyrone, NY December 25, 1872

Brown Squire 87 at Millport, NY December 19, 1872

Reed Truman 82y 7m at Italy, NY December 22, 1872

Loomis Mrs. Samuel at Jacksonville, NY December 15, 1872. Leaves husband and son George W. Loomis

Pierson Emily 20y 5m 7d wife of Warren A. and daughter of Richard W. **Shriner** at Hector, NY December 21, 1872

Berry Mrs. John D. 48 wife of Sargeant at Watkins, NY December 17, 1872. Leaves husband and son. Buried Elmira, NY

Hewett Dr. Judson 72 in Watkins, NY December 18, 1872. Born November 25, 1800 in Waterbury, Vermont. Wife died December 18, 1863. 5 children, Mrs. Fred **Davis** Jr., widow of Josiah **Davis**, Mrs. Captain **Davis** of Erie, Pa. Mrs. Harvey **Walter** of Watkins and son Judson, unmarried

Washburn Elizabeth 67y 10m wife of Rev. Daniel and daughter of John **Diven** at Watkins, NY December 14, 1872. Married April 1823.

Smith Orville son of late Chauncey of Hector, NY at Millport, NY December 20,

1872

Case Mary Emeline daughter of Joseph at Burdett, NY December 25, 1872

Woodward Horatio in 65th year at Burdett, NY December 20, 1872

Newton Squire 73 in Elmira, NY January 15, 1873

Ellsworth Elizabeth at Penn Yan, NY January 17, 1873. Born August 8, 1803 in Flanders, NJ youngest of 10 children to Dr. Robert R. **Henry** a surgeon in Revolutionary War and Mary **Hillard** of Danbury, Conn. Married September 7, 1822 Abraham P. **Vosburg.** Married (2) March 17, 1834 Samuel Stewart Ellsworth who died January 4, 1863 in 73rd year. 3 children, Mary Elizabeth died August 17, 1837, Henry died infancy and Samuel born 1839.

Wheeler Everal H. 65 wife of Thomas in Watkins, NY January 21, 1873. Born September 5, 1807, married February 27, 1837 in Dresden, NY. 3 daughters and 1 son. 1 died in Horseheads, NY and 1 in Oregon. Buried in Glenwood cem.

Bennett Henry M. abt 50 in Painted Post, NY January 10, 1873

Conderman Jacob 79 in Fremont, NY January 22, 1873

Partridge Erastus at Seneca Falls, NY January 20, 1873

Whiting Mary 93 in Binghamton, NY January 30, 1873

Denning Mary Jane 20y 11m 16d in Watkins, NY January 23, 1873

Bennett Bella Louisa 8m dau of Dr. M. L. in Watkins, NY March 1, 1873

Fenton John W. in 31st year at Hector, NY March 7, 1873

Kellogg Hattie A. wife of Charles and daughter of Hiram **Fausett** of Hector, NY in Palo, Michigan March 6, 1873

Mc Quillan Peter abt 25 in Watkins, NY March 16, 1873

Ewing James in 67th year at Tyrone, NY March 17, 1873

Brien Ann in 62nd year wife of William at Tyrone, NY February 24, 1873 and eldest daughter Mary Jane 42 died February 14, 1873

Hammond Ransom R. 48y 13d at Reading, NY April 2, 1873

Allen Mary L. 43y 2m 25d wife of Ephraim at Perry City, NY March 28, 1873

Williams Agnes daughter of Solomon funeral in Watkins, NY March 25, 1873

DEATH NOTICES

Magee John son of John in Watkins April 25, 1873. Brother G. J. Magee and sister Mrs. S. S. **Ellsworth** of Penn Yan, NY

Diven William 84 at Reading, NY April 27, 1873. Born 1789 in Perry Co. Pa.

Hicks Hattie K. in 3rd year at Watkins, NY April 26, 1873

Olmstead Clarissa in 70th year at Pine Grove, NY April 19, 1873

Terryberry Thomas age 103 in Dix, NY March 28, 1873 and wife age 93 died May 2, 1873

Griffith Stephen 35 at Madison, Ohio May 5, 1873. Born Livingston Co. Michigan lived mostly in Schuyler Co. Wife was daughter of late Alvin C. **Hause**. Buried Tyrone, NY

Kies Henry 63 in Watkins, NY May 7, 1873

Nichols Amasa 79 in Reading, NY May 4, 1873

Brunson Alson in 67th year at Watkins, NY May 27, 1873

Heist Mary wife of Dr. William at Townsend, NY May 23, 1873

Houghtaling John abt 60 at Monterey, NY June 10, 1873

Green Mrs. Mary 55 at Alfred, NY June 8, 1873

Calkins Mrs. Betsey 80 at Painted Post, NY June 24, 1873

Slaughter Jonathan 85 at Painted Post, NY June 24, 1873. Served in War of 1812

Howell Robert R. 30y this May 3 at Mother-in-law's Mrs. Robert **Burge** in Burdett, NY June 24, 1873

Frost Charles killed by train in Elmira, NY July 5, 1873

Smith Isaac 75y 11m at Reading, NY June 20, 1873

Harmon Julia 56 in Watkins, NY July 8, 1873

Thomas E. H. suicide at Moreland, NY July 12, 1873

Kirkendall Austin 32 formerly of Burdett, NY at Dubuque, Iowa July 14, 1873

Card Rev. H. S. 55 at Watkins, NY July 23, 1873. Born January 4, 1816 in Nelson, NY. Leaves wife, son and daughter

Havens John 57 formerly of Watkins, NY at Elmira, NY July 16, 1873. Son of

Hiram **Raymond** of Havana, NY

Boardman Russell in Tyrone, NY July 25, 1873. Brother Douglas

Mc Carthy Sarah L. 42y 2m 21d at Reading, NY August 18, 1873

Van Vechten Dr. Herman 77 in Havana, NY August 30, 1873

Watkins Walterman in 73rd year at son-in-law's Daniel **Tracy** in Havana, NY September 4, 1873

Parks Adelia 16y 9m at Sugar Hill, NY September 13, 1873

Squires Selah 93 at son's Theodore in N. Hector, NY September 27, 1873. Wife died 1848, buried Farmerville, NY

Wentz Justis 77 formerly of Dix, NY in Union, NY October 4, 1873, son of Rev. W. S. Wentz of Mecklenburgh, NY

Smith Nettie 27 at brother-in-law's Benjamin **Robbins** in Watkins, NY October 4, 1873

Miller Harvey of Danby, NY brother of late Dr. Miller and Sherman at Moreland, NY October 1, 1873

Berry Daniel 70 at son-in-law's Jonathan **Page** in Watkins, NY October 25, 1873

Kendall Silas 74 of Altay in Tyrone, NY November 5, 1873

Dyer John 94 at Orange, NY October 17, 1873. Born 1789 in Newport, Rhode Island

Campbell Adam G. 58 at Havana, NY October 28, 1873, son of Robert who died 5 yrs ago. Born 1815 in Ireland and came to US age 14. Married 1842 Ursala **Catlin** of Odessa, NY daughter of Phineas. Wife died 1864 leaving 3 daughters and 2 sons. Married (2) 1868 Jane G. **Lawrence** daughter of Samuel

Hager Frank M. 22 at Reynoldsville, NY October 31, 1873

Magee Jane A. 36 at sister's Mrs. Daniel **Beach** in Watkins, NY October 29, 1873

Babcock Job 90y 7m 6d at Barrington, NY October 19, 1873

Gage Mrs. Amos 100y 6m at Little Falls, NY October 10, 1873. Born near Cherry Valley, NY

Woodruff Reuben suicide in Tioga Co. Pa. September 23, 1873

Hoare Mitchell 26y 3m 9d at Watkins, NY November 6, 1873. Born England

DEATH NOTICES

Arnot John 80 in Elmira, NY November 17, 1873. Born September 25, 1793 in Donn, Scotland. Married 1824 Harriet **Tuttle** daughter of Stephen.

Leary Joseph abt 14 son of Cornelius in Watkins, NY November 5, 1873

Goldsmith Katie Downs 30 in Mecklenburgh, NY November 25, 1873. Buried in Monticello, NY

Parks Mary Jane 20y 1m 22d at Sugar Hill, NY November 25, 1873

Skinner Grace 7m daughter of Homer D. and Frank at Watkins, NY November 29, 1873

Barto Gen. Henry D. 50 son of H. D. at Trumansburg, NY December 15, 1873. Leaves wife and 4 sons

Mc Clure Thomas 77 at Havana, NY December 7, 1873

Vaughn Johnson 47y 7m 8d at Montour, NY December 13, 1873

Howard Joseph 81y 3m at Reading, NY December 23, 1873

Doane Ezekiel P. 49 in Elmira, NY January 13, 1874

Estelle William 22y 6m 26d in Watkins, NY January 16, 1874

Haight Silas died January 25, 1874. Born September 11, 1812 in Stanford, NY. Married (1) Fanny **Welply** daughter of Rev. Samuel, (2) Hester Ann **Maxwell** daughter of Thomas and (3) Joanna **Calkins**. 3 children, Maxwell, Mrs. H. H. **Purdy** and Rida.

Sage Alzada wife of J. L. of Mitchellville, Iowa and daughter of Samuel **Ross** in Reading, NY January 27, 1874

Mack Joseph L. 24 of Watkins, NY February 15, 1874. Born January 23, 1850 in Ulysses, NY

Sunderlin J. Lewis 34y 9m 15d son of D. J. in Barrington, NY February 13, 1874

Nichols Daniel funeral February 4, 1874, buried Glenwood cem.

Brown Dr. Edmund 75 in Burdett, NY February 17, 1874

Van Allen Sophia L. (**Downer**) 42 wife of John J. in Watkins, NY February 15, 1874

Millage Mrs. 84 Mother of Merritt **Wheeler** in Perry City, NY February 15, 1874. Married twice, several children unknown where

Covert Abraham 65y 1m 11d at Sugar Hill, NY February 18, 1874

Hunter Deborah 79y 9m 27d at Wayne, NY February 28, 1874

Hurd Sophia 94 Mother of Mrs. Ezra White in Tyre, NY February 27, 1874

Smith Dr. Norman 85 in Elmira, NY March 7, 1874

Graham Henry 74 in Seneca Falls, NY March 3, 1874

Gardner Bessie 18 suicide in Owego, NY March 16, 1874

Waugh Lucinda 14y 3m at Sugar Hill, NY March 25, 1874

Crawford Judge John in 79th year at Moreland, NY April 12, 1874. Born 1796 in Wallkill NY. Married 1820 Mary Catlin daughter of Judge Phineas, 12 children

Ferris Nathan 78y 11m 29d at Weston, NY April 21, 1874, native of Dutchess Co.

Hallock Able 55 suicide in Crystal Springs, NY April 2, 1874

Fero John H. 40y 4m in Dix, NY April 17, 1874. Leaves wife and 3 children

Wedgewood James 81 in Dix, NY April 17, 1874. Born Burslem, Staffordshire, England. Leaves wife, 2 sons and 3 daughters

Hager Abigail in 81st year widow of Peter and sister of Rev. Adams Platt in Watkins, NY April 19, 1874. Buried Peach Orchard

Slaght Mrs. John in Watkins, NY April 23, 1874

Priest Benjamin in 76th year in Orange, NY April 24, 1874. Wife died 2 months ago.

Eldred Joseph of Hector, NY at dau in Covert, NY May 14, 1874

Holden Heman 77y 3m at daughter's Mrs. William Frost in Reading, NY May 18, 1874. Born Lansing, NY and buried Genoa, NY

Hinman Guy C. at Catherine, NY June 8, 1874

Lewis Dr. J. De Los of Trumansburg, NY May 12, 1874

Ellison Edward 11y 11m in Tyrone, NY May 15, 1874

Butler William in 81st year at Big Flats, NY June 13, 1874

Spaulding Tennie 51 wife of Major E. C. at Mecklenburgh, NY June 12, 1874

Chapman Louisa 5y 9m 15d daughter of David and Annette in Altay, NY June 19, 1874

DEATH NOTICES

Bennett Emma Annette 35 wife of Charles H. in Lemars, Iowa. Formerly Miss **Wilcox** of Dundee, NY

Slosson Barzilla in 64th year at Geneva, NY June 27, 1874

Love Mary Jane 43y 6m 15d wife of Joseph in Reading, NY July 3, 1874

Sheardown Rev. Thomas S. at Troy, Pa. July 30, 1874. Pastor at Moreland, NY for 40 years. Born November 4, 1791 Co. of Lincoln, England. Married (1) Esther **Grassam** in England who died in Southport, NY. Married (2) Mrs. Loren **Alexander**

Van Etten Ruth 23 fell at Glen in Watkins, NY July 16, 1874

Crippen Mrs. John at Dix, NY July 29, 1874

Brown Rev. Amos at Havana, NY August 19, 1874

Jacobson Isreal 47 of Syracuse, NY in Watkins, NY August 19, 1874. Leaves wife and 5 children

Bennett Morris son of late Comfort in Horseheads, NY August 7, 1874

Gates Nellie May 9m 14d daughter of M. W. & E. A. at Watkins, NY August 29, 1874

Sackett Azuba 48 wife of S. W. and daughter of Col. William **Vaughn** in Watkins, NY August 21, 1874, Married October 19, 1845. Only son died 3 years ago.

Palmer Zimri 72 in Watkins, NY August 28, 1874. Born March 8, 1802 in Green Co. NY. Leaves wife and 7 children.

Quinby Mrs. Jonathan abt 75 of Caton, NY in Alpine, NY August 5, 1874.

Smith William N. 63 ex-sheriff of Steuben Co. in Bath, NY September 6, 1874

Hughey Martha Jane 24y 3m 7d eldest daughter of Robert at Sugar Hill, NY September 8, 1874

Williams Margaret 71y 6m 22d at Tyrone, NY September 10, 1874

Conover Howard F. 7m 13d son of Madison and Sarah G. at Wayne, NY September 20, 1874

Adem John 45y 7m 14d at Hector, NY October 6, 1874

Frank John of Virgil, NY October 18, 1874

Beecher Hannah 66y 11m at Beaver Dams, NY September 27, 1874

Phinney Mary suicide in Dix, NY October 6, 1874

Jackson George abt 70 years at Havana, NY October 13, 1874

Wood Leroy of Cayuta, NY at son-in-law's Jefferson T. **Beckwith** in Rutherford Park, NJ October 15, 1874. Buried Cayuta

Ely Mrs. Mother of Hector Ely in Hector, NY October 30, 1874

Corbett Walter abt 26 son of Otis in Reading, NY October 31, 1874. Buried Cleveland cem.

Chapman Noah 73 at Townsend, NY October 30, 1874. Came from Saratoga Co. Married 1821 Eliza **Himrod** of Lodi, NY

Kinnan Abigail in 89th year widow of John late of Hector, NY at son-in-law's J. D. **Winterstein** in Farmerville, NY November 15, 1874. Oldest of 8 children.

Mosier Samuel in 55th year at Havana, NY November 11, 1874, native of Switzerland. Leaves wife and 3 children, Louis, Kate, and Mrs. Charles H. **Page** of Worcester, Mass.

Boyer Belinda in 78th year wife of Derrick at Watkins, NY November 14, 1874. Born Conn. Married (1) Jeremiah **Townsend** from Delaware. He died 1842

Becker Leroy 47 at Hector, NY November, 28, 1874. Leaves wife and 5 children

Williams Asa in 84th year at Altay, NY November 27, 1874. Born November 15, 1791 in Groton, Conn. 1 of 11 children. Brother John, sister Mrs. Lydia **Brink** survive, 2 sons and 2 daughters

Rutledge Mrs. Mathew 74 at Rock Stream, NY November 20, 1874

Winton George in 55th year youngest son of Samuel at Catherine, NY November 25, 1874. Married 1848 Anna **Fanton** dau of Thomas L. of Havana, NY. Leaves wife & three children

Jackson Milton at Tyrone, NY December 1, 1874. Leaves wife, 2 children and brother Ethan

Vickery Ebenezer 82 at Catherine, NY November 24, 1874

Cowing Rhoda 92 wife of Caleb age 90 at Eddytown, NY November 22, 1874. Born Vermont nee **Royce**. Married 1810, no children

Lapham John H. 72 in Penn Yan, NY December 8, 1874

Spencer Caroline 61 relict of Rev. Horace at Penn Yan, NY December 6, 1874

DEATH NOTICES

Longwell James C. 60 at Penn Yan, NY December 6, 1874

Sloan Mrs. Julia 26 at Dundee, NY December 9, 1874

Bramble Parker 28 at Omaha, Nebraska December 11, 1874, 2nd son of Charles of Havana, NY. Buried Prospect Hill cem. Omaha

Lowrey Albert, colored, 30 at Havana, NY December 17, 1874. Born a slave in Virginia

Jones Timothy in 94th year funeral at Rock Stream, NY December 29, 1874

Aber Sidney abt 60 in Dix, NY January 1875

Baldwin Johnie H. in 4th year son of W. H. and Louise E. of Watkins, NY in Horseheads, NY December 29, 1874

Patten Submit 88 widow of Alexander of Barrington, NY at daughter's, Mrs. **Feagles** in Watkins, NY December 28, 1874

Bement Maria S. 24y 8m 12d wife of Porter and daughter of Bernardus and Polly **Swarthout** at Clifton Springs, NY October 8, 1874

Maring Dr. Andrew 64 at Hall's Corners, NY January 8, 1874

Shelton Almira in 78th year wife of John in Catherine, NY January 18, 1875

Mc Millan George 30 of Starkey, NY in Pulaski, Florida January 13, 1875

Ayers Lucy in 61st year at Rock Stream, NY February 1, 1875

Morehead Mrs. James in Starkey, NY January 24, 1875. Leaves husband and 3 children. Daughter of late Henry **Davenport**

Brown Lorenzo 66 in Havana, NY February 2, 1875

Knapp Netta Adell 2y 3m 9d daughter of Lucius E. & Ella (**Coats**) Knapp February 24, 1875

De Mont Judge James in 81st year at Ovid, NY February 18, 1875. Born June 17, 1786 in Shannock, NJ. 3rd wife Mrs. Rachel **Covert**, widow of Peter. No children.

Leonard William in 85th year at Orange, NY February 23, 1875

Bailey John S. 83 in Wayne, NY February 17, 1875. Served War of 1812

Bryant Persis abt 60 widow of George W. formerly of Watkin, NY at Bradford, NY February 7, 1875

Mc Elheney Rev. Theodore in 65th year at Burdett, NY March 23, 1875. Born Dryden, NY. Leaves wife and 6 children, names 1 - Mrs. George **Downing** of Watkins, NY

Beers Mrs. N. N. 46 in N. Hector, NY March 19, 1875. Buried in Catherine, NY

Nugent Jimmie 15y 23d son of Charles N. and Annette at Burdett, NY April 28, 1875

Huey Willie 4y 1m 19d son of James M. in Reading, NY July 22, 1875

Forshee A. G. son of Catherine formerly of Tyrone, NY in Crescoe, Iowa July 8, 1875

Denning Robert 59 at Sugar Hill, NY July 26, 1875

Osgood Albert 21 son of Hiram at Bradford, NY August 9, 1875

Allen Ephriam 48 in Perry City, NY August 16, 1875. Leaves wife and several children

Chapman Ida M. 20y 4m daughter of George and Sarah at Reading, NY August 13, 1875

Davison Lewis 80 at son-in-law's John **Osmun** in Starkey, NY September 5, 1875

Sebring Jane H. 34y 1m 11d at Altay, NY September 3, 1875

Cleveland Mary A. in 36th year wife of Nathan B. in Dix, NY September 9, 1875

Kellogg Emma 16 at Bennettsburg, NY September 28, 1875

Bristol Mrs. Laura 76 in Watkins, NY October 2, 1875

Mc Neil John 71 in Watkins, NY October 3, 1875. Son Smith now of Chicago, Ill.

Coville Elmina in 76th year widow of Miles in Elmira, NY October 11, 1875

Bassett Allen in 79th year at Barrington, NY September 29, 1875

Vosburg Kendrick in 40th year at Starkey, NY October 2, 1875

Spink Ezra 54 at Starkey, NY October 5, 1875

Carly Catherine 88y 2m widow of Abraham who died 18 years ago, at residence of John Carley in Hector, NY October 31, 1875. Born Pittstown, NY. Married age 15 at Johnstown, NY. 12 children, 7 living, 1 sister Mrs. Jemima **Fraser** age 84 of Glenora, NY

Harpending Minor 63 at Tyrone, NY November 6, 1875

DEATH NOTICES

Booth Dr. Winthrop E. 73 at Watkins, NY November __, 1875. Born January 1, 1802 in Catherine, NY. Married 1842 daughter of Col. Ebenezer **Thayer**. Leaves 2 sons John and Ebenezer and 1 daughter Mrs. E. B. **Stull**

Scudder Frank T. in Waverly, NY November 14, 1875

Haring William 67y 22d in Watkins, NY November 21, 1875. Born October 29, 1808 in Genoa, NY son of Garrett, 1 of 10 children. Married 1836, leaves widow and 2 sons Charles and George of Watkins, NY

Waterman Betsey R. 89 at Potter, NY November 29, 1875. Born 1786 in Rhode Island a lineal descendant of Roger Williams.

Simonds Sarah 50 at Starkey, NY November 17, 1875

Hall Sally 90 widow of Nathan at grand-son's Franklin Hall in Farmer Village, NY November 2, 1875. From Dutchess Co. NY. Leaves 3 children, 22 grandchildren and 53 great-grandchildren

Tuttle Charles G. 67 formerly of Schuyler Co. NY at Ithaca, NY December 6, 1875. Buried Greenwood Cem. New York City.

Hackett Clarissa 86y 2m 11d widow of Jacob at neice's Mrs. David **Clapp** in Starkey, NY December 26, 1875

Harpending Mehetable 88y 9m 5d widow of Peter formerly of Tyrone, NY in Hinsdale, NY December 28, 1875. Born March 23, 1787 nee **Northrop** in Dutchess Co. Married (1) Mr. **Frost**, 3 children. Married (2) Deacon Lewis **La Fever** of Reading, NY no children (He had 1 son Lewis J.) Married (3) Samuel **Kress** Sr. of Starkey, NY. Married (4) Peter Harpending

Magee Mrs. Hugh 74 at son-in-law's Daniel **Beach** January 13, 1876

Christopher Daniel at Farmer Village, NY January 13, 1876

Skiff Russell 83y 6m 7d at Reading, NY January 14, 1876. Born July 7, 1792 in Sharron, Conn. Married June 23, 1814

Weller Catherine 57 wife of T. V. Weller at Horseheads, NY January 18, 1876. Leaves 2 sons, Edwin and J. M. of Havana, NY

Hoare Mary 70 wife of James M. at Watkins, NY January 25, 1876. Native of England. Leaves 2 sons and 3 daughters.

Lewis Jane 60 wife of John L. and daughter of Dr. Andrew F. **Oliver** of Penn Yan, NY at Penn Yan January 23, 1876

Treman James son of late Jonathan and Anna of Trumansburg, NY at sister's Mrs. George **Grant** in Mecklenburg, NY January 28, 1876

Wakeman Esther 74 widow of Solomon in Trumansburg, NY January 28, 1876

Bodle James in 81st year at Mecklenburgh, NY January 26, 1876. Native of Orange Co. came to Hector 1819, youngest of 12 children. Leaves 4 children one Mrs. Madison **Treman** of Watkins, NY

Hagerman Mrs. P. V. in 61st year at Trumansburg, NY February 1, 1876

Craig Charlotte L. in 30th year wife of Stephen at Covert, NY January 28, 1876

Williams Ansel 50 at Tyrone, NY January 30, 1876. Leaves wife and 1 child

Conklin Julia A. 72 at Tyrone, NY January 22, 1876

Tuttle Daniel at Reading, NY February 9, 1876. Born March 31, 1797 in Boston, Mass. Married October 18, 1828 Lydia **Watkins** daughter of Charles of NY, neice of John and Dr. Samuel Watkins of Watkins, NY. Leaves 2 sons Adrian and S. Watkins

Walker Charlotte 66 in Havana, NY February 10, 1876

Coolbaugh David aged resident of Watkins, NY February 13, 1876

Brokaw B. of Hector, NY February 6, 1876

Tinker J. F. 35 at Lodi, NY February 10, 1876. Wife died 2 years ago, 2 children

Smith Benjamin 72 at Tyrone, NY February 7, 1876, buried Mc Dowell cem. in Wayne, NY. Formerly of Prattsburg, NY

Tuttle Samuel Watkins of NY son of Daniel Tuttle February 20, 1876. Leaves widow and 1 child

Coon A. M. formerly of Hector, NY in Springfield, Ohio February 24, 1876. Buried in Hector

Davis Lydia widow of Nathaniel of Milo, NY in Ovid, Michigan February 11, 1876

Gulick Louisa 60 wife of Hon. William, daughter of Aaron **Couch** of Ovid, NY in Watkins, NY February 21, 1876. Leaves 2 daughters

Skellenger Mary in 66th year widow of William in Havana, NY February 28, 1876. Born 1811 in Freeburg, Pa. 1 of 6 children none surviving. Married 1830. 2 sons and daughter deceased, 3 grandchildren survive

Spink Martha widow of Ezra in Starkey, NY March 5, 1876

Farrington Henry in Trumansburg, NY March 6, 1876

DEATH NOTICES

Hager Harriet O. 20 wife of Peter in Orange, NY March 8, 1876

Curry Mrs. E. L. 65 in Watkins, NY March 17, 1876

Dodson Catherine Elizabeth in 42nd year wife of N. T. nee **Munger** at Watkins, NY March 16, 1876

Sanford Bella 67 at Dix, NY March 16, 1876. Born Conn.

Lott Mrs. H. C. at Reading Center, NY March 25, 1876

Hoag Charles 9y 1d son of Augustus and Caroline March 13, 1876

Hoag Mary C. 6y 3m 21d March 20, 1876, Anna E. 2y 11m 9d April 2, 1876 and Rodney F. 12y 6m 15d March 25, 1876, all children of Marble B. and Margaret K. Hoag of Perry City, NY

Parker Rev. O. in Havana, NY March 14, 1876. Born October 9, 1800 in Metheren, (now Lawrence) Mass.

Comstock Ida in 55th year at Pine Grove, NY March 16, 1876

Dickeson Charles A. 23 in Wayne. NY March 10, 1876

Mills Jacob 89 an early pioneer March 22, 1876, leaves 4 sons and 4 daughters. Buried in family plot near Glen Creek, NY

Porter Thomas in 84th year at Tyrone, NY April 2, 1876. Born Fermanaugh, Ireland. Came here 1851, leaves wife and 2 children

Conklin Wilmer 50 at Starkey, NY March 25, 1876. Leaves wife, mother and 3 children

Miller Mary M. 81 at Bearytown, NY March 14, 1876. Leaves sons Henry **Hendricks** of Bennettsburg, NY and Jacob **Hendricks** of Montour, NY. 2nd husband died 19 years ago

Brokaw Jennie R. 18y 9m 20d daughter of Phillip F. and Martha E. April 2, 1876

Hatfield Martin F. 1y 5m son of Joseph and Deborah April 6, 1876

Sanford Charlotte 73 widow of Morris in Moreland, NY April 5, 1876

Sayre Jonas 92 in Horseheads, NY April 11, 1876

Curry Amos in 75th year at Enfield April 17, 1876

Duryea Louise 24y 5m daughter of James M. and Kezia Duryea at Mecklenburgh, NY April 13, 1876

Conkling Guy J. 24 in Ovid, NY April 18, 1876, Buried in Seneca Falls, NY

Bassett Sheldon in 97th year April 22, 1876. Born 1780 in Conn. Married at age 54 sister of Major **Roscoe** of Starkey. NY, 3 children, Joseph, Charles G. and Mrs. **Hurd**

Burch John 88 in Trumansburg, NY May 10, 1876. Served War of 1812

Ayres Lewis S. 65 at Penn Yan, NY May 15, 1876

Mosher Jonathan B. 67 in Horseheads, NY May 30, 1876. Leaves wife & 5 children

Smith Gen. George 73 in Ovid, NY June 3, 1876. Born February 6, 1803 in Romulus, NY son of Samuel Moore Smith. 1st marriage 12 children, 2nd marriage 4 children, 3 survive

Jackson George A. 24 of Toronto, Canada in Watkins, NY June 21, 1876

Bassett Mrs. Pierrepont 59 daughter of Richard **Woolsey** in Covert, NY June 16, 1876

Burlew Samuel in 82nd year of Waterburg, NY in Ulysses, NY June 22, 1876

Baker Elijah in 64th year at Lodi, NY June 29, 1876. Born Lodi, leaves 3 children, C. S. of Dundee, NY, F. E. of Syracuse, NY and Mrs. A. G. **Everts** of Havana, NY

Harmon George at Wellsburg, NY July 20, 1876

Caton Elizabeth wife of Joseph in Watkins, NY July 24, 1876. Born 1832 and married 1854

Culver Lewis H. on Wednesday evening (date of newspaper July 27, 1876). Born 1809 in Covert, NY son of Azariah C.

Bennett Edmond B. 21m son of Dr. and Mrs. M. L. at Watkins, NY August 12, 1876

Bailey Grover S. abt 61 in Hector, NY August 13, 1876

Hazelton Levi in 79th year at Starkey, NY August 26, 1876

Thompson William 58 formerly of Watkins, NY in Jackson, Michigan August 29, 1876

Mathews Sarah in 94th year widow of David in Reading, NY August 19, 1876. Born July 23, 1783 in Dutchess Co. Married 1801 in Delaware Co. Husband died 1863, 11 children 9 living

Smith James at Reading, NY September 8, 1876. Born 1793 in Scipio, NY 1 of 9 children

Huntley Russell 57 in Reading, NY September 12, 1876

DEATH NOTICES

Cornell Hiram W. 68 in Dundee, NY September 14, 1876

Guinnip A. Morgan in 56th year son of late George B. in Elmira, NY September 25, 1876

Coon Thomas 19y 8m son of William C. at Burdett, NY September 23, 1876

Wilson Ella M. 12y 24d daughter of Alexander in Watkins, NY October 19, 1876

Dodson Torry in 7th year son of N. T. at Watkins, NY October 27, 1876

Wilmot Alice in 7th year dau of Newton in Watkins, NY October 30, 1876. Son Frank died October 30, 1876

Mack Nathaniel in 12th year at Watkins, NY October 28, 1876

Horton Daniel T. in Tyrone, NY October 13, 1876

Jackson child of Lyman 2y in Altay, NY October 14, 1876

Brooks Eulillie 9y 9m 12d dau of Rev. C. W. and E. A. in Watkins, NY October 19, 1876

Wheeler Sarah of Farmer Village, NY in Corning, NY October 1, 1876

Wolcott Dr. Walter 85 in Dundee, NY October 10, 1876

Minier Samuel 71 in Big Flats, NY October 18, 1876

Phinney Joseph colored of Watkins, NY November 1, 1876. Leaves wife and several children

Beach George C. in 75th year at Watkins, NY October 31, 1876. Born December 6, 1801 in Scipio, NY. Names 1 son John N.

Goldsmith David 74 in Hector, NY November 4, 1876

Treman George B. 44 at Mecklenburgh, NY November 3, 1876

Brown Nellie 7y 9m dau of John in Watkins, NY November 5, 1876

Freer Sadie 3 daughter of George F. and Jennie in Watkins, NY November 12, 1876

Birdsall James E. in 49th year at Watkins, NY November 13, 1876

Bailey Mrs. Russell 32 in Reading, NY November 10, 1876

Baldwin Anna 6y 9m 10d dau of James K. in Watkins, NY November 11, 1876

Sleeper Harry 6y 1m 20d son of J. W. and Jennett in Reading, NY November 20, 1876

Roberts Maryland E. 4y 7m dau of Gilbert & Elizabeth in Reading, NY (date of newspaper November 23, 1876)

Speed Belle in 7th year dau of Daniel H. and Sarah in Watkins, NY November 16, 1876

Van Vleet Jared 85y 7m 16d at Romulus, NY November 16, 1876. Son of Peter Van Vleet, oldest of 12 children, 7 living. Married (1) age 21 Miss **Swarthout** daughter of Barna, 9 children. Married (2) Miss **Clarkson** of NJ, 3 children. 6 of 1st marriage living and 1 of 2nd marriage.

Woodward Banjamin Brooke 3y 10m 8d son of Benjamin W. and Helen E. in Watkins, NY November 18, 1876

Dolan Harry 8 son of Michael in Watkins, NY November 17, 1876

Grady Mary 16 at Watkins, NY November 16, 1876

Baldwin Phebe infant dau of James K. at Watkins, NY November 16, 1876

Caton Nellie C. 11y 6m 3d dau of Joseph in Watkins, NY November 15, 1876

Payne Marion Dewitt 4y 6m 27d dau of J. D. and Mary A. in Watkins, NY November 16, 1876

Clark Willie 12y 16d at Monterey, NY November 21, 1876

Bailey Eliza 73y 10m 3d in Watkins, NY November 29, 1876. Dau Mrs. L. H. **Durland**

Williams Annie 17y 6m 19d daughter of M. C. and Ruth Annie in Watkins, NY November 26, 1876

Vaughn Anna 79y 9m widow of Samuel in Burdett, NY November 27, 1876. Came from New Jersey. 8 of 12 children living

Shelton Mary Jane in 64th year wife of Joseph at Catherine, NY November 30, 1876

Smith Cynthia E. in 36th year wife of John in Ovid, NY November 20, 1876. Born February 5, 1841 in Hector, NY

Eldrich Thomas S. of Himrod, NY killed by train in Penn Yan, NY (date of newspaper December 14, 1876)

Feenaughty Edward 3y 3m 26d son of Rodger and Margaret in Watkins, NY November 30, 1876

DEATH NOTICES

Gabriel Permelia 78 widow of Alanson in Starkey, NY November 28, 1876

Craver Georgie Louise 4y 3m 20d dau of T. A. and Dorlestia in Watkins, NY December 3, 1876

Eveland Nettie 6y 8m 11d dau of Andrew and Margaret in Monterey, NY December 8, 1876

Clark Georgie 7y 11m 14d in Orange, NY December 6, 1876

Rose May 2y 1m 19d dau of William and Lucette in Watkins, NY December 5, 1876

Edgett Edna 6y dau of M. L. and Sarah in Watkins, NY December 7, 1876

Crandall Donnie A. 8m 22d son of Jason and Lucy in Watkins, NY December 9, 1876

Davenport Ada 1y 2m dau of Charles and Ella in Dresden, NY December 14, 1876

Dodson Kathleen in 5th year dau of N. T. Dodson in Watkins, NY December 15, 1876

Baldwin Donna M. 8y 8m at Mott's Corners, NY son of William H. and Louise of Watkins, NY

Cook Susan 39y 2m 26d in Sullivanville, NY December 4, 1876

Secor Robert in 78th year at Potter, NY December 3, 1876

Mekeel Anna H. 20y 5m 2d daughter of late Isaac D. in Hector, NY December 15, 1876

Smith George H. formerly of Horseheads, NY in Knoxville, Tenn. December 20, 1876. Son-in-law of Isaac **Wintermute**

Norton Philander 70 formerly of Watkins, NY in Elmira, NY December 25, 1876. Born Cambridge, NY

Whitney Lucinda 103y 5m 26d in Enfield, NY December 23, 1876

Tompkins George W. 72y 1m 15d in Hector, NY December 31, 1876

Bronson Horace formerly of Watkins, NY in Geddes, NY December 31, 1876

Roberts Jane 36y 8m wife of Timothy in Watkins, NY January 1, 1877

Enos Rebecca R. wife of B. Franklin in Dundee, NY January 1, 1877, daughter of David **Clark** of Jerusalem, NY

Rogers James 48 formerly of Watkins, NY in China December 20, 1876

Lyon Jannette (Sherman) 65 wife of Isaac in Havana, NY January 4, 1877

Sebring Metta 32 wife of Philo in Tyrone, NY January 2, 1877

Keyser Mary E. 13 dau of Alpheus and Maria in Havana, NY January 7, 1877

Brown Asa 96 in Jerusalem, NY January 2, 1877. Names 1 dau Mrs. John B. Harris

Chambers Thomas 74 in Starkey, NY January 8, 1877. Leaves 2nd wife and several children by first marriage

Mettler Elizabeth 79 in Horseheads, NY January 1, 1877. Children Mrs. Peter Keyser and Mrs. L. M. Conklin of Havana, NY and sister Zilpha Ayers of Havana. Buried Montour, NY

Youngs Benjamin 83 in Torrey, NY January 8, 1877. Came from Sussex Co. NJ in 1802 with father Isaiah, one of 9 children. Married Mary Haggerty

Gulick Samuel 86 in Lodi, NY January 20, 1877

Gray William D. in 12th year son of James and Cornelia in Watkins, NY January 13, 1877

Johnson Thomas 70 in Townsend, NY January 24, 1877

Pratt Daniel 70 in Elmira, NY January 28, 1877

Buckley Abel 75 in Mc Gregor, Iowa January 25, 1877 and wife age 77 died same place January 20, 1877, daughter of Isaac Bogart of Dresden, NY. Abel born September 5, 1799 in Seneca Co. Married at age 27

Weaver Josephine 12y 8m in Monterey, NY January 23, 1877

Haskell Freddie 10 son of late William and Sarah and grandson of Valentine Oldfield in Dundee, NY January 23, 1877

Strader Madison 63 in Peach Orchard, NY January 25, 1877

Wait Nattie 4y 17d son of William H. and Mary E. in Watkins, NY January 26, 1877

Disbrow Adeline in 28th year wife of Charles P. and dau of Joel A. Taylor of Starkey, NY in Dundee, NY January 29, 1877

Palmer George W. 32y 11m son of Zimri & Jane in Watkins, NY January 24, 1877. Brothers James D. of Montour, NY and W. C. of Dix, NY

Vosburg Margaret abt 67 at Beaver Dams, NY January 29, 1877

DEATH NOTICES

Littell Mary abt 58 at Dundee, NY February 4, 1877

Clute Charles E. 34 in Corning, NY February 9, 1877. Served Capt. Todd's Co. 23rd Reg. NY Vol.

Gray Rev. John at Moreland, NY January 31, 1877. Born September 21, 1799 in Dorset, Vermont. Wife died December 3, 1863, 5 children

Beardsley Sophia 72 relict of Phillip in Montour, NY February 13, 1877

Beardsley Caroline M. in 51st year wife of Scipio C. at Catherine, NY February 10, 1877

Allen Anna Mary 5m 12d dau of John S. and Sarah B. at Hector, NY February 10, 1877

Van Dorn Thomas 86 in Hector, NY February 13, 1877. Leaves widow, sons John T. in Michigan, Horatio W. of Burdett, NY and dau Leah at home

Secor J. M. abt 60 at Reading, NY February 19, 1877

Stothoff Louis J. 24y 3m brother of Mrs. George J. Magee and A. S. in Antrim, Pa. February 15, 1877

Sunderlin Mary A. 70 wife of A. W. in Wayne, NY February 6, 1877. Born December 6, 1807 in Hector, NY 3rd dau of William and Anna **Wortman**, 1 of 12 children. Married October 1825

Cole Nathan 96y 5m 24d in Covert, NY February 10, 1877

Voak Abram 84 in Watkins, NY February 20, 1877. Born May 12, 1793 in Wyoming, Pa. Leaves widow age 82, 7 children, 4 living, J. W. of Wilmot, Wis., Joel of Watkins, Job of Belton, Ill. and Mrs. W. A. **Spence** of Watkins

Barto Mrs. Charles P. of Trumansburg, NY in Dubuque, Iowa on way to California February 18, 1877

Phillips Nellie 6y 28d dau of George A. and Augusta in Watkins, NY February 21, 1877

Bennett Mary N. 33 wife of Dr. M. L. and dau of William **Hurd** in Burdett, NY February 18, 1877

Overhizer Nathan 10 in Orange, NY February 21, 1877

Hungerford Simeon in 80th year at Hornby, NY February 21, 1877

Overhiser Lelia in 7th year in Monterey, NY February 16, 1877

Alden Ettie 2y 8m daughter of Alonzo and Elvira in Monterey, NY February 18, 1877

Lockwood Dr. Jonathan of Tyrone, NY in Saratoga Springs, NY at brother's February 11, 1877

Stanley Gertie 5y 1m dau of Wesley and Charlotte in Odessa, NY February 6, 1877

Estabrook Aseneth 87y 2m relict of Hobart in Havana, NY February 25, 1877

Swick Tunis L. 86 in Covert, NY February 20, 1877. Wife died 1 year ago age 91. Children John H. and George of Hector, NY

Mc Lean George 54 at Prattsburg, NY February 24, 1877. Leaves wife and 4 children names 1 dau Mrs. A. T. **Skinner** of Watkins, NY

Hughey Minnie 3m 2w dau of Andrew and Delia in Sugar Hill, NY February 27, 1877

Taylor Charles Verner 1y 6m son of John & Estelle in Lodi, NY February 26, 1877

Chapman Charlotte 53 wife of Richardand dau of James **Bigelow** in Tyrone, NY February 22, 1877. Leaves husband and daughter

Mekeel Joshua 82 in Perry City, NY February 24, 1877. Born Westchester, Co. 1 of 6 children, 4 living, A. V. Mekeel of Hector, Caleb, Arthur and Mrs. Elizabeth **Mc Lalland** all of Iowa. Eldest, Isaac D. died recently

Patten Teeples abt 66 at Starkey, NY March 2, 1877

Coon Zackariah 75 in Jerusalem, NY March 3, 1877

Twist Charles Dell in 28th year in Watkins, NY March 8, 1877

Mc Clure Warren 85 in Altay, NY March 10, 1877. Leaves widow and 4 children

Smith Julia 15m 9d daughter of Harmon L. and Julia A. in Watkins, NY March 7, 1877

Burgess Benjamin in 80th year at Watkins, NY March 6, 1877. Born 1797 in Seneca Co. Leaves widow age 78 and 5 children, 2 are deceased. John C. of Ovid, Michigan, Mrs. M. **Killman** of Alleghany Co., Mrs, R. **Hoare** of Watkins, Mrs. S. A. **Mapes** of Horseheads, NY and Mrs. E. **Rundle** of Havana, NY. Buried Town Line cem.

Stillwell Ira 69 in Perry City, NY March 9, 1877. Born 1808 in Hector, NY son of James who came from Ulster Co. in 1801. 5 brothers and sisters living, Jacob, John, Col. M. D., Mrs. Susan **Secor**, and Mrs. James **Gibbons**. Leaves widow and 7 children, Mrs. Susan **Brown**, Mrs. Harriet **Wortman**, J. Wesley, E. R., Mrs. Eveline **Smith**, Mrs. Eunice **Potter** and Ira.

Smith Phillip 79 in Pine Valley, NY March 10, 1877. 13 children 9 living

Kennedy Patrick 33 in Dix, NY March 13, 1877

Comstock Nathaniel in 72nd year at Pine Grove, NY March 11, 1877

Banker Phebe M. in 66th year at Havana, NY March 12, 1877

Pattison Raymond J. 4y 3m son of Orville and Susie in Watkins, NY March 17, 1877 and Thurman 1y 3m died March 21, 1877

Norman Mrs. George D. 39y 9m in Watkins, NY March 18, 1877

Egbert Mrs. Morgan L. of Havana, NY at dau Mrs. George **Burris** in Elmira, NY March 19, 1877

Mc Whorter Silas in Ovid, NY March 18, 1877

Deming Aaron 75 in Barrington, NY March 27, 1877

Donohue Joseph 2y 2w son of Jeremiah and Bridget in Watkins, NY March 24, 1877

Quick Nellie age 2y 5m dau of Mrs. Hannah in Watkins, NY March 22, 1877

Harrington Monroe 42 in Ovid, NY March 24, 1877. Buried Watkins, NY

Sharp Stephen in 71st year at Starkey, NY March 20, 1877 Dau Mrs. M. J. **Sunderlin**

Page Fitzroy 3y 5m 22d son of Edwin A. and Viola J. in Watkins, NY March 30, 1877

Baker Frances wife of Isaac and dau of James **Mapes** of Orange, NY March 20, 1877 and son Leon L. died March 17, 1877

Reynolds Smith 82 in Reynoldsville, NY March 30, 1877

Pinch Jennie L. 15 daughter of William H. and Maria in Watkins, NY April 6, 1877

Moreland Chauncey 58 in Van Etten, NY April 3, 1877

Van Vechten Jay 5y 2m in Watkins, NY April 9, 1877

Voak Alice 30 wife of James in Watkins, NY April 17, 1877

Miller Charles in 69th year in Hector Falls, NY April 14, 1877

Stevens Betsey 90 in Lodi, NY April 15, 1877

Westcott Mrs. Mary 65 in Dundee, NY April 16, 1877 native of De Ruyter, NY. Married 1832

Dean John 89y 4m in Veteran, NY April 17, 1877. Came from NJ in 1815

Mc Swain Benjamin L. 70 in Himrods, NY April 18, 1877. Born Kentucky and buried in Starkey, NY

Culver Cyrus 18 son of Chancey hit by train in Havana, NY April 18, 1877

Bloomer Hiram in Trumansburg, NY April 26, 1877

Ellis Don H. 6y 11m 10d son of Joseph & Estella L. in Watkins, NY April 25, 1877

Smith Isabel in 84th year wife of James late of Reading, NY at son's Isaac H. in Montour, NY April 28, 1877. 9 children

Van Liew I. V. 64 in Tyrone, NY April 18, 1877. Born 1813 in Lodi, NY. Leaves widow and 8 children, Mary, Mrs. Charles Shafer, Mrs. Lee Weller, Mrs. W. Howell, Edson, Alden, Ira and Henry

Burritt Frederick 10y son of George R. & Susan in Watkins, NY April 23, 1877

Rarrick William in 98th year at Orange, NY April 30, 1877. Born 1779 in Dutchess Co. Wife died 11 years ago, 9 children 6 living, A. H. of Alpine, NY, Mrs. R. Griswold of Mitchellville, NY, Mrs. James Scofield of Addison, NY, Mrs. Clarkson Boyce of Weston, NT, H. S. of Orange and Mrs. George Cooley of Barrington, NY

Golden Sarah 26y 9m 24d dau of John Dickson in N. Tonawanda, NY April 29, 1877

Palmer Banjamin in Watkins, NY April 28, 1877. Born November 15, 1818 in New City, NY son of Jonathan. Married May 8, 1839 Caroline Bogert, dau of Henry G. of NY. Leaves wife, 1 son and 2 daus. Eldest sons died young

Favill Daniel 63 in Reading Center, NY May 7, 1877. Born Herkimer Co. 6 brothers, 6 sisters only 1 living

Labar Mrs. John in Burdett, NY May 6, 1877

Hausner Mary in 52nd year wife of Martin at Hector, NY (date of newspaper May 17, 1877)

Evans Helene L. 37 dau of George Paine in Watkins, NY May 6, 1877

Burt Mrs. Dorcas 78y 2m in Big Flats, NY May 1, 1877

Dunn James son of William in Elmira, NY May 7, 1877. Born January 27, 1804. Brothers & sisters, Charles, Thomas, William, Susan wife of Lyman Covell, Alice wife of Isaac Baldwin. Married April 28, 1827 Elizabeth Tompson of Goshen, Conn. 5 children living, D. Tompson & Henry in Georgia, Isaac & Mrs. F. H. Atkinson in Watkins, NY & Thomas Root of Philadelphia, Pa.

DEATH NOTICES

Bartlett Collins in 68th year at Moreland, NY May 6, 1877. Born 1809 in Amenia, NY, married age 23

Pope Chester D. in Havana, NY May 7, 1877. Wife Dr. Elizabeth D.

Reno Peter in 86th year at Dix, NY May 17, 1877 born Herkimer Co.

Woodward John step-son of Cyrus Barber in Searsburg, NY May 13, 1877

Everts Mary Ann (Wightman) in 87th year at Logan, NY May 27, 1877. Born Dutchess Co. Married Daniel Everts who died 1828, 6 children, Rollin of Orange, NY, Curran and Benjamin F. of Hector, NY, Emily and Harriet unmarried

Wilkin William 70 of Townsend, NY formerly of Dundee, NY May 12, 1877

Jessop Sarah 41 wife of John in Starkey, NY May 19, 1877

Hopkins Jeremiah 76 in Starkey, NY May 26, 1877

Jessop John Jr. 17 son of John in Dundee, NY May 27, 1877

Briggs Elizabeth wife of William S. at Penn Yan, NY May 25, 1877

Longwell Mrs. William 48 in Monterey, NY June 3, 1877

Covell Mrs. M. D. 45 in Starkey, NY May 29, 1877

Squires Harriet in 89th year near Stanley Station, NY May 19, 1877

Hendricks J. W. in 4th year son of William May 16, 1877

Bailey Gilbert D. 15 youngest son of Dr. Gilbert D. in Havana, NY May 23, 1877

Mathews Mrs. Alanson abt 60 in Hector, NY May 27, 1877

Grady Edward 65 suicide in Branchport, NY May 27, 1877. Born Ireland, leaves wife 2 sons and 1 daughter

Hunter Lorenzo 83 in Rushville, NY May 21, 1877

Gifford Jeannette 10y 4m daughter of Nelson and Mary June 2, 1877

Coykendall James S. 20 son of Anthony and Ruth in Dundee, NY June 1, 1877

Harrington Maria 62 wife of William in Dundee, NY June 3, 1877

Miller Mary 74y 6m in Monterey, NY June 6, 1877

Baskin William 60 in Starkey, NY June 7, 1877. Son of William, 1 of 12 children,

9 living. Married December 10, 1851 Eliza A. **Groves** of N. Hector, NY. Wife, 2 sons and 3 daughters survive.

Van Lone Richard 70 in Alpine, NY (date of newspaper June 14, 1877)

Barkman Mina in 60th year wife of Orville in Monterey, NY June 28, 1877, eldest daughter of Ezra **Chapman**. Married 4 months

Gaylord Leon 7y son of Leroy in Monterey, NY June 29, 1877

Osterhout Polly 79 in Catherine, NY June 24, 1877. Came from Kingston, NY in 1812. Husband died 1821, 4 children living, Mrs. Fanny **Owen** and Mrs. Peter **Cooper** of Catherine, Mrs. Samuel **Mitchell** of Ithaca, NY and Mrs. Abigail **Frost** of Havana, NY

Batty Mrs. John 33 in Starkey, NY June 29, 1877

Burr Louisa 45 in Lodi Center, NY June 15, 1877

Collum Jesse Sr. 91 in Barrington, NY June 28, 1877

Sloan Elizabeth (**Scott**) 82 in Penn Yan, NY July 1, 1877 Came from Maryland in 1807

Haring Mrs. William 65 in Watkins, NY June 24, 1877

Downing Sarah 35y 9m wife of George W. in Watkins, NY June 29, 1877

Shearer Maria 54y 9m 24d wife of Sylvester B. and dau of Dr. Marcus **Jones** in Havana, NY July 4, 1877. 1st husband Sidney S. **Decker** died August 26, 1849, 2 children, Sidney S. Jr. of Havana and Sarah wife of J. Milnor **Decker** of NY City

Brown Alice E. in 29th year wife of Norman and sister of W. E. and C. **Evans** in Hector, NY July 10, 1877

Keeler Esther 87y 10m 10d in N. Reading, NY July 7, 1877. Born August 27, 1789 in Fairfield, NY daughter of Stephen and Mary **Jacobs** youngest of 12 children. Married Elmer Keeler and moved to N. Reading in 1812. No children

Green Paris 87y 9m 25d in Horseheads, NY July 10, 1877. Born September 15, 1779 in Burlin, NY. Married at age 21 Sarah **Smith** who died June 1843, 9 children, names Mrs. Caroline **Mosher** of Ill.

Cowing Caleb in 93rd year at Eddytown, NY July 18, 1877. Born March 1785 in Saratoga Co. 4th son (9th child) of James who had 21 children. Married 1808 Rhoda **Royce** who died 2 1/2 years ago

Ogden Otto in Monterey, NY July 18, 1877. Born Monterey and married September 30, 1874 Mary A. **Hollingshead** in Chicago, Ill., 2 sons one age 2y and one age 8m

DEATH NOTICES

Agard Catherine in 90th year consort of Eaton at N. Settlement, NY August 13, 1877. Born Dutchess Co. NY and married 1816

Beers Anna 78 in Dundee, NY August 10, 1877. Born Mahoning, Pa. nee **Hendrickson**. Married (1) William **Smith** who died in Pa. 4 children. Moved to Starkey, NY in 1822, married (2) Joseph **Campbell**, several children. Married (3) Mr. Beers. Names 1 child, Mrs. George W. **Barnes**, 1st wife of late Thomas **Chambers** of Dundee

Smalley Isaac 77 shot himself in Weston, NY August 18, 1877. Wife died 10 years ago, son and dau in Weston, 1 son in Horseheads, NY and dau in Farmer Village, NY

Baker Olive 70 wife of Zalmon in Mecklenburgh, NY August 25, 1877. (newspaper gives date as October 25, date of newspaper August 30, 1877)

Call Gracie 5m 23d dau of Joseph and Ida August 23, 1877

Hause William in 49th year at Watkins, NY September 4, 1877. Born February 28, 1877 in Tyrone, NY. Married 1853 Maria **Kinney** dau of Judge Henry Kinney. Leaves wife and son, Henry K. Buried Dundee cem.

Mc Intyre Ada 22 wife of A. S. and dau of Isaac and Sarah **Rusco** in Monterey, NY September 4, 1877. Married 2 years, 1 child 2 months old

Lawrence Margaret 78 widow of William T. and dau of late R. F. **Muller** of NY City in Cayuta, NY September 1, 1877

Wheeler Elvira 25y 4m wife of John and only dau of Morgan **Freer** in Watkins, NY October 6, 1877. Leaves 1 child

Howell Jacob 81 in Watkins, NY October 14, 1877

Allen Frances 66 in Watkins, NY October 14, 1877

Kress George 35-40 suicide in Starkey, NY October 31, 1877

Coon Tillie 20 dau of Eli in Watkins, NY October 24, 1877

Coon Eliza Clark at Tyrone, NY October 14, 1877. Born May 8, 1790 in NY. Married 70 years this November Thomas Coon who died January 1858. 10 children 3 living, William C. of Burdett, NT, David K. of Tyrone and Amariah of Hematite, Missouri

Wood Jemima 68 wife of Rev E. in Reading, NY November 4, 1877

Ingersoll Charlotte M. 54 wife of Oliver in Watkins, NY November 17, 1877. Leaves husband and dau

Miller Clarence 8y 9m son of George W. and Nancy E. in Watkins, NY November

18, 1877

Hastings Libbie A. 16y 8m 19d dau of M. M. and M. A. in Watkins, NY November 24, 1877. Buried Ithaca, NY

Van Vleet John in 80th year at Monterey, NY November 28, 1877

White Captain William in Monterey, NY December 14, 1877

Pinch Bessie A. 3y 11m dau of William H. in Watkins, NY December 18, 1877

Smith James A. in Mecklenburgh, NY December 28, 1877

Couch Mary Ann 38y 2m 28d in Canandaigua, NY December 22, 1877

Smith Sarah wife of Erie and dau of George R. **Burritt** in Watkins, NY December 26, 1877

Hall Ida age 12 dau of Jerome and grand-dau of Dr. **Wager** in Monterey, NY December 22, 1877

Harvey Lydia in Enfield, NY December 29, 1877

Horton George Romain 29 only son of James and son-in-law of E. P. **Smith** in Monterey, NY January 1, 1878

Doty Isaac 67 in Enfield, NY January 4, 1878

Rumsey Samuel L. abt 76 in Dix, NY January 7, 1878

Beach Mary 72 wife of Obadiah and dau of Robert and Mary **Lang** from Westchester Co. at Tyrone, NY January 13, 1878

Rowlee John H. abt 70 at Sugar Hill, NY January 10, 1878

Stamp Lois E. in 9th year dau of A. N. and Frances A. January 10, 1878

Swick Julia wife of William at N. Hector, NY January 30, 1877

Doane Rufus 71 at Orange, NY February 2, 1878

Wakely Russell in 91st year in Dix, NY February 6, 1878

Lewis William abt 25 son of Alonzo suicide in Tyrone, NY February 10, 1877

Fleming Margaret 65 in Havana, NY February 11, 1877

Hazlett Bertha age 1y today dau of James R. in Peach Orchard, NY February 12, 1878

DEATH NOTICES

Carson Elizabeth in 70th year at Burdett, NY February 19, 1878

Crouch William T. 76 formerly of Painted Post and Watkins, NY in Topeka, Kansas February 9, 1878

Allen Mrs. David 25 dau of Mr. **Mosier** of Millport, NY at Monterey, NY February 16, 1878

Swarthout Benjamin in N. Hctor, NY February 14, 1878

Ellison Thomas in 85th year at Hornby, NY March 2, 1878. Born 1792 in Co. Tyrone, Ireland. Children, Mrs. A. **Wasson** Jr. and Andrew

Nye Alice 24 dau of Algernon in Watkins, NY March 6, 1878

Hazard Estella in 15th year dau of G. V. in Watkins, NY buried March 20, 1878

Hurd Fanny 78y 4m widow of Harry formerly of Starkey, NY in Watkins, NY March 19, 1878

Rogers Phineas 92 in Chemung, NY March 26, 1878

Shannon James in 70th year at Barrington, NY March 26, 1878

Ingersoll Oliver in Watkins, NY March 31, or April 1, 1878

Horton Thomas P. 86 in Monterey, NY April 1, 1878 at dau Mrs. Ruth **Evelette**, 2 sons James of Montour, NY and Daniel of Barrington, NY

Morse Mrs. Abner 66 in Monterey, NY April 2, 1878. Mother of Mrs. L. **Barnes** and Mrs. James **Jessop** of Tyrone, NY

Bennett James L. 84 in Watkins, NY April 5, 1878. Born November 4, 1807 at same residence only son of James who died November 5, 1858 age 85, one of the first settlers in 1792 from Great Bend on the Susquehanna. Leaves widow and 4 children, Mrs. C. L. **Turner** and Mrs. D. E. **Comstock** of Norwich, NY, Mrs. J. J. **Van Allen** of Watkins and son James H. on homestead.

Smith Betsey of Reading, NY in Co. Poorhouse at Bath, NY April 7, 1878

Nares Georgie 1y son of Tunis D. in Watkins, NY April 12, 1878

Freer George in 70th year at Watkins, NY April 17, 1878. Leaves wife and 3 children

Knapp Miss Abigail in 93rd year in Hector, NY April 28, 1878. Born August 1785 in Orange Co. Moved to Tyrone, NY with brother William

Morris Charles M. in 4th year son of William and Libbie of Watkins, NY in Odessa,

NY May 4, 1878

Foot Judge Samuel May 11, 1878. Born 1796 in Watertown, Conn.

Beecher Catherine in 78th year in Elmira, NY May 12, 1878

Watson Abigail in 95th year in Montour, NY May 15, 1878. Born 1783 in Vermont

Brooks Elijah P. in 60th year in Elmira, NY May 19, 1878

De Witt Chauncey age 42 in Monterey, NY May 16, 1878. In Civil War 141st Reg. NY Vol.

Slaght George in N. Hector, NY (date of newspaper June 20, 1878)

Tompson J. Leonard 27 in Watkins, NY May 18, 1878

Lewis Mrs. Leon of Penn Yan, NY in Rochester, NY May 20, 1878

Thompson Frank A. 43 son of Calvin and son-in-law of George **Vine** in Monterey, NY June 21, 1878. Leaves wife and 2 children

Gilmore John 27 in N. Hector, NY May 29, 1878

Taber Mrs. Sally in 62nd year at Peach Orachard, NY May 27, 1878. Dau of James & Elizabeth **Dickerson**, 1 of 11 children from NJ, 6 living, John of Hector, NY, 1 in Washington Terr., 1 in Mi., 2 in NJ

Drake James 63 in Watkins, NY June 14, 1878. Born February 4, 1815 in Dix, NY

Beach Obadiah in 74th year at Tyrone, NY June 24, 1878. Born January 8, 1804 in Marcellus, NY. Children, Lewis of Tyrone and Daniel of Watkins, NY. Wife died 6 months ago.

Orcutt Rev. Asa 82 in Sonora, NY June 17, 1878

Vann Samuel 105 in Ulysses, NY March 19, 1878

Quick Peter in Havana, NY July 3, 1878

Luce Hervey in Elmira, NY July 6, 1878. Born March 21, 1794 in Berkshire, Mass.

Littell Amos 22 suicide by hanging in Tyrone, NY July 4, 1878

Peck John in 49th year at Reading, NY July 19, 1878

Hoyt Mrs. Matilda 50 at Monterey, NY July 21, 1878

Graham John in 66th year at Watkins, NY July 25, 1878. Born July 28, 1813 in

Suffolk, England

Cheney Dr. T. Apolean 48 in Milo, NY August 2, 1878

Adamy E. T. 75 in Odessa, NY August 4, 1878

Eddy Daniel 64 at Reynoldsville, NY July 29, 1878. Leaves wife, son and dau

Hebermith Nora 30 in Monterey, NY July 29, 1878

Lockwood Anna 82 in Monterey, NY August 8, 1878. Children, William, Charles, George and Mrs. A. B. **Webber**

Hanmer Harry R. 16m 4d at Pine Grove, NY August 10, 1878

Badgley George H. in 40th year at Watkins, NY August 13, 1878

Hollister Ida M. 19 dau of O. A. J. and Sarah L. at Reynoldsville, NY August 27, 1878

Shay Deacon B. L. of Watkins, NY in N. Hector, NY September 2, 1878. Born December 27, 1816 in Conn. Leaves wife and 5 children

Babbit Stella step-dau of John S. **Swartwood** at grandfather's Col. H. A. **Newcomb** in Dix, NY August 23, 1878

Roblyer Garrett abt 50 in Reading, NY August 31, 1878

Shay B. L. of Watkins, NY in N. Hector, NY September 2, 1878

Ellis Mrs. Jennie dau of Solomon **Williams** in Bennettsburg, NY September 8, 1878. Leaves 4 young children

Wallenbeck Jennie A. 9y 4m 9d dau of John and Amelia in Watkins, NY September 5, 1878

Wood Jane 50-55 in Reynoldsville, NY September 15, 1878

Perry James 99y 4m in Himrods, NY September 1, 1878

Everts Alfred in Hector, NY October 2, 1878. Born August 2, 1812 in Hector. Leaves 6 children

Woodward Sophia wife of George & dau of Mrs. **Bolt** of Townsend, NY at Sugar Hill, NY October 14, 1878

Shearer Catherine L. wife of George C. and dau of Dr. William **Turk** and Eliza **Livingston** in Watkins, NY October 10, 1878. Brothers and sisters, Mrs. William **Plume** of Newark, NJ, Connaughty of Waterford, NY and Rear Admiral John L.

Livingston. Married (1) Joshua **Bloor**, 1 daughter, Mrs. Orville **Pattison** of Watkins. 2nd marriage, 2 sons, William A. of Reading, NY and Charles S. now of NY

Halleck Mrs. abt 50 suicide in Starkey, NY October 9, 1878

Sherman Jennie 21 at Bennettsburg, NY October 15, 1878

Kempton Jennie dau of Frank in Watkins, NY October 20, 1878

Rapplee Frances 25 in Monterey, NY October 21, 1878

Woodward Emma A. wife of Arthur C. in Peach Orchard, NY November 19, 1878

Myres Thomas J. in 75th year at Reading, NY November 1, 1878. Married Angeline **Taylor** in Penfield, NY. Leaves widow and 1 child, Mrs. Ellis **Putnam** of Reading

Clawson Sally 56 wife of Gerritt in N. Hector, NY November 13, 1878

Smith Winfield in Bennettsburg, NY November 16, 1878

Tompson George 68 in Watkins, NY December 5, 1878

Dean R. C. 4y in Altay, NY December 3, 1878

Howard Charles abt 59 in Watkins, NY December 5, 1878. Born 1820 in Reading, NY

Lawrence Abraham 60, unmarried, in Catherine, NY December 18, 1878. Born June 1, 1818 5th son of Samuel, grandson of Jonathan who was great-grandson of Thomas that immigrated to Long Island about 1635 from Herferdshire, England. He died 1703, Jonathan born October 4, 1737 and died September 4, 1812. Samuel born May 23, 1773 and with brother Joseph, settled in Catherine 1814. He married Elizabeth **Ireland**, dau of John and had 6 sons and 5 daughters, and died October 20, 1837. Names Abraham and sister, Mrs. Jane G. **Campbell** wife of Adam G. Buried family cem.

West Jonathan A. in 80th year at Logan, NY December 23, 1878 at son-in law's William **Gardiner**. Born Bedford, Mass., married Mary **Bennett** who died 14 years ago. 1 sister, Mrs. George S. **Whippy** and 2 brothers

Stothoff Mrs. George 28y 3m dau of M. S. **Converse** of Elmira, NY in Burdett, NY January 7, 1879. Buried Glenwood cem.

Webb William in 90th year at Monterey, NY January 5, 1879. 3 sons, Daniel of Orange, NY Bradford of Townsend, NY and Barnet of Geneva, NY

Griswold John in 76th year at Southport, NY January 9, 1879

Baldwin Mrs. Willis 52 in Watkins, NY January 13, 1879

DEATH NOTICES

Hodgekins Mrs. Abel 40 in Watkins, NY January 15, 1879

Everts Margaret 96 widow of Aranthus and dau of Amasa **Mathews** in Hector, NY January 23, 1879. Came from Shawangunk, NY, 1 of 9 children. Married 1802, Aranthus son of Daniel born Salisbury, Conn. 1779 and died 1867, had 5 sons and 1 dau

Chase Rev. Daniel 65 in Bennettsburg, NY February 1, 1879. Leaves wife, 2 sons and 1 daughter

Dean Horace 81 in Tyrone, NY February 6, 1879. Born May 29, 1798 in Putnam Co. Married 1824 Euphemia **Doty** who died 3 yrs ago

Clawson Peter in N. Hector, NY February 18, 1879

Van Nortric Mrs. 85 in N. Hector, NY February 9, 1879. Names 1 dau, Mrs. Orville **Townsend**

Rockwell Esther 78 wife of Samuel in Monterey, NY February 15, 1879. Leaves husband and 5 children

Andrews Phoebe in 97th year relict of Hamerst in Reading, NY February 12, 1879. Born December 23, 1782 in Chatham, NY. Married age 16, 6 children 1 living, Jesse of Dundee, NY. Buried Dundee

Kels Wilson 61 in Orange, NY February 18, 1879

Tyler Sarah 72 wife of Daniel in Burdett, NY February 19, 1879

Jackson Gen. Daniel 83 in Watkins, NY February 28, 1879. Born 1796 in Minisink, NY. Married Mary **Starkweather** who died in winter of 1870. Children surviving, George, Fred W. and Mrs. Dr. J. W. **Thompson**

Bronson Elizabeth 42 wife of Freegift and dau of William **Mc Donald** of Havana, NY in Watkins, NY February 21, 1879

Ely Harry 90 in Hector, NY March 3, 1879. Born May 3, 1788 in Salsbury, Conn., moved to Hector age 3. Married 1811

Lewis Fred H. 61y 5m in Rochester, NY March 1, 1879

Littell Miranda 82 at son Isaac's in Monterey, NY March 4, 1879

Hill George Jr. 4y 3m 22d in Watkins, NY March 5, 1879

Burke Albert H. in Havana, NY March 8, 1879

Shelton Mrs. Dithy 78 at son Calvin's in Havana, NY March 10, 1879

Keefer Henry L. in Monterey, NY March 12, 1879

Coon Mrs. Elias in Monterey, NY March 11, 1879

Tracy Willis H. abt 27 in Havana, NY March 21, 1879

Story Mrs. wife of Rev. 71 in Hector, NY March 18, 1879

Newcomb Cora A. 22y 6m in Monterey, NY March 24, 1879

Maxwell Mrs. Thomas abt 72 in Elmira, NY March 31, 1879

Ellison Mrs. Andrew funeral in Orange, NY April 1, 1879

Bennett Col. Green over 82 in Dix, NY April 8, 1879

Crawford Samuel in 80th year at Havana, NY April 4, 1879. Born July 4, 1799 6th son of James and Mary in Montgomery, NY. Great grandfather, Samuel Gillespie Crawford born 1730 in Ireland. Married March 1818-19 Elizabeth **Davis**, 4 sons and 2 daus, Medorum, John D. and Elizabeth born in Orange Co. Came to Catherine, NY in 1825. Medorum moved to Oregon in 1842, 2 younger sons followed. Brother John of Moreland, NY dec

Barkman Elizabeth 66 in Monterey, NY April 12, 1879

Skinner Aurelia widow of Arasmus of Prattsburg, NY at son's Robert in Cinncinati, Ohio April 15, 1879. Born April 23, 1789 in Shaghticoke, NY. Married December 25, 1815, 8 son & 1 dau

Swartwood Stella 26y 8m dau of John S. in Watkins, NY April 21, 1879

Mc Dowell Andrew funeral in Dix, NY April 23, 1879

Budd Mahlon in 78th year at N. Hector, NY May 13, 1879. Names son John S. and son-in-law Peter **Hager** of Watkins, NY

Wager Dr. E. B. in Havana, NY May 9, 1879

Aber Elias 61 formerly of Dix, NY in Odessa, NY May 20, 1879

Hopkins J. C. 71 in Bennettsburg, NY May 24, 1879

Adriance Mrs. in N. Hector, NY May 14, 1879

Gaylord Philena widow of Alonzo at dau Mrs. John **Kimball** in Elmira, NY May 14, 1879

Fleet Henry S. 71y 7m 26d in Watkins, NY May 17, 1879. Born Tyrone, NY. Leaves wife and 2 children, Albert H. and Mrs. Azuba A. **Bolhmer** of NY, a brother

DEATH NOTICES 109

Abram in Missouri and William of Tifflon, Ohio

Mc Cennor Phillip 82 in Lodi Center, NY May 21, 1879. Born Ireland. Leaves 7 children

Miller Isaac 78 of Ovid, NY in Watkins, NY May 30, 1879. Born Lodi, NY. Names son George W.

Bassett Mary E. in 27th year wife of L. R. in Dundee, NY June 3, 1879. Leaves husband and 2 children aged 6 and 4

Rice Mrs. 83 in Monterey, NY June 18, 1879

Staring Henry D. 54y 8m 11d formerly of Watkins, NY in San Francisco July 5, 1879

La Coste Elizabeth would be 94 on July 8 wife of Francis in Crystal Springs, NY July 6, 1879. Husband survives, age near 100

Drake Thomas W. 84y 8m 11d in Reading, NY July 5, 1879. Born October 26, 1794 in Mt. Hope, NY. Married (1) October 11, 1822 Mary Ann **Swezey**, who died July 24, 1841, 10 children. Married (2) April 11, 1842 Sally Ann **Culver** who died May 8, 1845, 1 dau. Married (3) May 6, 1840 Louisa **Cook** who survives. Served War of 1812

Tum George 56 in Catherine, NY July 16, 1879. Born in Wurtemburg, Germany, migrated 1847. Leaves wife and 2 children

Brown Allen 55-60 suicide in Millport, NY July 26, 1879

Abby Lizzie B. dau of Rev. D. A. of Schuyler Co. in Shokan, NY fell through bridge July 2, 1879

Blaine Theron 25 son of Amos in Logan, NY August 1, 1879. Married at age 19 Helen **Gerow** dau of G. F.

Bennett Mrs. Henry A. 64 in Watkins, NY August 5, 1879

Mapes William E. funeral in Monterey, NY August 25, 1879

Dates Ella 12 dau of George in Reynoldsville, NY August 30, 1879

Palmer Helen M. 24 wife of Rev. Noble in Havana, NY August 15, 1879

Mapes M. E. in Townsend, NY August 22, 1879

Hanmer David 67 in Townsend, NY August 27, 1879

Wideman Miles 56 in Townsend, NY September 1, 1879

Hurd Sarah 93 next October 18 widow of Gen. Timothy of Starkey, NY in Watkins, NY September 2, 1879

Mc Donald James H. 63 in Watkins, NY September 12, 1879. Born March 3, 1816 in Fairview, NJ. Married September 29, 1836 Elizabeth A. who survives. Leaves 3 brothers, Jeremiah, David and Rodolphus R. and 1 sister Mrs. Sarah Marie **Demorest** all of NJ

Reynolds Joel in 66th year at Reynoldsville, NY September 6, 1879. Born June 4, 1814 in Reynoldsville. Leaves wife and 1 dau Mrs. Rev. Samuel **Saylor** of Grand Traverse, Michigan

Campbell Abram in N. Hector, Ny September 14, 1879

Nye Sylvanus 92 buried in Mecklenburg, NY September 8, 1879

Goldsmith Lavina 57 relict of David and dau of Thomas **Spaulding** in Hector, NY September 17, 1879. Born July 5, 1822 in Hector. Married September 17, 1851

Stout Morgan 67 in Watkins, NY September 21, 1879 Leaves wife and 2 sons, Albert A. of Cal. and Thomas of Watkins

Ayres Esther 69 widow of Lewis S. of Penn Yan, NY at Johnston, NY September 10, 1879. Adopted dau Helen

Mc Lafferty G. D. 66 in Havana, NY September 21, 1879

Brien William in 83rd year at Reading Center, NY September 30, 1879. Born January 1797 in Co. Fermanagh, Ireland

Starkey Dr. John C. formerly of Watkins, NY in Owego, NY October 10, 1879. 1 brother William. Buried in Dundee

Conklin Miranda 54 wife of Isaac in Reading Center, NY October 14, 1879. Buried in Glenwood cem.

Horton Mrs. Thomas 89 at Sugar Hill, NY October 5, 1879

Hildreth Paul 30 in Glenora, NY October 9, 1879

Barrett James W. son of Mrs. James of Watkins, NY buried in Utah October 10, 1879

Hallock Elizabeth 42 wife of Edwin and dau of Alonzo **Williams** in Tyrone, NY October 18, 1879

Barnes Emma L. 32 wife of Lewis in Monterey, NY October 14, 1879

Phelps Wallace 63 in Beaver Dams, NY October 21, 1879. 4 children, Mrs. Charles **Stevens** of Reading, NY, sons Henry and Asa and daughter Nettie at home

DEATH NOTICES 111

Kress John Starkey 62 in Reading, NY October 31, 1879. 1 of 13 children, son of John J. and Rachel **Rial** Kress, dau of Anthony B. 3 brothers and 6 sisters survive

Birge Mrs. Samantha 34 in Hector, NY October 30, 1879

Ellsworth James S. 55 in Havana, NY November 2, 1879

Holmes Farley abt 60 in Penn Yan, NY November 27, 1879

Wilmot Mary 26 dau of Isaac W. funeral in Rock Stream, NY November 25, 1879

Roberts Elizabeth E. 46 wife of Gilbert & dau of William **Sprowl** in Reading, NY November 30, 1879

Chapman Ruth in 69th year wife of Porter in Watkins, NY December 4, 1879 nee **Aldrich** from Rhode Island. Married June 1831, 3 sons and 2 daughters. Son died in Civil War

Kels Elnora 28 in Monterey, NY December 2, 1879. Born May 21, 1851 only dau of William **Snow**

Chapman John 60 killed by train near Campbell, NY December 12, 1879, brother of Daniel and Ezra of Monterey, NY

Fletcher Charles H. 31 in Denver, Col. funeral in N. Hector, NY December 9, 1879

Thayer Col. Ebenezer 93 formerly of Watkins, NY in Bloomsburg, Pa. Buried Glenwood cem. August 21, 1880

Fillmore Rev. A. N. 72y 9m in Watkins, NY August 23, 1880. Born October 19, 1807 in Paris, NY. Married (1) 1833 and (2) 1837

Swartwood Glennie 10m 3d son of C. E. in Monterey, NY September 2, 1880

Mathews Captain Manly Tooker 42 eldest son of David of Reading, NY at Little Rock, Arkansas September 11, 1881. Married 1864 Sarah **Ostrander** dau of late John, 5 children

Hulett Charles 54 in Townsend, NY November 19, 1881

Kingsley Mrs. Jane 24y 3m 2d in Reynoldsville, NY December 24, 1881

Robinson Stella dau of Oliver and Maria at Hector, NY December 28, 1881

Goodwin Alfred 8y in N. Hector, NY January 1, 1882

Mc Manus Father James C. January 11, 1882. Born December 1841 in Ireland. Came here in 1862

Everts Mrs. Alfred 67 in Peach, NY Orchard January 6, 1882. Children, Mrs. J. A. and Mrs. A. C. **Woodward** of Watkins, NY

Hurd A. B. 68 in Monterey, NY January 11, 1882

Robinson Anna 14 in Hector, NY January 6, 1882

Tuthill Rebecca in 82nd year widow of Benjamin at Penn Yan, NY January 19, 1882. Children E. D., Captain H. of Penn Yan, Joshua E. of Saginaw, Michigan and Mrs. A. W. **Franklin** Of Penn Yan

Carman Adrian E. 17 in Watkins, NY January 21, 1882

Creighton Anna 13 dau of J. H. in Hector, NY January 12, 1882

Wagner Charles F. 26 in Altay, NY January 23, 1882

Skuse Samantha 53 wife of Philetus S. in Reading, NY January 30, 1882, dau of John and Clemenia **Drake** sister of James and George of Irelandville, NY, Mrs. B. L. **Shay**, Mrs. Steven **Warren** of Watkins, NY, Mrs. James **O'Daniels**, Mrs. Oliver **Ellison**, Mrs. Daniel **Skuse** of Reading, and Andrew J. of Buffalo, NY. Married (1) Benjamin **Burgess**, 1 child Marion of Reading. Leaves children of 2nd marriage, Addie, Fred and Charles

Hager Chester M. 56 in Watkins, NY February 4, 1882, 1 of 8 children born to Peter and Amanda (**Smith**) Hager. Wife was sister of Judge Chauncey Smith. Brothers and sisters, Ermina, wife of Peter **Durland**, Hannah A. wife of Richard **Ely**, Julia, wife of Calvin **Ely**, Edwin died Peach Orchard, ny, Albert H. died NJ, Chester M., and Peter C. in Orange Co. Wife and 2 daughters reside in Jersey City, NJ

Humiston Sylvia 62 in Monterey, NY February 2, 1882

Palmer Amelia 53 wife of Rev. Noble Palmer formerly of Watkins, NY in Buffalo, NY February 15, 1882. Buried Montour cem.

Mathews Mary in 21st year at Logan, NY February 14, 1882

Washburne Weston unmarried son of Rev. Daniel, brother of John and Ella in Ft. Worth, Texas February 8, 1882. Buried Watkins, NY

Lyon Walter 84 son of Jesse in Catherine, NY February 2, 1882

Haight Mrs. George W. in Watkins, NY February 15, 1882

Saylor John suicide in Watkins, NY February 21, 1882, buried in Mecklenburgh, NY

Nichols Mrs. Amasa 65 a widow in Reading, NY February 28, 1882

Coon Dr. C. C. 88 in Ovid, NY February 28, 1882. Wife Sara M. died following

DEATH NOTICES

day age 86. Married July 20, 1817

White Nancy 69y 7m 24d widow of William E., who was born in NJ and died 6 years ago, in Watkins, NY February 19, 1882. Born June 25, 1812 nee **Minturn** in NJ. Married age 21, 8 sons and 1 dau. Buried Glenwood cem.

Stoll Daniel C. 71 at Bradford, NY February 23, 1882. Born September 30, 1812 in Sussex Co. NJ.. Married 1834 Lydia **Kays**. Wife, 2 sons and 4 daughters survive, D. H. and Mrs. George **Mosher** of Watkins, NY, James M. and Philetus died Civil War

Burritt George 62 in Watkins, NY March 2, 1882. Buried Burdett, NY

Merritt G. Albert 34 only child of Peter A. in Dundee, NY March 11, 1882

Loveless Mrs. O. T. 37 in Watkins, NY March 2, 1882

Dixon James 37 in Hector, NY March 5, 1882, unmarried

Saylor Mrs. Schuyler dau of Mr. **Topping** of Foot's Hill in Hector, NY March 7, 1882

Van Valer Andrew at Townsend, NY March 14, 1882. Born October 24, 1786 and married age 20. Wife died 1864. 1 sister Mrs. **Fosdick** of Buffalo, NY, 2 daughters, Mrs. **Hadly** of Cal. and Mrs. Edwin **Mapes** of Townsend

Smith Joseph C. 48 son of Thomas S. and Elizabeth T. in Hector, NY March 14, 1882. Born Hector. Leaves widow, 2 sons and 1 adopted dau. Buried Bennettsburg, NY

Barrows John 76 in Havana, NY March 19, 1882, buried Montour, NY

Peck Mrs. D. Sutton in 79th year wife of Tennant in Reading Center, NY March 19, 1882. Sister of late Nathaniel and Aaron **Sutton** and Mrs. Samuel **Lott**. Born December 1, 1803 in Lodi. 10 children, 5 living

Chandler Frances 23 at Logan, NY March 13, 1882

Woodworth James 66 this month at Moreland, NY March 19, 1882. Native of Onieda Co. oldest of 16 children. Leaves wife, 1 son and 1 dau. 1 dau deceased

Pickering Daniel F. 66 in Elmira, NY March 27, 1882. Born June 6, 1816 Middle Smithfield, Monroe Co. Pa.

Huntley Isaiah formerly of Reading, NY in Canton, Pa. March 27, 1882, buried Glenwood cem.

Rogers Mary 23 wife of Daniel in Watkins, NY March 22, 1882. Born Troy, NY. Leaves 6 months infant. Buried Co. Line

Jamison J. Emmett 38 in Muskegan, Michigan March 17, 1882. Parents live Ovid, Michigan, formerly of Watkins.

Mathews Daniel in 72nd year at Logan, NY March 26, 1882

Searles Mrs. Jason A. at Reynoldsville, NY March 28, 1882

Hollister Orleans Andrew Jackson 67 at Reynoldsville, NY March 31, 1882. Born March 31, 1815 in Genoa, NY. Married 1848, leaves wife and 2 children, Mrs. William Dean of Corning, NY and 1 dau at home, brother Samuel F. of Jamestown, Pa.

Vorhees Cordelia 39 at Logan, NY April 3, 1882

Elliot Hiram 62 at Burdett, BT April 6, 1882, unmarried

Treman Madison in 64th year at Watkins, NY April 2, 1882. Born 1818 in Mecklenburgh, NY son of Calvin. Leaves wife, 3 children, 3 sisters, Mrs. W. G. Goldsmith of Mecklenburgh, Mrs. Helen Wheeler of Castleton, Dakota and Mrs. J. B. Bodle of Chicago, Ill.

Grant Mrs. Crandall at Watkins, NY April 6, 1882

Deming Hiram 82y 4m 24d at Syracuse, NY April 10, 1882. Brother Charles died 1861 in Illinois, Samuel W. died 1881 in Jackson, Pa. and C. W. out west

Case Caroline Amanda 56 in Burdett, NY April 13, 1882

Chubbock Rev. A. E. at Watkins, NY April 15, 1882

Griswold Mrs. Squire 66 in Watkins, NY April 22, 1882. Married (1) 1835 Marvin Van Norman. Husband and 2 daughters died 1839. Married (2) 1841 Squire who died 1880. 1 son and 4 dau by 2nd marriage

White Frank 36 son of late Rev. W. E. in Corning, NY April 21, 1882. Leaves wife, former Miss Featherly and 1 child

Baker Fannie 5y 6m 6d dau of Edmund and Mary L. in Watkins, NY April 14, 1882

Marshall Edna 4y 6m dau of Elmer and Zelma in Jackson, Michigan April 23, 1882

Griswold Isabella H. 43y 5m 18d wife of Dr. T. L. and dau of Fox Holden in Watkins, NY May 5, 1882. Born November 17, 1838 in Reading, NY. Married August 18, 1859, 4 sons, 3 living

Carpenter Alvah in Bennettsburg, NY May 28, 1882

Woodhull Charles W. son of Calvin of Havana, NY in Elmira, NY May 26, 1882. Buried Havana

DEATH NOTICES

Breese John 92 in Horseheads, NY May 28, 1882

Henderson Abigail 74y 10m 7d wife of Rufus in Reading, NY June 3, 1882

West Elizabeth in 40th year wife of John in Watkins, NY June 3, 1882. 3 children Mrs. Georgianna **Ahart** of Millport, NY, Delos age 14 & Blanche age 8

Wheeler Harry Arnot son of Arnot formerly of Watkins, NY in Au Gres, Michigan May 23, 1882. Born April 17, 1881

Clark Owen in 70th year at Watkins, NY June 5, 1882. Born December 26, 1812 Co. Cavan, Ireland. Immigrated 1840. Married Mary **Ryan** in New Hampshire. 7 sons and 2 daus, James C. dec. Buried Watkins Catholic cem.

Haxton Clarence 47 in Burdett, NY June 8, 1882

Hudson Miss Mary S. 62y 1m 19d in Watkins, NY June 14, 1882

Best Annie 9y in Rock Stream, NY June 12, 1882

Bryant Grace A. 6m 6d dau of Henry G. and Mary E. in Watkins, NY June 23, 1882

Halliday Abbie A. 38y 6m 27d wife of Smith in Watkins, NY July 5, 1882. Buried Elmira, NY

Guthrie Rhoda widow of Joseph in Watkins, NY July 8, 1882. Born September 5, 1802 in Benton Center, NY dau of Ezra Cole from Litchfield, Conn. Husband died 1861. Children Myron A. and Mrs. George **Ringer**. Buried Benton Center

Manning Col. John Y. 87y 26d in Ovid, NY July 3, 1882. Came from Conn. in 1815. Served War of 1812

Clizbe S. C. 62 formerly of Watkins, NY in Athens, Pa. July 4, 1882

O'Daniels Jennie Vail 22y 2m only remaining dau of James in Reading Center, NY July 28, 1882. Buried Glenwood cem.

Green Erastus in Burdett, NY July 24, 1882

Roberts Elizabeth 75 wife of Lewis in Reading, NY July 15, 1882. Born Mottsville, NY nee **Miller**. Several children, names 1 Mrs. James **Hatfield**. Buried Glenwood cem.

Wedgewood Ellen Cummings 84 July 14, 1882. Born Highlands, Scotland, came to America age 5. Husband from Boslem, England. He died April 1874

Frost Ely C. Jr. 34 in Canandaigua, NY July 21, 1882. Married Mary E. **Roberts**. Buried Weston, NY

Hill Eunice 77 wife of Caleb in Havana, NY August 11, 1882, nee **Durfey**. Married 1825 in Smithfield, Bradford Co. Pa. came to Havana in 1829. Leaves husband and 3 sons, E. W. of Malden, Missouri, Dr. A. D. of Dexter, Missouri and Hon, D. B., mayor of Elmira, NY. 2 daughters deceased. Buried Montour cem

Broakman Vena Franc infant dau of Charles M. in Watkins, NY August 6, 1882. Grandparents, A. A. **Hemingway**

Compton Amiee E. 4m 19d daughter of William R. and Alice in Watkins, NY August 11, 1882. Buried Glenwood cem

Mc Elheney Eliza 68 widow of Rev. Theodore in Burdett, NY August 16, 1882. Leaves 6 married daughters, Mrs. W. M. **Lambert**, Mrs. C. **Haxton**, Mrs. F. **Benham** of Burdett, Mrs. George R. **Downing** of Watkins, NY, Mrs. Charles **Osborn** of Canandaigua, NY and Mrs. W. H. **Hunter** of Rochester, NY

Capell Daniel 67 at Penn Yan, NY August 25, 1882. Dau Mrs. E. A. **Gillett** of Watkins, NY

Mattison Mrs. Ella J. 32 in Hector, NY August 22, 1882

Webb Barnard in 63rd year formerly of Reading, NY at son-in-law F. M. **Clarke** in Dundee, NY August 26, 1882

Ganung Edward 75 in Dix, NY August 30, 1882. Children, Mrs. Nathaniel **Chapman**, Miss Sarah of Mecklenburgh, NY and E. K. of Elmira, NY

Lattin Everett in 79th year at son-in-law's Horace J. **Baldwin** in Watkins, NY September 1, 1882

Fish Dr. William H. at Mecklenburgh, NY September 2, 1882. Born April 4, 1826 son of Dr. Henry Fish. Married October 12, 1858 Eliza A. **Noyes** of Eddytown, NY. Leaves wife and son Fred age 14

Lovell Henry at Veteran, NY September 4, 1882

Tracy Theopholis 67 in Reynoldsville, NY September 20, 1882. Born Granville, NY. Married (1) Elizabeth **Reynolds** and (2) February 15, 1844 Eliza **Hager** who survives

Craver Theodore A. in 40th year at Watkins, NY October 2, 1882

Abrams Edna in 23rd year wife of John and dau of Edward **Ganung** October 3, 1882. Married January 1882. Buried Glenwood cem.

Paige Mrs. E. A. dau of G. C. **Shearer** in Geneva, NY October 9, 1882. Leaves husband, son age 13 and dau age 7

Reed Mrs. James B. formerly of Watkins, NY at son-in law's E. B. **Fenton** October 14, 1882. Dau Mrs. O. S. **Holden** of Watkins, NY

DEATH NOTICES 117

Rooney James 83 in Watkins, NY October 4, 1882. Born September 29, 1799 in Co. Westmeath, Ireland. Immigrated in 1853. Wife died 29 years ago May, 5 sons and 1 daughter

Murdock John in Elmira, NY October 8, 1882

Berry Mrs. W. H. in 29th year year dau of Charles F. **Everts** at Hector, NY October 19, 1882

Gulick Levi 32 son of N. T. in Watkins, NY October 24, 1882. Leaves wife and 2 children in Dallas, Michigan

Ryall Elder formerly of Reading, NY at Penn Yan, NY October 21, 1882

Gibbs Asgill 95 formerly of Ovid, NY in Rochester, NY October 25, 1882. Born June 27, 1787 in Pownul, Vermont. Names son James S. of Watkins, NY

Morris Ephraim 83 in Bennettsburg, NY October 21, 1882. Born England, came to Hector 57 years ago. Children, Andrew, Isaac, Mrs. Sherman **Beardsley** of Hector and Mrs. Erie **Vaughn** of Watkins, NY

Schuyler Mrs. Dorman 50 in Orange, NY November 2, 1882

Dickens Eli S. 81y 6m 28d buried Cayuta, NY November 12, 1882

Huey Stephen formerly of Dix, NY funeral at brother Eli's in Tyrone, NY November 26, 1882. Leaves 5 children

Swarthout Heman C. in Reading, NY November 15, 1882. Born April 20, 1813 in Benton, NY, 3rd of 8 children to John and Irene (**Chapman**) Swarthout. Married age 25 Sarah Ann **Monroe**, 9 children, Irene E. wife of H. L. **White** of Watkins, NY, John C. of Pine Valley, NY, Helen wife of G. C. **German** of Havana, NY, Eliza J. wife of G. C. **Phillips** and Alice L. wife of Morris **Roberts** of Brandon, Minn., A. D. of Valparaizo, Ind., Charles B., Martha A. and Fred R. at home. Buried Reading, NY

Bassett Eliza in 90th year wife of Sheldon nee **Ruscoe** in Peach Orchard, NY November 19, 1882. Husband died April 1876 age 96. Children, Joseph, Charles B. of Watkins, NY. Only dau wife of I. N. **Hurd** died in India 25 years ago, leaving a son Charles B. Hurd of Chicago, Ill.

Conklin Nathan 49 in Havana, NY November 25, 1882

Woodward Timothy 55 at Dix, NY December 1, 1882. Leaves wife and 5 children. Buried Old Co. Line cem.

Hill Caleb 80 of Havana, NY in Waverly, NY December 9, 1882. Born 1802 in Wyndam, Conn. Wife died 7 months ago, buried Montour cem. Son Hon. D. B. Hill Lieut. Governor of NY

Spencer Helen 58 wife of J. P. and dau of Chauncey **Smith** in Hector, NY December 12, 1882. Leaves 2 daus

Compton Sylvanus in Logan, NY December 1882. Born December 18, 1812 in Monroe, NY. Married January 1, 1834 in Hector, NY Deborah **Mathews** who survives, also Mother age 90. Children, Jacob, Ezekiel, Charles Fremont and Betsey wife of Maxfield **Huston**

Heath George N. 15 son of Charles drowned in canal at Watkins, NY December 26, 1882

Tuttle Lydia widow of Daniel in Reading, NY December 29, 1882. Born October 1, 1795 in NY daughter of Charles **Watkins** (brother of Dr. Samuel founder of Watkins) and Susan **Marshall**. 5 daus, 1 died infant, Ann Marie died 1880, Mrs. **Williamson** and Mrs. **Lewis** both of Elizabeth, NJ. Brothers and sisters, John W., Charles, Lydia, Elizabeth and Duncan all born England except Samuel. Married October 28, 1828, husband died February 29, 1876 in 80th year. 8 children, 5 died young. Charles died age 18, Samuel died February 20, 1876. Adrian survives. Buried Glenwood cem.

Robinson Squire in 74th year at Reynoldsville, NY December 24, 1882. Born Putnam Co. Married 1831 Patty Ann **Leake** who died 1873. Resided with son Martin

Deyo Peter 53 in Orange, NY December 31, 1882

Hause Lyman in Minneapolis, Minn. December 23, 1882, buried Tyrone, NY

Peck Benoni 77 formerly of Watkins, NY at son's J. B. in Niles, Michigan January 2, 1883. Sister Mrs. George B. **Guinnip** and a brother Tenant age 81 of Reading, NY

Byram Abbie Jane wife of Charles in Watkins, NY January 6, 1883. Born December 6, 1825 in Dix, NY eldest dau of Solomon and Anna **Hicks**. Married March 25, 1845, 3 children, Henry G., William H. and Anna H., also Mother, 2 sisters and 2 brothers

Scobey Augustus 54 formerly of Sugar Hill, NY in Norwalk, Ohio January 6, 1883. Brother Andrew S. of Townsend, NY

Secord Barney 66 in Searsburg, NY January 12, 1883

Dilliston John 69y 3m 5d in Tioga, Pa. January 15, 1883. Born October 10, 1813 near Dundee, NY. Married 1837 Elizabeth **Sheardown** daughter of Rev. T. S.

Sutphen Jonas 10y son of Peter O. & Nettie in Burdett, NY January 16, 1883. sister Clarissa age 12 & brother John age 5y

Smith George son of Robert in Dix, NY January 18, 1883

Wickham Erastus January 13, 1883. Born February 3, 1812 in Tompkins Co. now Schuyler Co. eldest son of William Jr., grandson of William, 1st settler of Hector,

NY. Married 1834 Amelia **Everts** who died January 1, 1875, 8 children 6 living. Married (2) Mrs. Ruth A. **Tyler**

Tum Michael in Montour, NY January 21, 1883. Born Germany immigrated 1854. Leaves wife and 2 children

Newcomb Hiram A. 72 in Townsend, NY February 1, 1883

Townsend Mrs. Orville in Hector, NY February 11, 1883

Case Hannah B. 46 in Millport, NY February 13, 1883. Born February 1837 in Ludlowville, NY. Leaves husband and 2 daus

Moore Mercy 86y 3m 8d wife of Paul in Logan, NY February 21, 1883. Married nearly 67 years, husband 1 week older

Johnson Elizabeth nee **Estell** in 80th year widow of William at son-in law's Edward **Tompson** in Watkins, NY February 25, 1883. Born September 10, 1803 in Monmouth, Co. NJ. Married about 60 years, husband died December 20, 1882, age 82. Leaves 1 son and 2 daus, Mrs. Mary **Wagner** of Ottawa, Can., Edward of Barton, NY and Dr. George Johnson of Lewistown, Illinois

Vaughan Lavinia 76 in Burdett, NY March 12, 1883, dau of William **Martin**. Children, Erie of Watkins, NY 1 dau in Hector, NY and 1 dau Mrs. Samuel **Sackett** dec.

Smith George Jr. 43 in Watkins, NY March 13, 1883. Born 1840 in Mt. Vernon, Ohio. Leaves wife, 3 children, widowed Mother, 3 brothers and 2 sisters

Roberts Lewis 76 in Dix, NY March 4 1883. Born Reading, NY eldest son of John. Married Elizabeth **Miller** who died June 1882. Large family, 7 survive

Hill Jane 69y 15d wife of George G. in Watkins, NY March 12, 1883. Sister of late George D. **Freer** of Watkins, Dr. Jacob **Freer**, Mrs. **Hungerford** and Mrs. **Bange** of NY. Born February 27, 1814 in Marbletown, NY. 7 children, 5 living, Josephus in NJ, Aaron in New Mexico, George G. of Watkins, William P. in Onieda, NY and Fred D. in NY

Catlin Phineas in 89th year at Odessa, NY March 15, 1883. Born January 30, 1795 in Chemung, NY. Married February 1814 in Orange Co. Hannah **Lee** who died 1867. 7 children, Caroline **Miller** of Odessa, NY, Henry B., Lucy Louise wife of Thomas B. **Campbell** of St. Paul, MInn. Married (2) 1875 Deborah **Kimble**

Nickerson George Vincent 6y son of John in Watkins, NY March 26, 1883

Hoes James D. 36 in Watkins, NY March 28, 1883

Royce Amos in 80th year at Watkins, NY March 22, 1883. Born September 23, 1823 in Cayuga Co. 1 of 10 children to Samuel and Keturah (**Somerton**) Royce. Married

February 25, 1825 Marilla **Baker**, born 1809 in Vermont. Children, Charles I. died in 23rd year at Townsend, NY, Francis L. died Civil War and Harvey D. died age 19 in Townsend. Buried Montour cem.

Hatfield Joshua in 80th year at Reading, NY April 7, 1883. Sons survive, Oscar and John of Reading, James and George elsewhere

Bolt Daniel H. 82 in Townsend, NY April 5, 1883. Born 1801 in Saratoga Co. Leaves 2nd wife and 5 children, Mrs. John **Mills** of Watkins, NY, Mrs. Bennett **Ellis** of Bradford, NY, S. of Elmira, NY and D. A. of Harrisburg, Pa.

Miller Fannie Annette 13y 7m 25d in Watkins, NY April 8, 1883

Armstrong Abigail T. in 84th year at Watkins, NY April 22, 1883. Born December 6, 1799 in Saratoga Co. nee **Moulton**. Husband died 1823, remained widow over 60 years. 1 dau Mrs. Joel **Voak**, 1 sister and 3 brothers

Woodruff Mrs. Ann in 54th year at dau Mrs. **Peterson** in Watkins, NY April 23, 1883. Buried Co. Line cem

Collins Mrs. Eleazor nee **Updike** 40 in Watkins, NY April 30, 1883. Married 1873

Lynch Maurice 63 at Coal Point, NY April 25, 1883

Cressman Charles in Hector, NY April 25, 1883. Born January 1809 near Quakertown, Pa. Married 1830 Nancy **Owen** daughter of Nathaniel and Mehetabel who came from Orange Co. 1798

Bell Mrs. John 38 in Searsburg, NY April 18, 1883. Leaves husband and 11 children

Culver Chauncey 57 in Hector, NY May 5, 1883

Wager Mary E. 30 wife of Joshua formerly of Hector, NY in Veteran, NY May 19, 1883

Huey Mrs. Edward abt 30 in Watkins, NY May 22, 1883

Dann Fannie 71 in Penn Yan, NY May 17, 1883, buried Starkey, NY

Chapman Rev. Charles 79 in Rock Stream, NY May 25, 1883

Haring Charles in Watkins, NY May 25, 1883. Born February 11, 1838 in Reading, NY son of William & Elizabeth (**Cox**). Father died November 21, 1875 & Mother died June 24, 1877. Married 1864 Jane M. **Shepard** of Reading. 2 sons John S. & William S.

Lawrence Mrs. John L. at Asylum in Canandaigua, NY June 9, 1883. Suicide by hanging. Daughter Lizzie of Havana, NY

Thompson Elizabeth wife of Thomas near Mecklenburgh, NY June 9, 1883. Born 1819 eldest daughter of John W. and Dorcas **Mathews** from Waterbury, Conn. 8 children 7 survive, Charles died age 6m, Headly, Maggie wife of James **Higgins**, Delia B. wife of F. A. **Keeton**, Frank L., William A. and Bird M. all of Elmira, NY and Fred A. of Socorro, N. Mexico

Whippy Davis W. of Havana, NY in Downsville, Del. June 13, 1883. Born February 29, 1820 in Hudson, NY 1 of 8 children, 6 survive. Married April 13, 1845 Sarah **Rightmire**, 1 child Mrs. H. O. **Chambers**. Buried Montour cem.

Miller Sargeant 14y 11d son of Jabez in Reading, NY June 12, 1883

Pangborn Mrs. Eugene dau of late Robert **Huey** in Dix, NY June 19, 1883. Leaves husband and 4 children

Fero Mrs. Isaac 33 at Beaver Dams, NY June 17, 1883

Allen Mrs. Mercy in 90th year at Watkins, NY July 5, 1883

Drake Nancy nee **Vail** in 86th year widow of Thomas at Orange, NY June 26, 1883. Born October 5, 1797 in Mt. Hope, NY. Married 1834 (his second wife). Husband died November 1, 1839, 1 son Sylvester. Buried Sugar Hill, NY

Vine George 75 in Monterey, NY June 22, 1883. Wife died 2 years ago, leaves 1 son

Van Dyke Jacob abt 53 in Reading, NY July 4, 1883

Clark Loesa 29 wife of Hartwell J., dau of James M. **Shelton** in Reading, NY July 11, 1883. Married January 9, 1878

Drake Richard W. in 62nd year at Odessa, NY July 28, 1883. Born January 23, 1821 in Mt. Hope, NY son of Thomas W. and Mary Ann (**Swezey**) Drake. Married Rachel **Freeman** who died 1881, 1 dau Rachel only survivor

Huey John 76 in Tyrone, NY July 30, 1883. Children, Dr. Lyman Huey of Watkins, NY, Vernon C. and Lullie of Tyrone, James M. and John A. of Reading, NY, Mrs. C. W. **Sellen** and Mrs. George **Wellover** of Dix, NY, Edward in Clinton Co., Mrs. F. C. **Swift** of Branchport, NY and Mrs. E. B. **Campbell** of Nelson, Pa.

Cook Mrs. E. W. abt 70 of Havana, NY at dau Mrs. H. H. **Doty** of Wellsville, NY July 29, 1883. Buried Havana

Baldwin Willie H. 3y 8m son of W. H. at Watkins, NY July 27, 1883

Lockwood William 73 at Tyrone, NY August 10, 1883

Higgins John H. 21y 1m 15d son of D. H. at Watkins, NY August 31, 1883. Born July 16, 1862 Castile, NY

Grover Mason 9m 7d son of H. J. in Watkins, NY September 7, 1883

Gilbert Matilda in 62nd year near Havana, NY September 8, 1883. Born March 19, 1822 dau of Chester and Sally **Corbett.** Married age 22 S. K. Gilbert. 5 of 6 children survive, Mrs. J. E. **Ross,** Mrs. Ellison **Mc Intyre,** Sarah, Ida and Charles

Roberts Eliza O. 59 relict of Henry and dau of Rochester **Hurd** at Rock Stream, NY September 4, 1883

Mc Neil Sarah 73 formerly of Watkins, NY at dau Mrs. **Betteridge** in Elmira, NY September 9, 1883. Son M. W.

Hause Henry K. son of late William of Watkins, NY in Guaymos, Mexico September 12, 1883

Smith Phebe E. 70 September 9, 1883. Born Caroline, NY. Children, Mary, Fanny, Mrs. **Franklin** out West, Benjamin in Philadelphia. Pa., Dewitt of San Francisco and William in Caroline

Swim Samuel S. in Watkins, NY September 16, 1883. Born June 30, 1801 in Cornwall. Married April 24, 1830 Lydia Jane **Williams** in NY City, sister of William R. of Watkins. 1 dau Mrs. Leander S. **Chapman**

Mc Intyre John in 82nd year at Hall's Corners, NY September 11, 1883. Born Tyrone, Ireland. Married 1824-5 Elizabeth **Sproul** of Tyrone, NY, 11 children. Buried Tyrone

Knox Rev. William Eaton of Elmira, NY at Blue Mountain Lake September 17, 1883. Born October 16, 1820 in Knoxboro, NY. Married Alice Woodward **Jenks** who survives

Mathews Anjeannett in 38th year dau of George and Amelia at Burdett, NY September 15, 1883. Buried Peach Orchard, NY

Tower Harry 7y 2m 10d son of Rev. C. M. and M. E. Tower in N. Hector, NY September 17, 1883

Call Catherine 67 widow of Chauncey L. at son's J. C. in Watkins, NY September 30, 1883. Born 1817 in Seneca Co. NY. 5 children survive, 2 daus in Chicago, Ill., 1 in Iowa, 1 in Florida

Phelps Joel (date of Newspaper October 18, 1883). Born December 20, 1829 in Dix, NY. Married 1851 Nancy E. **Weller.** 5 children, oldest son lives Michigan

Gabriel Mrs. Harriet 80 in Reading, NY October 29, 1883

Stamp John Aaron 41 in Havana, NY October 28, 1883

Hoare Richard 83 in Watkins, NY October 29, 1883. Born January 31. 1831 in

Chartham, Kent Co. England, came to US in 1854. Married (1) Mary **Lawrence** who died August 1866 leaving 3 children, Emily wife of Henry De **Munn**, Gracie and Minetta. Freddie died 2 years ago age 3. Married (2) Mrs. Rachel **Smith** dau of Benjamin **Burgess** of Dix, NY. Other survivors, father James M. 3 sisters, Mrs. George G. **Freer**, Mrs. George G. **Hill** and Mrs. George H. **Ellas** all of Watkins, NY.

Osmun Eunice at Rock Stream, NY October 27, 1883. Born November 10, 1792 in NJ daughter of Daniel **Shannon**. Came to Starkey, NY in 1806, married January 21, 1809. Husband died 1855, 12 children, 9 reached maturity, 5 survive

Platt Brewster in 83rd year at Townsend, NY November 22, 1883. Born December 25, 1800 in Unadilla, NY. Married ca 1835 Betsey **Hovey** dau of Maj. Ebenezer. Leaves wife and 1 widowed dau Mrs. Mary **Graham**. 1 son died

Perry Sally abt 60 widow of Harrison in Altay, NY November 5, 1883

Demund Sarah H. 57y 2m 25d in Watkins, NY November 20, 1883. Children James V. and William N. **Prebasco** of Watkins. Buried Sheldrake, NY

Love William S. 39 in Sugar Hill, NY November 28, 1883

Laraby Charles 78 in Watkins, NY November 26, 1883. Born November 1805 in Vermont. Married age 19 Hannah **Wanzo** in Reading, NY who died October 3, 1875. Children, Henry, John and Mrs. H. C. **Miller** of Watkins, William of Dundee, NY, Mrs. A. J. **Coykendall** of Reading. Buried Lake Rd. cem in Reading

Knapp Mrs. M. V. in 50th year suicide in Wayne, NY December 31, 1883

Moran James 62 in Watkins, NY January 9, 1884. Born Ireland. Leaves wife and 6 children

Decker Simon 77 in Havana, NY January 5, 1884. Born January 2, 1807 in Deckertown, NJ. Married twice, son Hiram by 1st wife. Married (2) August 12, 1869 Harriet E. **Badgely**, 1 son Simon. Brother Sidney died 1849

Barton Fanny 75 widow of Nathan in Watkins, NY February 14, 1884

Johnson Levi in Dix, NY February 13, 1884

Sprowls William C. abt 74 February 11, 1884. Born April 10, 1809 in Sussex Co. NJ, 4th child of James and Susannah (**Cornelius**) Sprowls. Father died July 22, 1853 and Mother died January 9, 1854 ages abt 74. Brothers and sisters, Christian born 1803 married Elias **Westfall** and died in Michigan. Caty born 1805 married Lewis **Fitzsimmons**, resides in Oak Hill, NY. Peter born 1806 died wealthy in Hillsdale, Michigan abt 2 yrs ago. William C. born 1809, dec. Mary born 1811 married Dr. Daniel **Wilson**, died in Branch Co. Michigan about 7 years ago. Daniel born 1816 of Starkey, NY, Effaline born 1823 married Lorenzo **Chubb** of Pewamo, Michigan. Married 1827 Agnes **Wood** born 1810 in Geneva, NY dau of Thomas and Nancy (**Goundry**) Wood. Children all born in Starkey, NY, James L. born November 28,

1828 and died December 9, 1868, Elizabeth born September 26, 1835 married Gilbert L. **Roberts** of Reading, who died about 4 years ago leaving 2 daus Agnes and Alice who married Charles Love. D. S. born May 3, 1838 at home. Willie H. born February 12, 1845 and died age 3. M F. born September 5, 1850 of Meriden, Iowa.

Rooney Andrew 10y 6m son of William and Kate in Watkins, NY February 14, 1884

Barnum Warren in Elmira, NY February 13, 1884. Born September 11, 1838 son of Samuel B. who died 6 years ago age 77. Mother was Polly **Reynolds** who died 1 year ago age 75. Brothers and sisters, Eli of N. Barton, NY, Reynolds of Binghamton, NY, Mahala wife of E. M. **Hutchings** of Spencer, NY, Matilda **Shipman** of Owego, NY and Malvina M. **Weed** of Smithfield, Pa.

Brokaw John 34 in Watkins, NY April 15, 1884. Married twice, son by 1st wife died young, dau Fleety by 2nd wife

Thompson Frank P. eldest son of Dr. J. W. and Cordelia in Watkins, NY June 21, 1884. Born May 5, 1852 in Burdett, NY. 3 sisters and 1 brother, Mrs. Mary D. **Gardner** of Tully, NY, Bertha D. and Addie C. of Watkins, NY and John M. of Michigan

Hager Charles suicide in Logan, NY June 21, 1884. Born October 1827 in Beaver Dams, NY

Mead John C. 80y 10m in Burdett, NY September 14, 1884

Coyle Carrie dau of Rev. Michael and Phebe September 6, 1884. Born February 5, 1867 in Jacksonville, NY

Pope Alice 8m dau of Horace G. in Reading, NY September 19, 1884

Arnwine Peter 22 killed by train in Tyrone, NY September 18, 1884

Woodward Mrs. K. in Enfield Falls, NY September 12, 1884. Born January 20, 1803 in Ovid, NY

Prosser David B. in 80th year at Penn Yan, NY September 17, 1884

Buck William C. at Sugar Hill, NY September 18, 1884. Born May 2, 1809 in Ulster Co. Married 1828 Elizabeth **Allen** who died 1841. 2 sons, William L. died age 19. Married (2) Susan **Hanmer**. She had 3 sons and 2 daus.

Cole Asahel in Havana, NY September 25, 1884. Born June 5, 1814 in Carmel, NY to Joseph and Phebe 1 of 6 children. 1 sister survives, Mrs.Minerva N. **Patchen** of NY. Married June 23, 1836 Mary Ann Savory at Post Creek, NY. Wife and 3 children survive, Harlem of Watkins, NY, Ira S. of Havana, and Mrs. Charles **Bennett** of Dix, NY. Buried Montour, NY

Rich Alfred 3y 6m son of Charles B. and Estella in Reading, NY September 29, 1884

DEATH NOTICES

Beardsley Elam 87 in Havana, NY September 29, 1884

Norton Willis W. in 83rd year at Reading, NY September 27, 1884. Born June 28, 1802 in Goshen, Conn. son of Jesse. Married March 11, 1829 Phebe **Gregory** sister of Mrs. Betsey **Catlin** of Watkins, NY and Harman L. of Altay, NY. 7 children, 2 died young, Miles B. died 1879, Oscar Orlando of Lodi, NY, William Leroy of Watkins, NY, Francis Marion of Carbondale, Kansas, Mary Elvira wife of Rev. L. D. **Worth** of Reading

Beardsley Mrs. Asa in Hector, NY October 5, 1884. Son Elmer killed by falling tree September 11, 1884

Bartholomew Eliza in 63rd year at Dix, NY October 10, 1884. Born Co. Tyrone, Ireland to Samuel and Jane **Love**. Brothers, William N. Love of Watkins, NY, Joseph B., sisters Mrs. Thomas **Jack** of Reading, NY and Mrs. Martha **Campbell** of Iowa. Son Charles

Maloney John in 26th year at Watkins, NY October 12, 1884. Born January 9, 1859 in Corning, NY son of Patrick and Eliza. Leaves 4 sisters, Nellie, Maria, Eliza and Kate, 3 brothers, Daniel, William and Frank. Buried St. Mary's cem.

Hamilton Peyton R. in 86th year at Watkins, NY October 12, 1884. Born November 19, 1798 in Hudson, NY. Buried Glenwood cem.

Roof Phillip 68 in Starkey, NY November 18, 1884

Carpenter Mary Dubois in Watkins, NY February 7, 1885. Born January 22, 1800 nee **Westlake** in Blooming Grove, NY. Married February 20, 1883 Zeno Carpenter who died March 17, 1876 in Horseheads, NY. 9 children, Mrs. Phebe E. **Greeman** died last January in Horseheads, NY, William Henry of Monsey, NY, Mrs. Hannah Mc **Henry** of Southport, NY, George D. of Penn Yan, NY, Mrs. S. M. **Marriot** of Watkins, NY, Mrs. Phila A. **Marshall** of Horseheads, Zeno of Penn Yan, NY, Mrs. Sarah F. **Hewitt** of Tifflin, Ohio, and John L. of Horseheads. Buried Horseheads

Rice Louisa wife of W. D. of Hinton, Michigan at Sugar Hill, NY February 18, 1885. Born November 5, 1854 to William and Nancy **Caldwell**. Father died Spring of 1883. Surviving husband, Mother, brothers and sisters, William and Robert of Sugar Hill, John of Texas, Mrs. David **Wasson** and Sarah of Sugar Hill. Married December 18, 1882

Haring Cornelius 80 in Orange, NY February 18, 1885. Born September 7, 1805 in Genoa, NY son of Garrett and Phebe 1 of 6 children, late William of Watkins, NY, Mrs. Polly **Johnson**, Mrs. Anna B. **Johnson** and Mrs. Dr. **Bell** of Monterey, NY and Mrs. Deborah **Horton** of Savona, NY. Married (1) (**Johnson**) 3 children, 2nd wife was sister of 1st wife, 7 children. Married (3) February 14, 1855 Mrs. Freelove **Townsend** who survives. Children Elizabeth wife of W. M. **Payne**, Wealthy wife of Henry **Wood** of Cal., Martha wife of Thomas **Lewis** of St. Croix, Wis., Charlotte wife of C. W. **Hurd**, Garrett, William, Mary wife of Mortimer **Crum** & Alice wife of J. E. **Anthony**

Gilbert Frances nee **Youngs** 34y 5m wife of Baxter in Watkins, NY March 20, 1885

Reynolds C. F. Sr. 70 in Burdett, NY March 25, 1885. 2 children, C. F. Jr. and Mrs. Norman **Hubbell** of Boise, Idaho

Carpenter Mrs. Charles 21 adopted dau of Enos **Horn** of Monterey, NY in Starkey, NY March 23, 1885. Married November 7, 1883

Beattie Jane H. 66 dau of Caleb **Huson** of Dundee, NY in Watkins, NY March 21, 1885. Sisters, Mrs. Uriah **Hair** of Watkins and Mrs. John **Gray** of Lakeville, NY. 2 children, Mrs. George M. **Sayre** of Watkins and John E. of Starkey, NY. Husband James died 1874 in Hall's Corners, NY. Buried Hall's Corners

Carpenter Mrs. George W. in Abilene, Kansas June 7, 1885. Born April 13, 1852 in Havana, NY dau of Elijah S. and Clara **Hinman**. Married October 1, 1872, 7 children

Kendall Lyman 72 in Tyrone, NY June 8, 1885. Born Mass. to Abel and Erva 1 of 11 children, 2 living Abel Jr. age 93 of Altay, NY and Mrs. Erva **Sunderlin** of Rochester, NY. 1st wife Rosetta **Clark** dau of Joseph, who died when children were infants, Edward of Yates Co. and Lewis in Rochester. Married (2) Mary J. **Carpenter**, 2 children, Wayland died youth and Erva widow of Albert H. **Booram**

Huey Eugene in 20th year suicide June 22, 1885. Son of Stephen who died 2 years ago Mother died 6 years ago

Knapp Mrs. Albert in Watkins, NY June 24, 1885. Has 2w old child

Sellen Sarah 81y 3m 2d widow of John in Reading, NY June 24, 1885. Born Orwell, Pa. to Leben and Esther **Roberts**, 3 sisters and 4 brothers, 1 survives Mrs. Belinda **Sellen** of Watkins, NY widow of Wesley. Married 1824, husband died 4 years ago age 80, last of family of 10. 3 children, Rosetta widow of Willett **Purdy** who died in Civil War, Melissa wife of Henry **Tabor** of Watkins, Rev. Philemon of Castile, NY and Mrs. Isaac **Conklin** of Reading

Stevens Mrs. William 57 in Beaver Dams, NY June 30, 1885

Pease Norman 61 of Hector, NY at son-in-law's F. M. **Stoughton** July 18, 1885. Wife died July 8, 1883, 2 sons and 4 daus

Freer Mathew Dewitt in 61st year at Watkins, NY July 29, 1885. Born March 23, 1825 in Marbletown, NY son of Solomon and Polly (**Cass**) Freer of French Huguenot descent, 1 of 12 children only 3 survive, Mrs. **Hungerford**, Mrs. **Bange** and Dr. Jacob S. all of NY. 1st wife Melissa **Bloomer** dau of John L. of Ulster Co. 3 sons Robert of Havana, NY, Morgan and Fred of Western Territory. Married (2) Julia **Bull** of Tompkins Co. her 2 children Frances H. and William B. Buried Glenwood cem.

Harpending John 78 in Altay, NY September 11, 1885. Born Beech Woods, Sullivan Co. Married August 28, 1831 Eunice **Teller**. No children

DEATH NOTICES 127

Conover Clarissa 84y 7d widow of Peter H. in Watkins, NY September 13, 1885. Children Sarah J., Maggie A. and Anna E. of Watkins, C. J. of Orr, Dakota and Mrs. Myra **Van Horn** of Groton, NY

Hager Theodore F. in 42nd year at Odessa, NY September 12, 1885

Nutt Mrs. Nancy 91 in Dresden, NY November 16, 1885

Ross William 78 in Reading, NY November 22, 1885. Born 1807 in Perry Co. Pa. Married age 26 Theresa **Frost** at Eddytown, NY

Blaisdall Louisa M. 38 wife of Charles H. and dau of John J. and Mary **Smith** in Watkins, NY November 20, 1885. 2 sisters Caroline deceased and Ella. Married 13 years, 1 son Charles H. Jr.

Jamison John formerly of Reading, NY in Ovid, Michigan November 13, 1885. Brother Cyrus of Watkins, NY

Overhiser Casper 73 in Monterey, NY December 11, 1885

Thompson Abram 86 in Catherine, NY December 25, 1885

Russell Harriet in 75th year at Watkins, NY December 27, 1885. Born February 10, 1811 in Henniker, New Hampshire nee **Whitcomb**. Married April 1837 Benjamin, only surviving children E. B. and Mrs. G. L. **Nobles**. Buried Glenwood cem.

Lewis Dr. Edwin W. in 77th year at Watkins, NY December 26, 1885. Born January 30, 1809 in Dresden, NY to John L. Lewis native of New Haven, Conn. and Lora native of Vermont. Brothers and sisters surviving Judge John L. of Penn Yan, NY, Rev. Martin B. of Red Wing, Minn. and Mrs. Sarah E. widow of Fidus **Livermore** of Jackson, Michigan. Married 1837 Mary C. **Gardiner**, 7 children 5 survive, Charles C., Caroline S. of Watkins, Edwin A. of Franklin, Mass., Martin B. of Blossburg, Pa., John L. of Corning, NY and Mary E. of Watkins. Emma died November 1864

Gleason Ida 23 nee **Loveridge** wife of Ezra Jr. in N. Urbana, NY January 1, 1886

Sears Deacon in 81st year at Mecklenburgh, NY January 4, 1886

Allen Sarah 80 in Burdett, NY January 4, 1886. Born September 22, 1805 in Warren Co. NJ. 2 children William and Mary

Whitney Mrs. Lewis at Enfield, NY January 8, 1886

Burgess Delilah 87y 8m widow of Benjamin in Havana, NY January 11, 1886. Buried old cemetery west of Watkins, NY

Bower E. P. 25y 8m in Watkins, NY January 16, 1886

Stamp Abner abt 87 in Thurston, NY January 16, 1886

Gilbert Rachel 71 in Dix, NY January 14, 1886

Havens Charles in 72nd year at Watkins, NY January 17, 1886. Born March 6, 1814 in Dresden, NY. Married abt 50 years Hannah **Ellsworth**, 6 children, Mrs. G. V. **Hazard**, Mrs. Jedediah **Walker**, Franklin, Mrs. Alice **Hevener** all of Watkins, Mrs. Elizabeth **Whitmore** of Trumansburg, NY and Francis of Rome, NY

Jones William in 66th year at Havana, NY January 17, 1886

Tracy Elijah in Townsend, NY January 10, 1886. Born November 9, 1807 in Oxford, NY youngest of 13 children. Married 1832 Caroline **Harvey**. Leaves wife and 3 children, Mrs. James **Raplee** and John F. of Townsend, and Mrs. Rev. M. **Coyle** of N. Hector, NY

Thompson Nelson 74 in Penn Yan, NY January 20, 1886

Andrews Harriet 49 in Dundee, NY January 25, 1886. Dau of Lewis J. **La Fever**

Teeter Andrew 91 in Newfield, NY January 18, 1886

Halsey Anna 85y 10m widow of Gilbert in N. Hector, NY January 21, 1886. Born March 8, 1800 in Covert, NY to Rev. John P. **Woodworth**. Married January 1819, 12 children 7 living, Parker, Chauncey of Oregon, Fanny of N. Hector, Nancy of Albion, NY, Mrs. Mary Ann **Miller** of Lodi, NY, Mrs. Elizabeth **Hawes** of Watkins, NY and Mrs. Carrie **Curry** of Rochester, NY. Buried Lodi

Milliman James 47y 10m in N. Hector, NY January 23, 1886

Culver Albert 56 in Reading, NY January 27, 1886

Ellis Clara Jane in 16th year in Havana, NY January 23, 1886

Stanton Emmaline 84y 11m in Watkins, NY January 31, 1886. 2 children, Martha and Julia

Thynne Polly 77 wife of Nathaniel in Hector, NY February 7, 1886

La Fever Lewis J. in 73rd year at Starkey, NY February 10, 1886. Married Jane **Carpenter**.

Skinner Mulford Md. in Milford, Cal. February 12, 1886. Born January 27, 1815 in Covert, NY son of James 1 of 9 children, 4 living. Married July 19, 1843 Lufanny **Whitney** of Seneca Co. 1 son Homer D.

Gould Mrs. Sally 84 in Bennettsburg, NY February 23, 1886

King infant son of David in Mecklenburgh, NY February 21, 1886

Waugh James Sr. 95 at son-in-law's James **Scott** in Sugar Hill, NY February 18, 1886

DEATH NOTICES

Henderson William Rufus 46 formerly of Watkins, NY in Geneva, NY February 22, 1886. Buried Town Line cem

Lord William of advanced age in Penn Yan, NY February 26, 1886

O'Daniels Mrs. James 65y 7m in Reading, NY February 24, 1886

Culver Thomas 90y 10d in Reading, NY February 13, 1886. Born February 3, 1796 in Sussex Co. NJ. Married ca 1820 Anna **Fulkerson**. 9 children, 5 living

Hurd George R. 49 in Glenora, NY February 25, 1886

Scott A. H. 81 in Coopers Plains, NY February 27, 1886

Compton Mrs. Sylvanus in Logan, NY March 2, 1886. Husband and son died 4 years ago. Leaves 2 sons and 1 daughter

Scott Margaret in 84th year at Mecklenburgh, NY March 1, 1886

Hovencamp Charity 65 in Mecklenburgh, NY March 3, 1886

Bodle William abt 45 in Mecklenburgh, NY March 6, 1886

Goodrich Richard 5y in Townsend, NY March 12, 1886

Loncoy George in Watkins, NY March 17, 1886

Gilbert Willis 50y 5m in Reading, NY March 21, 1886. Born October 15, 1835 in Reading 2nd son of David and Clarissa (**La Fever**) Gilbert. She died October 8, 1881 age 72, Father now age 78. Brother Wakeman of Bath, NY. Married January 9, 1864 Mary J. **Drake** daughter of Thomas of Reading. Leaves wife and son Morris age 9

Golden Augusta 36y 5m wife of Frank formerly of Watkins, NY in Tonawanda March 22, 1886 a sister of Orville **Kees** of Watkins

Frost Horton 81 in Elmira, NY March 26, 1886 from Dutchess Co. in 1811. Married abt 60 years, Diantha **Cunningham**. Brother George of Watkins, NY and 2 brothers out west.

Downes John 12y 6m 11d son of Patrick in Watkins, NY March 30, 1886

Graham Anna Jane 63y 5m in Watkins, NY March 31, 1886. Born October 6, 1822 in Enfield, NY dau of Isaac and Elizabeth, sister of late George C. and John. Married February 22, 1843 Austin J. Graham at Enfield Center, NY. 5 children. Mrs. Ettie A. **Gray** of Denver, Col., George A. of Richmond, Ind. and Mary H. of Watkins

St. John Rev. Almiron 73 in Watkins, NY April 4, 1886. Born 1812 in Berne, NY. Leaves 2nd wife, son Montrose of Rockford, Illinois and 2 daus in Otsego Co.

Powell George 19 in Watkins, NY March 29, 1886

Ely Caleb 86 in Watkins, NY April 5, 1886

Thompson Demetrius in 47th year at Watkins, NY April 8, 1886. Born November 19, 1839 in Veteran, NY son of late Samuel H.

Wasson Jane in 89th year wife of Andrew age 84 at Dix, NY April 16, 1886. Born September 15, 1797 in Tyrone, Ireland. Married 1824, 6 sons and 2 daus. I dau died in Tyrone, Ireland, 3 sons served in Civil War, 1 died. Leaves husband, 5 sons and 1 dau

Johnson Betsey in Watkins, NY April 16, 1886. Born March 26, 1827 in Reading, NY 1 of 10 children to Moses and Betsey **Benham** from Vermont, 2 died recently, Farley in 1884, Moses February 1886. Surviving, S. S. and Mrs. Dyer **Robinson** of Watkins and Mrs. Madison **Marshall** of Reading. Married 1839 James A. Johnson who came from Conn. He died August 1874. 5 children, Mary E. wife of J. J. **Lane**, and Mrs. Susan M. **Meeks** of Watkins, Charles R. of St. Mary's, Ohio and Frank of San Francisco, Cal.

Van Liew Catherine 70 in Tyrone, NY April 16, 1886. Born June 1816 in Lodi, NY. Married January 1834 J. V. Van Liew who died 9 years ago. Surviving, 4 sons, 4 daus, 18 grandchildren

Gorton Alonzo H. in 58th year at Corning, NY April 26, 1886

Cleveland Eliza Lee in Reading, NY April 24, 1886. Born October 11, 1807 in West Town, NY dau of William and Betsey **Lee** 1 of 3 daus and 3 sons, 2 living, James of New London, Ohio and Joseph of Kansas City. Married 1823 Luther Cleveland born February 2, 1801 in Sugar Creek, Pa. family came from Conn. He died January 17, 1872, 6 children none living. Son Milton U. died 1881 in Ft. Scott, Kansas. Dau Bethia Lee died age 9y at Westown. Mary Lee wife of Hiram B. **Tuttle** died in Corning, NY age 21

Davenport Harry H. in Monterey, NY April 28, 1886

Ogden Ira 33 in Mecklenburgh, NY April 25, 1886

Wood Clinton 79 in Mecklenburgh, NY April 28, 1886

Boyce Mrs. Henry 73 in Mecklenburgh, NY April 30, 1886

Wheeler Freelove 43 wife of N. M. in Sodus, NY April 28, 1886, eldest child by 2nd marriage of Esquire and Fanny **Griswold** late of Dix, NY. Married 1866 Rev. N. M. Wheeler. Buried Glenwood cem.

Smith Hebe 9y 15d dau of Emmett C. in Reading, NY April 14, 1886

Logan Paul 90y 5m 27d at Logan, NY May 3, 1886

DEATH NOTICES

Franklin George 66 in Ovid, NY May 2, 1886

Andrews Etta M. dau of late Edwin C., sister of Mrs. Lyman **Ballard** of Watkins, NY in Dundee, NY May 12, 1886

Dumond Isaac at Danby, NY May 12, 1886. Born August 12, 1795, 1st child born in Danby

Reynolds Laura 68 formerly of Reynoldsville, NY in Gr. Traverse Co. Michigan at son-in-law's S. H. **Saylor** May 11, 1886. Born January 18, 1818 in Hector, NY dau of late Isreal **Pease**. Married age 22 Joel Reynolds who died September 6, 1879

Smelzer Phillip 72 in Lodi, NY May 11, 1886. Came from Germany age 5. Married age 20 Matilda **Meeker**, 8 children living, Cap. J. M. of Geneva, NY, Mary wife of Abram **Campbell**, Jane wife of Charles **Coleman**, Helen at home, Sarah M. wife of Warren **Hurd** of Watkins, NY, Lewis of Lodi, Dr. H. T. of Havana, NY, Addie wife of Samuel **Van Fleet** of Ovid, NY

Stilwell child of Peter 6y in Perry City, NY May 16, 1886

Hamilton George 50 in Burdett, NY May 14, 1886

Green Peter abt 60 in Watkins, NY May 15, 1886. Born a slave in Tenn. Served Confederate Army, released and joined Union Army under Col. Wells of Illinois. Arrived Watkins 1864

Williams William R. in Watkins, NY May 18, 1886. Born December 6, 1811 in Sullivan Co. Married February 1, 1835 Sarah **Thompson** now age 75. 3 children, Lewis, Elizabeth wife of Fred S. **Barrows**, Agnes wife of Thomas Mc Caul of Tomah, Wis.

Graham Mrs. Joseph in Monterey, NY May 21, 1886

Gabriel William E. at Starkey, NY May 21, 1886. 1 child Mrs. L. G. **Phinney** of Reading, NY

Carr Florence 3y 6m dau of Dr. C. S. in Reading, NY May 23, 1886

Gates Frank A. 32 in Rochester, NY May 29, 1886, son-in-law of N. T. **Gulick** of Watkins, NY. Leaves wife, son age 7 and daughter age 2

Worden Humphrey 27 in Cayuta, NY May 27, 1886

Chase Obed 84 in Searsburg, NY June 4, 1886

Bell Mrs. John in Burdett, NY June 12, 1886. Born Co. Downs, Ireland. Leaves husband, 1 son and 2 daughters

Stoll Hannah 56 in Watkins, NY June 14, 1886. Born May 29, 1830 in Sussex Co.

NJ daughter of Nathan **Cole**. Brothers and sisters Ramah of St. Paul, MInn., Mrs. Mary **Ryerson** of Muscatine, Iowa, and Mrs. Dr. **Miller** of Andover, NJ. Married April 7, 1848 Andrew Stoll in NJ, 4 children, Frank of Salt Lake City, Hattie wife of F. A. **Levine** of Ridgewood, NJ and Dora at home

Tyler Daniel in Burdett, NY June 18, 1886. Born April 18, 1806 in Westchester Co. Married age abt 40 Sarah **Beyea** who died 7 years ago. No children

Conklin Jane 89 in Reading, NY June 18, 1886, buried Thurston, NY with husband. Children, Mrs. Catherine **Crevelling**, Isaac and Smith. Samuel **Cole** son by 1st marriage

Burritt John G. 63 son of late Elder in Havana, NY June 22, 1886

La Fever Mrs. Nelson R. 44 formerly of Reading, NY in De Leon Springs, Florida June 29, 1886

Slocum Betsey 92 inmate of Townhouse at Dix, NY July 5, 1886

Stewart Samuel 22 in Peach Orchard, NY July 6, 1886

Bassett Eliza Bowlby in N. Hector July 8, 1886. Born November 3, 1808 in Hunterdon Co. NJ nee **Cranmer**. Married February 22, 1827 in NJ William **Bowlby**, 11 children. He died September 29, 1853. She married (2) 1856 John Bassett who had infant, Addie. Children, Mrs. Lydia **Doolittle** of N. Hector, NY, George F. Bowlby of Havana, NY, Ira R. and Susan A. of N. Hector, Mrs. Mary M. **Shelton** of Odessa, NY, Mrs. Sarah M. **Halsey**, Mrs. Samantha S. **Van Liew**, and Mrs. Charlotte W. **Stanley** of N. Hector, William T. of Willard, Mrs. Eliza M. **Curry** of Lodi Landing, Mrs. Ella **Howard** of N. Hector and Addie Bassett

Porter Jane in 81st year at dau Mrs. Isabelle **Mc Dermott** in Dundee, NY July 7, 1886, sister of Andrew **Wasson** Sr. of Sugar Hill, NY in 95th year

Hughey Daniel 60y 5m in Watkins, NY July 10, 1886. Born 1826 in Tyrone, NY son of William. 2 brothers Milton U. & C. B., 4 sisters living Mrs. Margaret **Drake** of Morenci, Mi., Mrs. Nancy **Eutermarks** of Tioga Co. Pa., Mrs. Daniel **Crandall** of Williamsport, Pa. and Mrs. Homer **Swick** of Lockport, NY. Married 1847 Rebecca Jane **Hurley**. No children

Jeffers Thomas abt 64 in Hector, NY July 11, 1886

Thompson Robert in Newfield, NY July 16, 1886

Mc Duffee Mrs. John 48 in Cayuta, NY July 14, 1886

Rose Mrs. William 41 in Watkins, NY July 27, 1886

Jackson Mary E. 65 suicide in Havana, NY July 28, 1886

DEATH NOTICES 133

Richards Mrs. Isreal in Watkins, NY July 27, 1886. Born June 1, 1800

Merrick J. S. 79y 10m in Watkins, NY July 31, 1886

Seaman Samuel 53y 3m son of late Orison in Watkins, NY August 1, 1886

Downes Michael 6m son of Patrick in Watkins, NY August 10, 1886

Wygant Phebe 71y 7m at the Dix Town Home August 10, 1886

Powers Bridget 27 in Rock Stream, NY August 8, 1886. Dau of John and sister of Thomas of Watkins, NY, Nicolas of Havana, NY & Michael of Rock Stream

Weaver Solomon D. 91 in Havana, NY August 5, 1886. Son of James Sr. who died age 92, grandfather Josiah died age 93. Leaves 2 brothers James Jr. age 86 and Hugh age 81 of Reading, NY

Sheardown G. W. in Plainfield, Wis. August 5, 1886. Born April 17, 1822 in Covert, NY son of late Elder. Brother S. B. now of Winona, Minn. Married January 1849 Maryette **Mitchell**

Van Cleef Joanna 91 in Seneca Falls, NY August 13, 1886. 1st white child born in Seneca Falls to John **Smith**, 1st settler

Norman Sarah Eliza in Watkins, NY August 24, 1886. Twin sister Emily Louise died August 18, 1886, daus of George D.

Brown Margaret 34 wife of Thomas formerly of Watkins, NY August 19, 1886

Hinman Dr. George T. 78 at Chase's Lake, NY August 19, 1886. Born June 21, 1808 in Catherine, NY son of E;lijah S. married December 1837 Irene **Benson**, 2 children Franc & Grover C.

Townsend Marcia 64y 4m at son-in-law's Charles A. **La Fever** September 5, 1886. Buried Hall's Corners, NY

Andrews Charlotte age in Townsend, NY August 8, 1886

Ames Harry 12 son of Thomas in Watkins, NY August 9, 1886

Feagles Willie 16 and Lee 12 sons of Robert S. in Monterey, NY August 13, 1886

Wagner Gen. George 71 son of pioneer Abraham in Penn Yan, NY September 5, 1886

Ellis Caroline M. 56 in Watkins, NY September 14, 1886. Born 1830 in Benton, NY 3rd of 4 children of Isaac **Voak**, 1 living J. D. of Watkins. Widowed Mother married B. B. **Hollett** of Watkins had 1 dau Jennie wife of J. D. **Bushnell** of Harford, NY. Married February 1853 Albert Ellis

Wigg Frances 69 in Watkins, NY September 18, 1886

Swarthout Darius in Wayne, NY September 16, 1886

Haas Deborah Varney 59 in Watkins, NY September 20, 1886. Born September 15, 1827 in Brandon, Vermont. Married January 1847 William T. Haas, 4 living children, Henry V., Carrie wife of James **Probasco**, Ella wife of George **Perry** all of Watkins, Fanny wife of George **Clapper** of Geneseo, NY. Eldest child Mary wife of William **Vanderpool** died May 1884 in Shelbyville, Ill.

Godard Mary 47 dau of late William of Dryden in Watkins, NY September 27, 1886

Palmer Caroline in 66th year at Watkins, NY September 26, 1886. Born February 7, 1820 in NY only child of Henry J. **Bogart**. Married Benjamin Palmer who died April 28, 1877 age 68. Children, Henry, member of 141st Reg. NY Vol. died in service, Jonathan died 1863 in Monterey, NY, S. H. of Watkins and Emma at home

Catlin Betsey in 85th year at Watkins, NY September 25, 1886. Born January 24, 1802 in Litchfield, Conn. Married 1821 Leman Catlin from Fairfield, Conn. who died 17 years ago. 10 children, 1 dau died age 24, 2 died infancy. Living E. S. of Saginaw, Mi., J. H. of Moreland, NY, George of Osceola, Pa., Brandt of San Francisco, Anna of Odessa, NY, Alva of Carson City, Nevada, Mrs. Mary G. **Pope** wife of Dr. H. G. Brother Burr **Gregory** of Iowa and sister Mrs. Phebe **Norton** age 82 of Reading, NY. Half brother H. L. **Gregory** of Altay, NY. Buried Montour cem.

Mettler Mary E. 28 of Elmira, NY at parent's H. W. **Sivern** in Watkins, NY. Born February 22, 1858. Married June 30, 1880 J. Milton Mettler. Leaves husband and 1 child Edith Belle age 5

Graham Mary nee **Gregory** 76 in Dix, NY October 6, 1886

Pope James in 80th year at daughter's Mrs. George **Drake** in Reading, NY October 6, 1886. Born July 26 1807 in Chenango Co. 1 of 17 children, 4 living. Married age 21 Caroline **Underwood** who died April 26, 1884 age 73, 8 children, Ahava wife of George W. **Drake** of Reading, Ophelia deceased, wife of Dr. Horace **Seamans** of Beaver Dams, NY, James A. of Cawku City, Kansas, H. G. of Watkins, NY, Charles U. killed in Kansas 15 years ago, Ellen E. wife of V. **Pope** of Chenango Co., Alice B. wife of George **Dean** of New Haven, Conn. and Horace of Pine Grove, NY

Coon Sarah A. 48 wife of John in Hector, NY October 2, 1886. Born Newfield, NY sister of Mrs. George **Prentiss** of Hornellsville, NY, Mrs. S. **Reynolds** of Elmira, NY and Mrs. Silas **Price** of Dundee, NY. Leaves husband, 1 son and 2 daus

Ellsworth John W. 82y 2d in Clyde, NY October 8, 1886. Born Old Paltz, NY. Married Lydia **Goltry** who died 1846, 3 children, Moses D., Eliza Jane who died 1856 and Ann wife of R. P. **Cooley** now in Seneca Co. Married (2) Lydia A. **Roushey**

Tompkins Hannah M. 83 in Doyleston, Wis. October 5, 1886. Born April 9, 1803

in Watkins, NY. Married 1821 Daniel Tompkins, moved to Wis. 1854. He died August 10, 1876, 11 children 8 living, E. D. of Watkins, C. S. of Hampton Wis., James of NY, Mrs. J. **Cotey** of Madison, Neb., Mrs. T. **Jones** of Columbus, Wis., Mrs. W. F. **Whitfield** of Blue Earth City, Minn., Lucretia and S. J. at home. Buried Otsego cem.

Crawford Arvilla 63 in Steamburg, NY October 12, 1886

Erway James M. 74 of Hector, NY in Horseheads, NY October 8, 1886

Fox James L. 74 2nd son of James in Dix, NY October 1, 1886

Tuell Melzer 90y 7m 18d in Penn Yan, NY October 2, 1886

Sharp Mrs. Mother of Mrs. M. J. **Sunderlin** in Dundee, NY October 12, 1886

Horton daughter of Alvah 5y in N. Hector, NY October 20, 1886

Arnold William in Tyrone, NY October 20, 1886. Born March 23, 1815 at Romulus, NY. Married (1) February 7, 1838 Mary Ann **Compton** who died May 11, 1871, 7 children, 6 living, James H. of Mecklenburgh, NY Mrs. M. T. **Murdock** of Dundee, NY Mrs. P. W. **Latier** of Grove Springs, NY, Edwin C. of Tyrone, NY, Mrs. D. R. **Perry** and Dewitt B. of Watkins, NY. Married (2) September 8, 1872 Sarah Maria **Mc Kinney** of Mecklenburgh, NY who survives

Russell J. M. son of Rev. Benjamin Russell of Watkins, NY in Philadelphia, Pa. October 11, 1886. Buried Glenwood cem.

Cooper Ashley 47 in Catlin, NY October 16, 1886. Born Catherine, NY

Nobles Mrs. Anson in 69th year at Cayuta, NY October 10, 1886

Snyder George 81 in Cayuta, NY October 9, 1886. Children Mrs. J. C. **Moot** & William of Cayuta & Mrs. E. W. **Reed** of Watkins, NY

Jones George W. in Ovid, NY October 17, 1886

Flanagan Thomas 58 in Watkins, NY October 24, 1886

Wheeler Rebecca in Au Gres, Michigan October 26, 1886. Born
March 17, 1860 in Burwell, England nee **Marsh**. Married 1878 Arnot Wheeler formerly of Watkins, NY. Funeral at Watkins

Fields Mary E. 42 at Willard Asylum Ocrtober 28, 1886 wife of "Tom" once prominent figure of NY City. Abandoned by husband a politician with Tweed Ring without support and an infant son in 1872. He fled to Canada with large amount of public funds. She was committed to Hudson River Hospital for insane and tranferred to Willard in 1879. Her husband died in St. Andrews, Canada leaving an estate of $50,000 in litigation, his wife unprovided for. Leaves 1 son abt 15 years in Canada

Hager Mrs. Tamah in Hector, NY October 21, 1886

Walters Daniel in 94th year at Urbana, NY October 30, 1886

Perkins Martha Raymond in 89th year at Benton, NY November 5, 1886. Leaves husband age 91. Married over 61 years

Clark Mrs. John abt 60 in Perry City, NY November 4, 1886

Herrick Frank formerly of Watkins, NY in Corning, NY November 5, 1886

White Benajah P. B. 33 in Watkins, NY November 11, 1886. Born August 26, 1853 son of Rev. William E. 6 brothers John W., Richard R. of Corning, NY, George R., Horace L., Charles W., and Henry of Watkins. Buried Glenwood cem.

Stilwell Mrs. Eunice at dau Mrs. Margaret **Hager** in Hector, NY last week (date of newspaper November 4, 1886)

Beahan Ada 34 wife of C. C. formerly of Schuyler Co. in Sioux City, Iowa November 17, 1886. 5 year old son died last week, 1 dau living

Arnot John 56 in Elmira, NY November 20, 1886. Born March 11, 1831 in Elmira son of John and Harriet (**Tuttle**) Arnot

Cornell Mary in 70th year at Monterey, NY November 20, 1886. 11 children, Rev. James of Webasha, Minn., Rev. George H. of Laramie, Wy., William of Himrods, NY, John, Albert and Charles of Monterey, Eliza wife of Peter M. **Norman** of Rochester, NY, Mary wife of Lewis **Supplee** of Himrods

Hatfield Ellen Warner in 70th year at Rock Stream, NY November 24, 1886 sister of John W. **Warner** of Reading, NY

Fillmore Mrs. A. N. 72 in Rock Stream, NY November 26, 1886 widow of Rev. A. N. who died 6 years ago. Only child Mrs. J. H. **Newman** of Rock Stream and dau of husband Mrs. Charles **Hunt** of Milo, NY

Putnam Daniel C. 32 in N. Reading, NY December 4, 1886

Harvey James in Bennettsburg, NY December 11, 1886

Stamp Abner M. 47 in Dix, NY December 9, 1886. Born Reading, NY son of Abner and Elizabeth (**Crandall**) Stamp. Married Frances **Mathews**, leaves 1 son

Morgan Mary Estelle 21y 6m at Watkins, NY December 10, 1886

Roberts Mrs. Horace at Mother's Mrs. **Pyle** in Glenora, NY December 19, 1886

Peck Norman 54 in Dix, NY December 17, 1886. Born August 14, 1832 in Reading, NY son of Jason. Married 27 years ago Sarah A. **Ayres** who died March 3, 1886, 1

son William J. Brothers Benoni of Monterey, NY, Leander of Steuben Co., Alanson of Seneca Co., Mahlon of Tioga Co. and Chilon of Reading, NY

Andrews Richard formerly of Hector, NY, son of Charles of Seneca Falls, NY in Cherokee, Iowa December 12, 1886

Rhodes Sarah S. at dau Mrs. **Bennett** in Syracuse, NY December 18, 1886. She was 1 of 10 children of Moses and Betsey **Benham**. Moses died Steuben Co. February 1886 age 82. Funeral at sister's Mrs. Dyer **Robinson** of Watkins, NY. Farley Benham died 2 years ago and S. S. out west

Howard Ann M. in Reading, NY December 15, 1886. Born June 19, 1818 in NY City 1 of 8 children to William and Abby **Crosby**. Married March 26, 1839 Henry S. Howard, 6 sons 3 living George O. of Reedsburg, Wis., John of Reading, Henry S. Jr. of Watkins, NY. 1 brother Alfred, 4 sisters, Mrs. J. W. **Merrifield**, Mrs. E. **Waldron** all of Yates Co., Mrs. Lydia **Sidway** of Geneva, NY and Mrs. J. W. **Brown** of Wis.

Norton Phebe in 84th year at Reading, NY December 14, 1886. Born October 30, 1803 daughter of Josiah and Abiah (**Hinman**) **Gregory** in Bridgeport, Conn. Mother died 1819 in Reading. Brothers and sisters, Mrs. Betsey **Catlin** died last September, Burr in Iowa age 86, half brother Harmon L. of Altay, NY. Married March 11, 1829 Willys Norton, 7 children 4 living, 2 died childhood, Miles B. died 1879, O. O. of Lodi, Cal., W. L. of Watkins, NY, F. M. of Carbondale, Kansas and Mrs. Elvira **Worth** of Reading

Platt Betsey in Dix, NY December 15, 1886. Born April 29, 1812 dau of Ebenezer **Hovey** at Niagara Falls, NY 1 of 4 children. Married Brewster Platt Jr., 3 children 1 living

Morehouse Harriet 86 in Bradford, NY December 23, 1886 at son-in-law's King **Foster**. Born 1800 in Romulus, NY dau of John **Waldron** 1 of 9 children, 1 living Mrs. Catherine **Smith** of Burdett, NY Married 1836 Silas Morehouse, lived Burdett

Hanmer Mrs. Peter 78 in Tyrone, NY December 29, 1886

Leffler Mrs. Phillip in N. Hector, NY December 29, 1886

Thompson Elizabeth 60y 6m widow of Samuel in Watkins, NY January 1, 1887. Children, George and Mrs. J. E. **Perry** of Watkins and Mrs. Fred **Barker** of Elmira, NY

Bailey Mrs. John in N. Hector, NY January 2, 1887

Voak Martha 91 in Watkins, NY January 8, 1887. Born October 1, 1795 in Warren, NY daughter of Joshua and Hannah (**Card**) **Payne** 1 of 10 children. Married April 29, 1818 Abraham Voak who died February 20, 1877. 8 children 4 living, Mary, Isaac, Nelson and Hannah all deceased. Living are Joel, Mrs. M. J. **Spence** wife of Dr. W. A. of Watkins, J. W. of Wilmot, Wis. and Job of Britton, Dakota

Honeywell Enoch in 99th year at Altay, NY January 13, 1887. 3 children Alba of Ill., Gilbert and Mrs. Emma **Fenno** of Altay

Pullen Albert 24 in Watkins, NY January 13, 1887

Dolan Bridget 76y 8m in Watkins, NY January 14, 1887

Agard Noah Jr. 20y 10m in Hector, NY January 15, 1887

Pierson Garria L. 84 at son-in-law's C. F. **Benjamin** in Southport, NY January 18, 1887 Born 1802 in Jackson, NY. Married 1826 Catherine **Heist**, leaves 2 daus

Updike Ada in Logan, NY January 24, 1887, buried Trumansburg, NY

Ayres Elias in Reynoldsville, NY January 22, 1887

Nichols John H. in Reading, NY January 29, 1887. Born April 3, 1816 in Balston Spa, NY son of Amasa and Martha (**Chapman**) Nichols. 4 sisters, 3 living Mrs. Eliza **Mathews** of Douglas Co. Dakota, Mrs. Charlotte **Coddington** of Reading, NY, Mrs. Lydia **Cady** of E. Williamson, NY. Married March 31, 1839 Esther Ann **Townsend** of Starkey, NY, 9 children eldest age 46 youngest 27, Amasa H. of NY Martha Z. wife of Dr. G. H. **Goltry**, Mary A. wife of L. A. **Randall** both of Reading, Henry T. of NY, Charlotte A. at home, Emma Jenette wife of Seward **Robson** of Seneca Falls, NY, Rev. John Richard of Garretsville, Ohio, Charles W. of Lynxville, Wis. and Louis L. at Oberlin College, Ohio

Sherer Hiram 56 in Hector, NY January 23, 1887

Shannon George 42 in Orange, NY January 25, 1887

Chapman Daniel 70 in Monterey, NY January 31, 1887

Reynolds Ralph 17 eldest son of Jefferson and Arvilla in Cayuta, NY February 3, 1887

Mc Donald 2y 4m youngest child of Isaiah and Maude in Watkins, NY February 2, 1887

Gay Matilda 96y 6m in Peach Orchard, NY February 6, 1887. Born August 15, 1790 in Putnam Co. Married (1) February 9, 1809 and (2) October 6, 1821. Buried Starkey, NY

Bull Susan Jane wife of Moses in Slaterville, NY February 3, 1887

Williams Lewis T. in Watkins, NY February 9, 1887. Born November 13, 1843 in Watkins son of William R. and Sarah (**Thompson**) Williams. Father died May 18, 1886. Leaves Mother, 2 sisters Mrs. Thomas **McCaul** of Tomah, Wash. and Mrs. Fred S. **Barrows** of Watkins

DEATH NOTICES 139

Meeker Anna 96y 6m in Catherine, NY February 19, 1887

Mc Intyre Daniel in N. Hector, NY February 20, 1887

Drake Judson A. abt 65 in Milo Center, NY February 26, 1887

Drum Mr. and Mrs. Barber formerly of Catherine, NY burned to death in home at Big Flats, NY February 25, 1887

Allen son of Ephraim 17m funeral in Mecklenburgh, NY February 26, 1887

Kimble Lucinda 55 in Watkins, NY March 7, 1887

Howell Mrs. Dewitt 29 in Burdett, NY dau of late Jackson **Strader**, funeral March 4, 1887

Strader Jacob 72 in Dix, NY March 6, 1887. Born January 17, 1815 in Sussex Co. NJ son of Peter and Mary (**Bunn**) Strader

Barrett Mary 60y 11m widow of James in Watkins, NY March 8, 1887. 10 living children Mrs. J. C. **Giles** and Mrs. M. **Grady** of Hornellsville, NY, Mrs. M. D. **Murphy** of Jersey Shore, Pa., Miss Maggie, Frances and Lizzie of Watkins, John J. and Charles S. of Oswego, NY and Rev. Thomas H.

Price Eliphalet in 79th year at Altay, NY March 5, 1887. Born June 8, 1809 in Ovid, NY son of Levi from NJ and Sarah **Clark** who was born November 10 1788 in Newford, Westchester Co. 1 of 13 children, Susan wife of Watson **Prentiss** of Hornell, NY, William of Grand Rapids, Mi., Sarah A. 1st wife of John **Force** died 1849 in Erie Co. Ohio, Elizabeth wife of Clark **Vaughn**, Helen C. died 1848, Levi died 1881, John D., Harvey E., Esther, Harriet and Edward V. all of Tyrone, NY. Married 1829 Anna **Vaughn** of Barrington, NY who died 1852. Her parents came from Rhode Island. 7 children, 2 daus died young, Jennie wife of H. B. **Sebring**, Hannah, Benjamin V. died Civil War. 2 sons survive John H. and William C. both served in Civil War, 179th NY Vol

Kendall Abel abt 95 of Tyrone, NY in Eddytown, NY March 7, 1887

Ingalls Ebenezer in Watkins, NY March 16, 1887. Born January 12, 1822 in Ellisburg, NY son of Edmund and Charlotte (**Dickenson**) Ingalls. Married 1846 Mary E. **Nutting** in Jefferson Co. Moved to Minn. and Wis. and back to Watkins 21 years ago. 5 children 2 living, Charles and Mrs. Ella **Baskin**

Roberts John 2nd in 79th year at Reading, NY March 10, 1887. Born May 1, 1808 eldest son of James who came here with brother John from Reading, Pa.

Pott Samuel J. in Reynoldsville, NY March 15, 1887. Born February 28, 1824 in Hector, NY. Married Caroline **Davis** sister of C. W. 2 sons David S. and Charles D. at home

Shelton Joseph 79 formerly of Schuyler Co. in Elmira, NY March 21, 1887. Born March 19, 1806. Leaves 1 son Charles, 2 sisters and 4 brothers

Van Deventer Stephen W. in Townsend, NY March 23, 1887. Born September 10, 1814 in Romulus, NY son of Abraham and Charry (**Wakeman**) Van Deventer. 3 brothers 1 sister, Isaac of Friendship, NY, Charles of Flower Creek, Michigan, John of Bolivar, NY, Anna Marie **Phillips** of Clay Banks, Mi. Married December 13, 1838 Eliza Mc **Elwee** of Watkins, NY 2 children A. F. of Townsend and Kate E. wife of O. R. **Haring** of Reading, NY an adopted son W. H. **Hunter** of Rochester, NY

Murray Patrick 76 in Logan, NY March 19, 1887. Born Co. Meath, Ireland, immigrated 1848

Tibbs Clemant 78 of Tyrone, NY in Roaring Branch, Pa. March 22, 1887, buried Tyrone

Quirk Edward 13 son of John in Watkins, NY April 8, 1887

Slaght Phebe at son-in-law's Augustus **Kimble** in Burdett, NY April 15, 1887. Born March 14, 1800 in Seneca Co. dau of John B. **Covert**. Leaves 3 sons and 1 dau

Beardsley Elizabeth abt 95 in Havana, NY buried April 14 1887 in Burdett, NY. Married (1) Mr. **Stone** and (2) Clark Beardsley

Guernsey Mrs. William in 63rd year in Windsor, NY April 14, 1887. Born near Hudson River, lived Havana, NY. Brother L. H. **Whippy** of Watkins, NY

Smith Mary J. 36 wife of George F. in Watkins, NY April 16, 1887

Eddy Mrs. Daniel in Dix, NY April 17, 1887. Buried with husband in Rock Stream, NY who died November 30, 1884

Andrews Mrs. Joseph in Watkins, NY April 20, 1887

Holmes James 68 in Dundee, NY April 18, 1887. Born March 31, 1801 in Seneca Co.

Kirkendall Mary A. in 81st year at Burdett, NY April 18, 1887. Born June 12, 1806 in Belvidere, NJ nee **Fisher**. Married 1829 Richard A. Kirkendall, children Mrs. H. M. **Baker** of Watkins, NY George died 1840 in Enfield, NY, John H. died 1861 in Chicago, Austin J. died 1872 in Dubuque, Iowa. Buried Enfield

Johnson Mrs. Derrick 80y 11m 24d in Logan, NY April 24, 1887. Came from Hoosick, NJ. 8 children survive

Mc Dowell Phebe 97 in Dix, NY April 24, 1887. Born January 1790 in eastern NY. Widow for 70 years. 2 sons dec, Stephen 26 years and Andrew 10 years ago

Wilkin Lewis J. 78 in Barrington, NY April 28, 1887

Burr Jane 79 in Searsburg, NY April 30, 1887

Speary Samuel in Sugar Hill, NY May 2, 1887. Born March 3, 1811 in Luzerne Co. Pa. Married Mary **Pennington** (now 78) 7 children living, Charles died age 16, Fletcher in Ill., Phebe wife of John **Brown** of Pa., Mary wife of Dr. **Simmons** of Iowa, W. A. at home & Permelia wife of Lewis **Littell** of Altay, NY

Mahoney Patrick 46 in Watkins, NY May 1, 1887

Green Orlando 55 in Watkins, NY May 16, 1887. Born Rush, NY. Served Co. B. 107th Reg. NY vol.

Rogers Mrs. John 75 in Mecklenburgh, NY May 9, 1887. Born May 4, 1812 dau of James **Mitchell**. Married age 22, 3 sons and 2 daus. Buried Johnson Settlement, NY

Bailey Mrs. John 31 only dau of Theodore **Lewis** in Mecklenburgh, NY funeral May 8, 1887

Tracy Sylvanus 67 in Reading, NY May 11, 1887. Born February 3, 1820 in Oxford, NY 1 of 9 children, 3 living Isaac J., Ebenezer and John G. Married (1) Maria **Hamilton**, 1 dau Mrs. Marion L. **Lybolt** wife of William of Antelope Co. Neb. Married (2) Miriam **Chapman**

Morgan Jane 74y 7m in Catherine, NY May 12, 1887. Dau of Jesse **Mitchell** and grand-daughter of John of the Revolution. 3 sons Henry of Portland, Ore., John of Odessa, NY and Charles of Pa. 2 brothers James and Burr of Saginaw, Mi., sisters Mrs. J. J. **Van Vechten** of Flushing, Mi. and Mrs. William V. **Smith** of Watkins, NY

Mathews William abt 86 at dau Mrs. A. **Tucker** in Monterey, NY May 17, 1887

Hicks Clara 53y 4m youngest child of Moses and Betsey **Benham** of Reading, NY in St. Louis, Mo. May 16, 1887. Living, S. S. and Mrs. Dyer **Robinson** of Watkins, NY. Reuben F. died February 1, 1884, Moses died February 28, 1885, Mrs. Betsey **Johnson** April 26, 1886 and Mrs. Sarah S. **Rhodes** December 18, 1886

Spencer Wheedon T. was 81 on June 10th formerly of Hector, NY at son's J. O. in Medina, NY May 18, 1887

Durkee Asher S. 81y 19d in Havana, NY April 22, 1887. Born Brutus, NY. Married 1830 Elizabeth **Lee** dau of David & Susan. She died 1850, married (2) Eunice **Lee** dau of Daniel & Sarah. She died 1872, married (3) widow of James **Sturdevant**. 2 children William & Emma

Caughlin Mrs. Daniel in W. Reading, NY May 28, 1887

Brother Henry 61 in Bath, NY May 20, 1887

Crommett Polly 96 in Starkey, NY May 2, 1887

Smith Lucinda in 79th year widow of Dr. Hervey Smith who died May 17, 1843, in Dundee, NY May 17, 1887. Buried Rock Stream, NY

Rusco Mrs. James 87 in Orange, NY June 4, 1887. Husband died 1870

Bassett Palmer H. formerly of Dundee, NY in Cleveland, Ohio June 4, 1887. Buried Dundee. Son Fred died in Florida, other son died in army

Curry Carrie (**Halsey**) in N. Hector, NY May 24, 1887. 2 sons Edwin W. & Clifford H.

Brown Miss Myra in Watkins, NY May 30, 1887. Born August 10, 1862 dau of Charles & Anna in Onieda, NY. Father died June 7, 1868. 1 sister Anna, 3 brothers Levi, Charles & George

Ely Emma L. wife of Charles R. in Moss Springs, Kan. (Kan. paper dated June 2, 1887). Born May 4, 1859 in Hector, NY dau of P. H. & Mary E. **Durland**. Married 7 years

Webb Mary M. 25 nee **Mc Creary** wife of Lee B. in Sugar Hill, NY June 6, 1887

Andrews Ursala widow of Zenas in Bradford, NY May 22, 1887. Born January 23, 1823 in Tyrone, NY. Married age 19. Husband died November 23, 1871

Kirkendall Nellie 22y 7m dau of Austin in Burdett, NY June 4, 1887. Buried Wilkesbarre, Pa.

Randall Nettie Millie 31 wife of Lyman and dau of William **Miller** in Orange, NY June 4, 1887

Charles Laura 98 at dau Mrs. Thomas **Charles** in Catherine, NY June 4, 1887

Jackson Morris in N. Hector, NY June 6, 1887

Durland Henry 70 in Hector, NY June 11, 1887. Surviving wife Henrietta sister of B. W. **Norris** of Reading, NY. D. C. of Chemung, NY, sisters, Mrs. Charles **Adriance** of Hector and Mrs. Harvey **Nichols** of Sugar Hill, NY

Welsh Rachel wife of L. in Hector, NY June 8, 1887

Clawson Abby funeral in Logan, NY June 12, 1887

Norris Miss Delia A. 77 in Chemung, NY June 18, 1887. Born Conn. dau of Daniel. Brothers D. C. of Chemung, NY, B. W. of Reading, NY and sister Mrs. Henry **Durland** of Hector, NY

Keep Mrs. Caleb widow in Logan, NY June 20, 1887. 2 daus at home, Carrie and Libbie

Kidder Mrs. W. E. 34 at sister's Mrs. S. H. **Ferenbaugh** in Watkins, NY June 23, 1887

Beam Eliza H. wife of G. Anson in Dundee, NY June 25, 1887. Born 1840 in Dundee dau of John **Compton**. Married June 10, 1868

Woodward Dr. William 70 in Big Flats, NY June 30, 1887. Born January 20, 1817 in Westlaigh Farms, Biddleford, Devonshire, England son of John and Sarah (**Venn**) Woodward. Married (1) Harriet **King** dau of John of Ithaca, NY. Children, William E., Helen, Charles M. of Watkins, NY, John and George H. 2 living. Married (2) Mrs. Margaret C. **Elwell** dau of Frederick **Vaughn** of Big Flats, NY, 1 dau Harriet

Winters Prof. A. C. in Griffin, Georgia July 3, 1887. Born September 20, 1835 in Barrington, NY son of late Daniel and Mary. Married Hattie **Payne**, 3 sons age 17, 15 and 8

Hibbard Mrs. George P. 60 in Watkins, NY July 5, 1887

Mapes Jonathan F. in 67th year at Dundee, NY July 2, 1887

Considine Elizabeth May 5m dau of P. H. in Watkins, NY July 9, 1887

Haggerty Harriet 61 in Rochester, NY July 14, 1887. Lived Burdett, NY 35 years. Husband William died Rebel Prison in Civil War

Teller Daniel in Altay, NY July 24, 1887

Georgia Mrs. E. P. in Altay, NY July 26, 1887. Leaves husband and 5 children

Mathews John abt 50 in Cayuta, NY July 28, 1887. Leaves wife and 6 children

Rice B. P. funeral in Altay, NY July 29, 1887

Havens Mrs. George 81 in Mecklenburgh, NY July 31, 1887

Cooper Phebe H. in 77th year at Mecklenburgh, NY August 3, 1887. Born February 11, 1811 dau of Samuel **Denton** of Orange Co. Married April 14, 1836 Jason Cooper of Long Island. 2 sons and 4 daughters survive, Mrs. Frank G. **Bodle**, S. Denton, Terzah L. **Fish**, George B., Amelia S. **Carman** and Adelia S. **Meeker**

Yapple Samuel at Post Creek, NY August 15, 1887. Born October 29, 1811 in Middleton, NY. Leaves wife, 1 son Herman I. and 1 dau Mrs. John S. **Huey** of Langdon, Pa.

Simmons Mrs. Alonzo 79 in Rock Stream, NY August 17, 1887. Born February 24, 1808 dau of Nathaniel and Elizabeth **Huson** in Hillsdale, NY. Married February 25, 1827, husband died 1875. 5 children 3 living, Mrs. C. W. **Barnes**, Mrs. Dr. D. A. **Johnson** of Dundee, NY and George of Elmira, NY

Bradley Edwin 72y 5m 12d in Montour, NY August 23, 1887. Leaves 2 sons Austin J. of Montour and L. H. of Watkins, NY

Hathaway B. G. H. 74 in Rock Stream, NY August 25, 1887. Born January 8, 1814 in Milo, NY son of Gilbert and Mary (**Hurd**) Hathaway. Leaves wife and 4 children, Mrs. J. M. **Archer** of Rock Stream, Mrs. E. R. **Kenyon** of Temple, Texas, George M. of Rock Stream and C. F. of Celina, Ohio

Shewman Omer J. 36 in Beaver Dams, NY August 24, 1887, unmarried

Page Mrs. Sally 72 in Mecklenburgh, NY August 27, 1887. 2 brothers John and Isaiah **Rolison**

Mickle Mr. 75 in Mecklenburgh, NY August 29, 1887

Osborn Belinda in 71st year at Mecklenburgh, NY August 28, 1887. Born December 25, 1816 dau of Henry R. **Winter** at Washington, NJ. Married July 2, 1839 B. C. Osborn of Springfield, NJ. 3 children, 1 died aged 1 year, 2 living, Charles E. of Washington, NJ and Elizabeth W. **Duryea** of Mecklenburgh

Van Arnum Bessie J. 7m dau of Charles in Watkins, NY August 31, 1887

Rich Abigail Caroline in Reading, NY September 5, 1887. Born August 11, 1825 dau of Thomas and Mary Ann (**Swezey**) **Drake** in Orange Co. Married January 16, 1850, Alfred Rich. 2 children Charles B. and Flora A. at home. 6 brothers and sisters living, John R., George W., Mrs. Mary J. **Gilbert** of Reading, Mrs. Harriet E. wife of Charles **Carpenter** of Starkey, NY, G. E. of Watkins, NY Frances L. wife of George **Dickerson** of Seneca Co.

Taylor Mrs. Margaret 88 in Watkins, NY September 5, 1887. 2 daus Mrs. **Chappel** and Mrs. David **Hurley**. Buried in Susquehanna, Pa. her former home

Wemple J. C. 60 in Brooklyn, NY September 7, 1887. Father of A. E. Wemple and Mrs. J. B. **Morris** of Watkins, NY

West Mrs. Sally at son's John E. in Watkins, NY September 8, 1887

Sunderlin Louisa 76 widow of Deliason at Grove Springs, NY September 4, 1887. Husband died September 8, 1871, 3 sons and 3 daus. Surviving Mrs. Ursala **Swarthout** wife of Derastus of Wayne, NY and M. J. of Watkins, NY

Stevens Abraham B. in Watkins, NY September 10, 1887. Born March 10, 1830 in Lodi, NY 1 of 12 children, 6 brothers living. Married 1844 Mary **Mc Cannon**. Served 148th Reg. NY Vol.

Horning H. A. 45 in Elmira, NY September 13, 1887

Mitchell Robert 87 in Watkins, NY September 14, 1887

DEATH NOTICES 145

Potts Jane E. dau of late James in Burdett, NY September 18, 1887

Kelly J. M. 72 in Mecklenburgh, NY September 21, 1887. Born March 23, 1815 in Seneca Co. Married May 7, 1834 Judith G. **Carman** of Hector, NY who died December 5, 1877. 11 children 4 living Mrs. A. S. **Burd**, Mary F., Warren O., and Charles A. Married (2) Ann **Treman** of Hector

Treman Abner in Trumansburg, NY September 20, 1887. Born same place, son of Abner who came from Conn. in 1792

Phelps John F. 78y 6m in Havana, NY September 23, 1887

Ladow N. C. 63 in Watkins, NY September 25, 1887

Hollett Dr. Arthur P. abt 40 in Havana, NY September 28, 1887. Born April 11, 1847 in Geneva, NY. Served Civil War 189th Reg. NY Vol

Wentz Justus in 68th year at Watkins, NY September 24, 1887. Born October 28, 1819 in Binghamton, NY. 1 brother Hiram. Wife died 18 years ago, 11 children 8 living, E. J., Frank H. of Little Falls, NY, John M. of Seneca Falls, NY, Mrs. Frank **Carron** of Sodus, NY, Mrs. Charles **Berry**, Mrs. Kate **Sayre**, Mrs. Porter **Ward** and Edward of Watkins

Tichenor Phebe 92 in Ithaca, NY October 5, 1887. Lived Searsburg, NY

Irvine Albert Taylor 7y son of Dr. and M. R. in Watkins, NY October 5, 1887

Burge Mrs. Robert 66 in Burdett, NY October 12, 1887. Leaves husband and 1 dau Mrs. H. B. **Howell** of Burdett

Van Allen Helen dau of Cornelius & Emma in Watkins, NY October 5, 1887

Beardsley Mrs. Cyrus 80 in Catherine, NY October 9, 1887

Wilkes Addie Vanette 10y dau of James in Watkins, NY October 16, 1887

Smith Eugene C. 18y son of S. D. in Reading, NY October 11, 1887

Huey Daniel S. 15y son of Milton V. and Henrietta October 16, 1887. Born July 21, 1872. Brother William Herbert age 9

Hovencamp John 84 in Smith Valley, NY October 18, 1887

Hollett Arthur 14 son of Dr. A. P. in Havana, NY October 17, 1887

Jamison Lavina nee **Newman** 64 in Hornellsville, NY October 22, 1887. Born Reading, NY, married 1845 Dr. J. S. Jamison then of Canisteo, NY. Only son Newman in Hornellsville

Cole Nancy T. 85 wife of Watson formerly of Dix, NY in Corning, NY November 4, 1887. Sons Nathan D. of Corning and Edwin out west

Sirine Abraham in Reynoldsville, NY November 9, 1887

Page Erastus in Searsburg November 7, 1887. Born April 19, 1824 in Litchfield, Conn. Sister Mrs. H. A. **Newcomb** of Dix, NY & dau Mrs. M. **Farrington** of Searsburg

Bradner James in Monterey, NY November 9, 1887

Atwater Mrs. Fedelia 47 wife of D. A. in Watkins, NY November 13, 1887. Dau of Zolmon W. **Lyon** of Hector, NY. 5 children

Vaughn Col. William 82 in Hector, NY November 18, 1887. Born February 3, 1806 in Knowlton, NY youngest son of Daniel and Hannah. Married April 28, 1825 Lavina **Martin** dau of William, 3 children Azuba wife of late Samuel W. **Sackett**. She died August 21, 1874, Erie & Ursala wife of Isaac **Morris** of Hector. He was Lieut. Col. in 145th Reg.

Bower Oliver P. November 22, 1887. Born Havana, NY son of Isaac. 1 dau Lottie E. **Swick** wife of William who died the following day age 25. Son died 1 year ago. Buried Montour cem.

Cook Col. E. W. in Havana, NY November 22, 1887. Born 1804 in Springfield, NY, 1 brother Charles. Married 1832, living children J. Paul of Springfield and Grace at home

Mead William funeral in Tyrone, NY November 26, 1887

Fisher Oscar 40 in Mecklenburgh, NY December 4, 1887

Spaulding William B. in 75th year at Hector, NY December 3, 1887. Born December 9, 1812 in Hector

Giles Margaret at Sugar Hill, NY November 25, 1887. Born June 10, 1830 in Schuyler Co. dau of David and Katie **Horning** 1 of 4 children, 2 living. Married 1851 William Giles, 6 children, Horatio R. of Sugar Hill, Arsala D., William H. died 1872, Plummer S., Citheria S. and Ida M. at home

Hill Charles F. 15y son of Fitch in Burdett, NY December 7, 1887

Fitzpatrick Mrs. John December 4, 1887, buried Elmira, NY. Children John, Joseph, Thomas and Charles of Havana, NY and Mrs. James **Moonan** of Elmira

Knapp Oliver C. 48 in Penn Yan, NY December 6, 1887

Mc Coy Frank 29 in Reynoldsville, NY December 15, 1887

DEATH NOTICES

Hurley Mrs. Holiday Mother of Warren in Reading, NY December 16, 1887

Moore Mrs. Levi dau of Ira Case in Reading, NY December 18, 1887

Price Miranda 62 in Altay, NY December 24, 1887. Born Altay. 2 sons and 2 daus S. A. of Dundee, NY, Floyd L., Charlotte A. **Gilbert** and Mary D. **Sproul** of Altay

Mathews Oliver 54y 10m 12d in Watkins, NY December 30, 1887. Born Reading, NY son of Whitman and Harriet

Rich Alfred in N. Reading, NY December 27, 1887. Born December 7, 1824 in Starkey, NY son of Alfred and Almy (**Roberts**) Rich. Married January 16, 1850 Abigail Caroline **Drake** dau of Thomas & Mary Ann (**Swezey**) Drake of Orange Co. 2 children Charles Byron & Flora Almy

Thomas Mr. 92 at son's Rev. Ira D. in Monterey, NY January 2, 1888. Buried Woodhull, NY

Ellis Mrs. Townsend abt 65 in Monterey, NY (date of newspaper January 12, 1888)

Hennessey Edward 28 son of Patrick in Watkins, NY January 16, 1888

Buck Mary Ann in Watkins, NY January 15, 1888. Born June 23, 1833 in Johnstown, NY to Jeremiah **Hapeman**. 2 daus Alcie at home and Helen wife of Charles **Sheldon** of Kirksville, Mo.

Phinney William in Reading, NY January 13, 1888. Born April 1, 1813 in Deerfield, Mass. Married July 2, 1834 Fanny **Nichols**, 3 children, Lewis G. of Eddytown, NY, Dr. Lorenzo N. of Norwalk, Conn. and Clarissa wife of Philander **La Fever** of Dundee, NY

Spencer Alvin T. in railroad accident, funeral in Elmira, NY January 18, 1888. Born May 25, 1862 in Rome, Pa. eldest son of A. G. of Reading. Married November 1885 Mattie **Lott** of Van Etten. Leaves 1 child 4w old, 1 brother and twin sisters

Allbright Catherine 72 in Hector, NY January 13, 1888

Seaman W. H. D. Md. 58 in Beaver Dams, NY January 13, 1888. Born 1829 in Reading, NY son of Patrick L. Mother was sister of Abiah **Newman**. Married age 26 Ophelia **Pope** who died 6 years ago. Leaves son Dean.

Weaver Lemi B. funeral in Reading, NY January 17, 1888. Son of James age 90 of Reading

Ellison Samuel 72 in Tyrone, NY January 23, 1888. Born Co. Tyrone, Ireland son of Andrew and came to America as babe. 3 brothers John and Andrew of Reading, NY and Thomas of Hornby, NY. Married Sarah **Van Duser**, 10 children, 3 died in 1 week about 30 years ago. Living, Henry of Tyrone, Monroe of Nelson, Pa., Mary wife of James **Baker** of Orange, NY, Lewis of Iowa, Susan wife of Isaac **Baker** of

Tyrone, Albert of NY, and Frank of Tyrone

Wynn Henry Ward 26 formerly of Watkins, NY in Erie, Pa. January 20, 1888

Keyser Alpheus in Hornellsville, NY January 23, 1888, buried Havana, NY

Murphy Mrs. John 76 in Watkins, NY January 22, 1888

Everts Eunice 85y 8m widow of Charles, who died 34 years ago, formerly of Peach Orchard, NY in Burdett, NY January 22, 1888. Born 1802 nee **Leavitt** in Conn. 1 son Alpheus

Goldsmith Libbie (**Jewell**) wife of George formerly of Schuyler Co. in Manistee, Mi. January 24, 1888

Robinson Emeline 76 in Torrey, NY January 23, 1888. Born May 31, 1812 dau of Ephriam and Rachel **Ensley**. 4 children, Mrs. Mary **White** of Watkins, NY, Alba H. of Rosendale, NY, Charles of Los Angeles and Elizabeth at home. Sister of J. S. **Ensley** of Reading, NY and Mrs. Angeline **Remer** of Gage, NY

Webber Henry Dixon 61y 11m 26d in Watkins, NY January 28, 1888. Born Suffolk Co. England. Buried Candor, NY

Spaulding Mrs. Edwin 53 dau of Lewis **Miller** of Moreland, NY in Corning, NY January 27, 1888. 2 daus Mary and Minnie. Sister, Mrs. S. B. H. **Nichols** of Corning

Brooks Mrs. C. W. 48 in Watkins, NY February 6, 1888

Berry H. Franklin 36 in Watkins, NY February 9, 1888. Born Reading, NY June 4, 1852 son of James

Smith Mrs. Hector W. 47 dau of Ebenezer **Boynton** in Watkins, NY February 13, 1888. Leaves husband and 1 dau Cora M.

Smith Hattie at J. W. **Mc Kiggen**'s in Mecklenburgh, NY February 11, 1888

Norris W. H. in Barrington, NY February 11, 1888

Aber Lucinda 83y 7m 7d formerly of Dix, NY at son's H. G in Carey, Ohio February 10, 1888. Born Ulster Co. Married Jehial Aber who died 1837

Howell Eleanor E. 90y 8m 12d in Watkins, NY February 26, 1888. Born NJ. Children, Mrs. William **Race** and Mrs. **Traverse** of Watkins

Wait Hannah 91y 7m 3d in Reading, NY February 29, 1888. Born July 26, 1796 in Saratoga, NY dau of James **Calvert**. Her grandfather John was drowned in Hudson River. Brothers and sisters, Alpheus died 1880 age 85 in Reading, George, John and Anna. Married March 7, 1815 Ahijah Wait born January 29, 1792 in Mass. son of

DEATH NOTICES 149

Daniel and Phebe (**Manchester**) Wait 1 of 5 sons and 7 daus. He died January 28, 1871 age 79 in Reading. 6 children, Mrs. Phebe **Parish**, Henry, Margaret, Sarah of Reading, Nancy wife of Frederick **Stamp** and Ebenezer of Illinois

Milliman Elvira 75 in N. Hector, NY March 10, 1888. 1 dau Sarah wife of W. B. **Shattuck** of Cincinnati, Ohio

Van Duser Nancy 70 in Altay, NY March 10, 1888

Spears Sarah in Townsend, NY March 17, 1888

Poppino Frances E. 86 in Watkins, NY March 12, 1888

Hicks Isaac 86 in Reading, NY March 14, 1888

Kimble Hannah 84 in Hector, NY March 17, 1888

White Mrs. George in Watkins, NY (date of newspaper March 22, 1888)

Miller Metta 12 dau of George in Watkins, NY March 25, 1888

Evans George 68 in Dix, NY March 25, 1888

Walker Jedediah age 54 in Watkins March 28, 1888

Pollis Susan in 18th year at Watkins, NY March 24, 1888

Smith Daniel K. 64 in Havana, NY March 27, 1888. Brother William V. of Watkins, NY

Pease Mrs. Peter in Pittston, Pa. March 18, 1888, buried in Corning, NY. Leaves son and 1 dau

Thompson Mrs. Ananias advanced age in Millport, NY March 26, 1888. Dau Mrs. Burr **Shelton** formerly of Catherine, NY and sister of late Col. William **Vaughn**

Huey Eli 39 in Weston, NY March 21, 1888

Wing Mrs. Hannah 95 in Corning, NY March 25, 1888

Roberts Samuel in Cayuta, NY March 19, 1888. Born March 1, 1804 in Livingston Co. Married Annie **Lindenberry** who died 1872, 6 children. Married (2) in 1874

Beecher Truman 56 funeral at Beaver Dams, NY March 30, 1888. Came from Vermont 40 years ago. Leaves wife and 5 children

Miles Samuel in Rock Stream, NY April 8, 1888. Born January 26, 1809 in Bainbridge, NY 7th of 8 children to Isaac Miles of Rev. War from Conn. and Mother Martha **Davis** of Mass., both of Scotch parentage. Brothers, Isaac of Scio, NY and

John of Cameron Mills, NY. Married October 14, 1840 Elizabeth **Day**, 9 children, 2 living

Rowley Mrs. Elizabeth in 92nd year at Scott's Corners, NY April 5, 1888. nee Scott, parents from Conn. Married (1) Bloomer, 4 children, E. J. **Bloomer** of Lenawee Co. Mi., Mrs. J. C. **Sackett**, Mrs. William **Jeffers** and Mrs. Truman **Parson** all of Hector, NY. Married (2) Nathaniel Rowley who survives

Moore Emily L. formerly of Watkins, NY at sister's Mrs. J. J. **Mc Wiliams** in Buffalo, NY April 14, 1888. Eldest dau of Philander and Jane E. **Norton** of Elmira, NY

Sterling H. A. formerly of Bennettsburg, NY fell from train near Painted Post, NY April 15, 1888. Leaves wife and children in Hornell, NY

Bateson Elizabeth nee **Dilliston** 58 in Mecklenburgh, NY April 9, 1888

Beers Mrs. Nelson 57 in Cayuta, NY April 19, 1888

Price Eli 21 son of Benjamin in Altay, NY April 26, 1888

Houck Mrs. Joseph 75 in Wayne, NY April 18, 1888

Calvert Alpheus 84y 4m 11d in Reading, NY funeral November 27, 1878

Slaght John in Watkins, NY December 3, 1878

Everts Mrs. Aranthus 97 recently in Hector, NY (date of newspaper September 7, 1881) 1 son Alanson

Wickham Nelson in 69th year at Burdett, NY January 25, 1882. Leaves widow and 4 children, Frank at home, Harris of Big Flats, NY, Mrs. S. J. **Lanternman** of Crookston, Minn. and Mrs. Otis **Ballou** of Durango, Col.

Hover Henry in Weston, NY March 20, 1886

Loncoy George 39 suicide in Watkins, NY March 17, 1886 at sister's Mrs. Louisa **Harrington**. Leaves widow

Hibler Zachariah in 70th year buried Bradford, NY February 4, 1889

Beckwith Charles S. in 80th year at Watkins, NY March 7, 1889. Born 1810 in Coldrain, Conn. son of Joseph and Lucinda eldest of 12 children, 3 living, Jasper of Burwell, Neb., William of Shiawasse Co. Mi. and Jason of Scranton, Pa. Married 1836 Sarah Ann **Foster** of Hector, NY, 9 children 8 living, Mrs. William **Collins**, Mrs. W. D. **Seaman**, Charles A., Mrs. W. S. **Longwell** of Corning, NY, William J., John S., Mrs. Sarah **Clauharty** and Mrs. Frank **Seaman** of Elmira, NY. Buried Glenwood cem.

DEATH NOTICES 151

Stackhouse Charles Jr. abt 25 in Havana, NY April 2, 1889

Woodward Emeline wife of Arthur C. in Watkins, NY April 5, 1889. Born August 15, 1852 in Hector, NY dau of Alfred and Emeline **Everts** and sister of Mr. Woodward's 1st wife. Married December 1, 1879. Buried Peach Orchard, NY

Walsh Mrs. James 31 in Watkins, NY April 6, 1889, dau of Phillip **Powers** of Reading, NY. Married 10 years, 2 daus and 2 sons. Sister Mrs. Mary **Long** of Watkins

Dimon Jerry at brother John's in Beaver Dams, NY April 13, 1889

Wasson Andrew S. 96y 11m in Dix, NY April 11, 1889. Born 1792 in Co. Tyrone, Ireland. Married 1824 Jane **White** who died April 10, 1886 age 88y 7m. 8 children, 6 living

Fitzpatrick Lawrence of Watkins, NY at sister's Mrs. Nicolas Fitzpatrick in Beaver Dams, NY April 16, 1889

Lovell George in Big Flats, NY April 13, 1889

Dunham Mrs. Eli in Havana, NY April 12, 1889

Lambert Della E. in 17th year dau of Wesley at Burdett, NY April 16, 1889

Sutton Aaron 75 in Reading Center, NY April 22, 1889. Born June 25, 1810 in Lodi, NY. 1 sister Mrs. Samuel **Lott**, 2 daus Mrs. **Horne** and Austa, sons Russell and Cassius. Son William died 1863

Stanley Benjamin 58 in Watkins, NY June 28, 1889. Leaves wife and 3 children, Mrs. **Williams** of Williamsport, Pa., Nettie of Binghamton, NY and James of Watkins. Brothers, Samuel of Clearfield, Pa. and Abijah of Potter Brook, Pa.

Langridge Frank Loss 15 in Watkins, NY May 2, 1889

Burch Mrs. Bridget 59 in Watkins, NY April 19, 1891. Born Ireland

Van Duzen David L. 56 in Watkins, NY April 15, 1891

Insco Hiram C. inf son of Martin and Elizabeth in Watkins, NY April 15, 1891

Schuyler Renssalaer in Logan, NY June 24, 1892

Freer Aaron 44 in Willard, NY June 25, 1892. Brothers, George F. and Charles of NY and sister Mrs. John **Booth** of Watkins, NY

Cratsley William Henry abt 40 eldest son of Abram of Monterey, NY in Starkey, NY June 26, 1892

Himrod Mrs. would be 91 in 10 days of Tyrone, NY formerly of Weston, NY buried June 29, 1892.

Hopkins A. R. widow of E. G. in Penn Yan, NY January 2, 1894. Would be 96 in February

Morgan D. A. 51 in Elmira, NY December 28, 1893. Brother M. W. of Watkins, NY

Franklin Susan A. wife of Augustus in Penn Yan, NY December 1893 formerly of Starkey and Watkins, NY, sister of late Cap. Henry and E. **Darwin** now of Chicago, Ill.

Hoffman Mrs. Samuel December __, 1893, buried Glenwood cem

Fitzpatrick John Sr. in Havana, NY January 17, 1894. Born 1824 in Milltown, Clare Co. Ireland. Wife died 7 years ago. 4 sons, John, Joseph, Charles and Thomas, 1 dau Mrs. James **Moonan**

Bramble Mrs. Sanford abt 50 in N. Hector, NY June 12, 1894, dau of Garrett **Clawson** who died in January. Leaves husband, 6 children, 1 sister and 1 brother

Elliot Omer 40 son of Daniel in Catherine, NY June 30, 1894

Wakeman Miss Sarah at William Wakeman's in Havana, NY July 3, 1894

Byram Charles 76 in Watkins, NY July 6, 1894. Born January 17, 1818 in Newark, NJ. Surviving 2 children, Henry of Watkins, Mrs. Eugene **Kies** of Elmira, NY, 1 sister in Penn Yan, NY and 3 in Waterloo, NY. 1 brother unknown where

White Samuel B. in N. Reading, NY July 5, 1894

Vanderhoof Albert in Weston, NY July 29, 1894

Forrester Eliza in Trumansburg, NY July 28, 1894, buried Dundee, NY

Ellis Daniel in Dundee, NY July 28, 1894

Berry Henry 71 in Watkins, NY July 30, 1894. Leaves 2nd wife, 5 sons, David of Cleveland, Stephen of Canandaigua, NY, George of Eddytown, NY, Lee and Fred of Townsend, NY, son Gordon died and 1 dau

Caldwell Herbert 7m son of Alexander and Nancy in Watkins, NY July 29, 1894

Moore Mrs. John in N. Hector, NY August 5, 1894

Everts Maria 72 widow of Charles in Burdett, NY August 5, 1894

Stoddard Mrs. Jesse 78 near Wedgewood, NY August 5, 1894. 1 son living, Richard

DEATH NOTICES 153

Peck Charlotte 75 widow of Benoni formerly of Watkins and Beaver Dams, NY in Elmira, NY August 5, 1894. Buried Glenwood cem

Wait Samuel Wrightley 81 in Watkins, NY August 8, 1894. Born Reading, NY. Married Hetty **Lewis** of Danby, NY who died 14 years ago. 8 children 6 living, George of Spencer, NY, Lewis, Henry, Nelson, John and Mary H. of Watkins. Buried Mitchell cem.

Hoagland Mrs. Francis 60 in Hector, NY November 15, 1894. Leaves 3 sons

Chapman David W. 54 in Reading, NY November 18, 1894. Born Columbus, Ohio 1840. Served in 161st Reg. NY Vol.

Ellison Nathaniel H. 84 at dau Mrs. Walter **Wells** formerly of Tyrone, NY in Barrington, NY November 16, 1894. Born Orange Co. came to Schuyler Co. age 16. Married Lydia **Williams**, 8 children, 5 living

Wait Henry in Reading, NY November 13, 1894. Mother Hannah **Calvert** came to Reading 1806, Father Ahijah and grandfather Daniel settled 1811. Born October 19, 1820 in Reading 3rd child of 6, 3 living Ebenezer of Ill., Margaret and Sarah at home. Married July 26, 1852 Hannah Maria **Case** who died April 13, 1885. Only child De Ett married October 7, 1885 John H. **Abrams**

Hutchins Lester in 72nd year at Townsend, NY November 19, 1894 at son-in-law's F. L. **Woodward**. Came from Herkimer Co. Other children Mrs. David **Hicks** and Mrs. James T. **Drake**

Yaw Mary Belle 3y dau of Phillip in Watkins, NY October 23, 1896

Moran Joanna age 32 wife of William J. and dau of John **Foley** in Watkins, NY January 28, 1900. Surviving 3 brothers, 3 sisters, husband, 2 daus age 5 and 2

Mosher Charlotte 60 widow of George in Watkins, NY May 1, 1900. 4 children, Grant and Jennie of Watkins, Frank of Penn Yan, NY, Mrs. Harry **Smith** of Reading, NY, a step-daughter Mrs. Burlock **Norris** of Reading

Corbett Charles M. son of Chester pioneer of Reading, NY in Pomfret, Conn. April 24, 1900. Born September 28, 1836. Brothers Otis R. and J. W. of Reading, sister Mrs. J. W. **Warner** of Watkins, NY. Married Mary A. **Brizzee** who died August 21, 1884, 2 children Ella wife of G. W. **Averill** of Rochester, NY and Edward E. who died July 21, 1891. Buried Watkins

Sleeper Mrs. J. W. 64 in Reading, NY April 26, 1900

Watkins Review March 28, 1896 - December 1900

Wickham Mrs. A. A. funeral in Elmira, NY March 24, 1896, buried in Hector, NY

Tyrrell Cornelia E. in Monterey, NY March 21, 1896

Wilkes Herman D. 30 son of James D. formerly of Watkins, NY in Jersey City, NJ February 17, 1896. 3 brothers and 3 sisters, C. J. of Bradford, Pa., T. G. of NY, Fred of Watkins, Mrs. M. D. **Insco**, Mrs. C. D. **Soper** of Elmira, NY and Edith of Watkins

Hern William in Catherine, NY April 25, 1896

Dunning Dr. Benjamin 82 in Trumansburg, NY April 21, 1896

Newall Charles over 60 in Watkins, NY May 4, 1896. Born April 22, 1836 in Lockport, NY. Married 1870 Elizabeth **Parker**, 6 children, Mrs. C. W. **Hathaway**, Lavina, James, Fred and William of Watkins and Charles of Buffalo, NY

White Henry E. at brother's Charles W. in Watkins, NY May 1, 1896. Born October 5, 1850 in Watkins son of late William E. Married Frances **Leonard** who died January 1892. 1 son age 10 living in Seneca Co. 1 sister and 5 brothers, George R., H. L., C. W. of Watkins, John W. of Tioga Co. Pa. and William R. of Wellsboro, Pa.

Sargeant Mrs. Watson in Tyrone, NY May 12, 1896

Supplee Lewis in Reading, NY May 12, 1896. Leaves wife and son

Thomas Alvah 88 died in Orange, NY last week (newspaper date May 15, 1896)

Ayres Andrus in Montour Falls, NY May 10, 1896. Born 1818

Harvey Edward 31 in Watkins, NY May 10, 1896

Kies Orville in Watkins, NY May 8, 1896. Born Canoga, NY. Surviving, widowed Mother, 3 brothers and 1 sister, J. K. and George of Mi., Eugene and Mrs. Frank **Coleman** of Elmira, NY

Broas Charles J. 78 in Farmer Village, NY May 9, 1896. Came from Dutchess Co., resided Havana, NY

Stacey Mrs. J. George 59 nee **Lewis** May 15, 1896. Born Elizabeth, NJ. 7 children, 1 died infant, Charlotte died 8-10 years, J. George Jr., Lewis, Annie, Susan and Theresa

Meddick Mrs. aged resident in Hector, NY May 31, 1896

Nye Algernon S. 80 formerly of Watkins, NY in Dundee, NY May 29, 1896. Leaves wife and 2 sons David late of Reading, NY, Sidney of NY. Daughter Allie died in Watkins, grand-daughter Eleanor W. with Mother Mrs. Fanny B. Nye

Berry Frederick 30 in Dix, NY June 8, 1896. Born January 19, 1866 son of late

DEATH NOTICES 155

Henry. 5 brothers and 2 sisters

Rapalee Martha in 90th year wife of Roswell in Watkins, NY June 9, 1896. Born February 5, 1807. Of 14 children only 1 survives, George who was 73 on June 10

Diven Gen. Alexander S. 87 in Elmira, NY June 11, 1896 son of Captain John of Revolutionary War and pioneer at head of Seneca Lake. Sister still resides at homestead 1 mile west of Watkins, NY. Born February 10, 1809 and married July 1834 Amanda **Beers** who died August 18, 1875. 8 children 5 living, George Miles, Eleanor, Mrs. H. C. **Silsbee**, Mrs. Col. **Liseum** of Dakota and John M. of Elmira, NY

Fenno Mrs. Willard J. at Altay, NY June 3, 1896. Born June 1831 only dau of Enoch **Honeywell**. Only son F. H. died 4 years ago

Martin J. Reeves in Watkins, NY June 6, 1896. Born September 18, 1849 near Burdett, NY 1 of 11 children to Archer and Almira. Sister Ellen died, Arvilla wife of Aranthus **Scoville** of Neb., Elizabeth wife of Charles **Dewey** of Chemung Co., William S. of Watkins, Archer D. of Mi., Oliver W. of Montour Falls, NY, John P. of Cal., Mark L. on homestead in Hector, NY, Aaron of Port Jervis and Peter of Burdett, NY. Leaves wife Addie E. nee **Brown** and 6 children, Raymond, Myron, Mabel, May, Reeve and Harold.

Wedgewood James of Dix, NY June 14, 1896. Born 1829 in eastern NY. Leaves wife, 2 sons Arthur at home and Oscar of Missoula, Mi.

Hemans Carrie A. 29 in Watkins, NY June 13, 1896

Campbell Mrs. S. A. 81 in Watkins, NY June 14, 1896. Leaves 1 son Charles. Buried Pine Valley, NY, former residence

Prentiss Polly 78 widow of Stephen in Watkins, NY June 18, 1896. Son Horace L. of Watkins. Sister of late Dyer **Robinson**

Crampton Simeon 79 in Tyrone, NY June 13, 1896

Raymond William Henry in 70th year son of Thomas B. at Reading, NY June 18, 1896

O'Connell Henry Francis 4m 2w twin son of Henry in Watkins, NY June 21, 1896

Brown James in Watkins, NY June 24, 1896

Gurnett John in Richland, NY June 18, 1896

Fordham Mrs. John in Rock Stream, NY June 23, 1896. Children, Dr. G. C. and Dewitt C. of Watkins, NY, Etta wife of Byron **Totten** of Mi., Abbie wife of Edward **Elliott** of Eddyville, NY, Hattie, Vinnie and Martin

Sherman Orra in Watkins, NY June 20, 1896. Born November 4, 1825 son of Elias D. of Rose, NY. Married 3 times, only son Urban died November 1895, 2 daus, Viola and Alice wife of Franklin F. **Irish**. 3 brothers, Elias D. of Watkins, Levi L. of Rochester, NY and Franklin of Three Rivers, Mi.

Huey Phineas in Tyrone, NY June 12, 1896. Born January 19, 1873 son of James

Hallett Mrs. Catherine over 60 wife of William drowned in Chemung Canal at Watkins, NY July 3, 1896. Leaves several children

Hawes Dr. Mathias D. 85 in Hector, NY July 20, 1896. Born 1811 in Hector oldest of 8 children son of Jonas and Rebecca, only 1 living Mrs. Gertrude **Rhodes** of Lodi, NY. Married 58 years to Isabelle **Palmer** surviving and 3 children, W. P. of Watkins, NY, Dr. James P. and Belle of N. Hector

Shillette Caroline in Bennettsburg, NY July 28, 1896

Sanford Lewis in Reading Center, NY July 25, 1896. Born June 1832 son of Ira. Married December 1874 Catherine **Lott** dau of Samuel, living age 83

Lewis Mrs. Mary in 74th year of Omaha, Nebraska while visiting relatives at Dix, NY August 4, 1896 . Born November 26, 1822 in NJ eldest child of Phillip and Anna **Gano**. Brothers J. Halsey and L. M. of Watkins, NY, J. D. of Dix, G. W. of NY, 3 sisters Mrs. Sarah A. **Davis** of Dix, Elizabeth **Catlin** of Tioga Co. Pa., Harriet **Heggie** of Potter Co. Pa. Leaves husband in Nebraska and son C. W. **Davis** of Washington DC

Swarthout Polly 84 widow of Bernardus at Perry City, NY August 9, 1896

Gottrey William Oliver in Kendaia, NY August 3, 1896. Born January 12, 1823 in Reading, NY

Sargeant Watson in Tyrone funeral August 8, 1896. Born 1844

Holden Miss Betsey August 13, 1896. Born April 6, 1820 in Lansing, NY. Brothers, Roswell deceased, Heman and Fox

Collins William August 20, 1896. Born 1836 in reading, NY son of Elijah. Leaves wife of 9 years, brothers Eleazor and John of Watkins, NY

Kies Martha B. 81 widow of Henry in Watkins, NY August 27, 1896. Born Canoga, Seneca Co. Leaves 3 sons and 1 daughter

Mc Connell John 82 in Tyrone, NY August 29, 1896. Leaves wife and 1 son Alfred, 4 daus, Mrs. D. **Lalor** of Havana, NY, Mrs. Fred **Zimmerman** of Gr. Rapids, Mi., Hattie and Florence

Osborn John W. 81 in Mecklenburgh, NY September 5, 1896. Born 1816 in NJ. Leaves 3 sons, John W. Jr. and W. F. of Rochester, NY, William of Mecklenburgh and 2 daus Mrs. B. C. **Smith** of Reynoldsville, NY and Lydia of Mecklenburg

Cure Mrs. Amos of Hector, NY funeral at Bennettsburg, NY September 5, 1896

Randall Addison in Monterey, NY September 8, 1896

Greenley Sarah L. 75 wife of William in Moreland, NY August 30, 1896. Born in Vermont dau of Thomas **Soper**, Married 1841 Russell **Osborn** who died 1866. Married 1880 to William. 1 son Thomas R. of Painted Post, NY, dau Sarah of Mi. and Mrs. Harriet **Lynch** of Corning, NY. 4 brothers and 1 sister survive

Wellover Eli M. 59 in Altay, NY September 3, 1896

Mead Mrs. John C. 91 in Burdett, NY September 15, 1896. Leaves 3 daus, Mrs. Mary **Willis**, Mrs. George **Snyder** of Burdett, Mrs. Charles **Osborn** of Waterloo, NY, 3 sons Garwood of Burdett, Luther of Poughkeepsie, NY and Edwin of Phelps, NY

Hazlitt James R. 57 in Hector, NY September 12, 1896. Born 1839 in Reading, NY son of David. Mother was dau of pioneer James **Roberts**. Married Mary **Miller** of Enfield, NY. 1 child Herbert age 17, 1 sister Mrs. Mary **Cotton** of Friendship, NY. Sister Mrs. Charles **Ingersoll** died a few weeks ago

Tabor Charles E. M. 57 in Detroit, Mi. September 11, 1896. Left Watkins, NY last June on trip to Gr. Lakes. Born Hillsdale, Mi. son of John D. and Adelpha B. Mother in 85th year lives Watkins. Father buried Broadalbin, NY. Married January 11, 1872 Mrs. Julia **Chester**

Clock Mary L. wife of Samuel R. in Trumansburg, NY August 16, 1896. Born Ulysses, NY dau of James F. **Letts** Sr. Married 52 years

Swarthout Lorenzo 65 in Wayne, NY September 26, 1896. 2 sons, Asa of Wayne and Robert of Bradford, NY

Cook Foster 15 son of H. C. and grandson of Mrs. S. C. **Beardsley** in Dundee, NY September 30, 1896

Bostwick William L. in Ithaca, NY September 22, 1896. Born March 13, 1837 in Tompkins Co. Married 1861

Carman Cornelius October 3, 1896. Born January 12, 1822 in Ulster Co. Married Matilda **Collins**. Leaves wife, son and dau

Bolt Polly 91y 9m in Townsend, NY October 11, 1896 dau of pioneer Hampton **Miller** of Reading, NY. Married (1) Jarvis **Dean** and (2) William Bolt of Reading. Leaves 2 sons and 5 daus

Faville Mrs. Daniel 73 in Reading, NY October 21, 1896. Born April 21, 1823 nee Mary A. **Cole** in Herkimer Co. Married about 50 years, husband died 1877. 2 children Daniel and Ella at home. 2 sisters 1 in Herkimer Co. and 1 in Clifton

Springs, NY

Yaw Mary Bell 3y 4m dau of Phillip in Watkins, NY October 23, 1896

Hynes R. J. formerly of Watkins, NY in Batavia, NY October 23, 1896

Woodward Dr. Charles 52 in Tecumseh, Mi. October 27, 1896. Born Hector, NY. Brothers A. C., B. W. and sister Mrs. O. H. **Budd**

Fero George in Moreland, NY buried October 28, 1896

Cooley White in Dix, NY October 27, 1896. Born Tioga Co. 1832. 1 dau Mrs. Oscar **Wedgewood**

Baldwin W. H. 58 in Beaver Dams, NY October 30, 1896

Case Ezra in Reynoldsville, NY October 27, 1896. Leaves wife and 2 sons

Chandler Mrs. Polly in 90th year at dau Mrs. John **Clawson** in N. Hector, NY November 29, 1896

Chapman Mrs. Samuel A. 73 in Watkins, NY November 18, 1896 at dau, Mrs. Charles **Fox** of Elmira, NY

Mc Donald Mrs. E. A. 82 in Watkins, NY November 28, 1896, widow of James who died 15 years ago. Adopted dau now wife of Deidrick **Willers** formerly Mrs. James H. **Randall**

Bong Herman 27 in Beaver Dams, NY November 10, 1896. Married 1895 Agnes **La Fever** dau of Lovett. 1 dau age 1m

Coger Henry in Corning, NY November 26, 1896. Born December 12, 1818 in Green Co. resided Watkins, NY 40 years. Wife died 3 years ago, 2 sons W. R. and Minard

Kimble Augustus W. 67 in Burdett, NY December 1, 1896. Born Burdett, 2 children John M. of Rochester, NY and Mary wife of William **Hager**

Parker George B. 33 in Burdett, NY November 28, 1896

Fletcher Julia W. 68 wife of Deacon in Tyrone, NY buried December 2, 1896 in Union cem.

Mathews Mrs. Daniel 80 in Burdett, NY December 14, 1896

Swick Mrs. D. C. in Steamburg, NY December 3, 1896

Swan George colored man of Odessa, NY December 12, 1896

Townsend William in 70th year at Glenora, NY December 11, 1896, son of Eli and

DEATH NOTICES

Betsey (**Huson**) Townsend. Married January 31, 1863 Julia **Weller** dau of Judge Noble Weller of Chemung Co.

Rudy Fred L. son of Minier suicide in Hector, NY December 14, 1896

Stannard Madison 65 in Hector, NY December 9, 1896

Bovier Charles 88 July 4th last in Bradford, NY December 12, 1896

Smith Molly 78 wife of George Sr. in Watkins, NY December 21, 1896. 3 children, Walter of Cincinnati, Ohio, James of Watkins and Mrs. L. M. **Carpenter** of Millport, NY

Pike Eleanor widow of David in Dix, NY December 22, 1896. Born February 1810 nee **Edwards**. Husband died 1885. Children, Mrs. Mathew **Case**, Sewall, Hiram E., Mrs. Noah **Squires**, Mrs. Albert **Beckwith** and Mrs. George W. **Ganung**

Hovey Hannah V. 76 widow of Erastus in Burdett, NY December 23, 1896. Born June 1820 in NJ nee **Snyder**. Married 50 years, husband died March 1875. Children all died infancy except J. P.

Love Joseph B. in Reading, NY December 21, 1896. Born April 1821 son of Samuel in Co. Tyrone, Ireland and came here 1844. Married (1) Mary Jane **Hughey** and (2) Mary **Sproul**. Children George W. out west, Emmett R. of Perry City,, NY Mrs. Levi **Sproul** and Miss Jennie of Dundee, NY, May, Ira, Sarah, Willie and Leon at home. Brothers and sisters, William N., Mrs. Ira **Bartholomew**, Mrs. Oliver **Mackey**, Mrs. William J. **Campbell**, J. B., John and Mrs. Thomas **Jack**. All died except Mrs. Campbell and Mrs. Jack

Swick Eugene 32 hunting accident in Hector, NY December 27, 1896

Mallerson Marcus 80 in Orange, NY December 24, 1896

Palmer Mary L. 39 wife of Loyal in Lodi, NY December 28, 1896. Born September 8, 1857 in Hector, NY dau of John D. and Sarah **Rogers**. Married November 10, 1883 in Middlebury, Pa.

Bassett Helen C. 54 in Dundee, NY January 4, 1897

Love child of John age 3y 10m in Watkins, NY January 13, 1897

Sutton Carlos Harrison in Reading, NY January 26, 1897. Born December 18, 1820 in Reading eldest son of Nathaniel who was born in Lodi, NY and Phebe **Peck** Sutton. She was born Windham, NY and died 1829. Nathaniel married (2) Susan **Humphries**, their children Mrs. Thomas **Ellis**, Edwin, Mrs. J. B. **Chase**, Leroy, Monroe and Anson, Loren deceased. Married May 3, 1848 Maria **Eggleston**, 3 children, Emma died young, Mary Lillian wife of George W. Mc Nemer, Harry E. who married Hattie G. **Phinney**

Simmons Eli funeral in Wayne, NY January 17, 1897

Sullivan Timothy 87 of Lyons, NY in Watkins, NY Janaury 23, 1897. Born Ireland. Leaves 1 son and 4 daus

Seymour Mrs. J. O. 68 formerly of Watkins, NY in Geneva, NY January 21, 1897. 1 brother, 3 sisters, Mrs. Gertrude **Howard**, Harriet **Hunt** and Sarah **Seymour**. No children, 1 dau died Waterloo, NY

Loveless Nelson in Catherine, NY February 5, 1897. Born 1820, leaves wife and 1 dau Mrs. Lewis **Carpenter**

Wood Joel 70 in Orange, NY February 8, 1897

Button Mrs. Jesse 20 in Orange, NY recently (date of newspaper February 12, 1898)

Hovey Mrs. Jacob C. 70 formerly of Monterey, NY in Orange, NY February 14, 1897

Hendrickson Mrs. Charles 30 in Watkins, NY February 6, 1897

Huey Edwin C. 53 in Dix, NY February 8, 1897. Born Orange, NY son of Andrew

Routlege Thomas 70 in Rock Stream, NY February 7, 1897

Edgerton Phebe Jane in 78th year at Rock Stream, NY February 2, 1897. Born Reading, NY dau of Ralph **Smith**. Married age 18 Andrew Edgerton who died 38 years ago in Wis. 7 children

Pearsall Mrs. Warren M. of Watkins, NY in Rochester, NY February 7, 1897. Born Waterburg, NY dau of Halsey **Wortman**. Survived by Mother, 2 brothers, several sisters, Mrs. Burr **Mitchell** and Mrs. Madison **Covert** of Watkins

Bronson Annie Bell 20 dau of Charles in Beaver Dams, NY February 10, 1897

Murphy Margaret 47 wife of Patrick in Salt Point, NY February 14, 1897

Dailey Harriet widow of James 87 in Burdett, NY February 13, 1897

Howard Mrs. Lewis in Watkins, NY February 10, 1897. Born February 17, 1825 in NJ nee Electa **Headley**. Married September 2, 1857 in Watkins, 2 daus Mary E. wife of Charles S. **Hoyt** of Dundee, NY and Helen L. wife of Frank **Gilbert**

Smith Miner in 61st year of Watkins, NY at Glenora, NY February 8, 1897. 5th child of Charles Smith and Hannah **Carley** in Smith Hollow, NY. Grandson of James. Leaves wife and son George

Sebring Eugene funeral at Tyrone, NY February 13, 1897

Bump Lucy in Orange, NY February 11, 1897. Leaves Mother, 3 sisters and 1

DEATH NOTICES

brother

Hutchinson Mrs. Emma in Orange, NY February 12, 1897

Mapes Sarah Ann widow of H. N. 66 in Watkins, NY February 20, 1897, dau of late Benjamin **Burgess** of Watkins. Husband died Mi. 3 years ago. 1 dau Mrs. Morris **Richardson**

Lockwood Clark in 51st year at Watkins, NY February 18, 1897. Born June 1846 only son of Robert. Surviving Mother Mrs. Jane Lockwood, 3 sisters Mrs. William M. **Pellett**, Mrs. E. B. **Russell** of Watkins and Mrs. Fenno **Wakeman** of Rico, Col.

Donovan child of Patrick age 12 in Orange, NY March 9, 1897

Hall Mrs. Mary E. 54 in Watkins, NY March 9, 1897

Townsend Rapplee 78 in Dundee, NY March 11, 1897

Smith Elizabeth 87 in Watkins, NY March 5, 1897. Buried Logan, NY

Rogers Henry H. in Watkins, NY March 2, 1897. Children, Elijah of Watkins, Charles of Corning, NY, Daniel of Jersey City, NJ and Mrs. Warren **Gregory** of Watkins

Mc Donnell Maurice 29 in Watkins, NY March 7, 1897. Born Springfield, Mass. came to Watkins when young with Mother Kate and Step-father Charles B. Mc Donnell. Buried Holyoke, Mass.

Magee Gen George J. of Watkins, NY at Nice, France March 11, 1897, buried Glenwood cem.

Coon Isreal L. in 70th year formerly of Watkins, NY in Phoenix, Ar. March 16, 1897. Leaves wife and children, George S. of Watkins, Charles and William of Phoenix and Mrs. James **Davy** of Geneva, NY

Tompson N. S. 94 at Foot's Hill, NY last week (date of newspaper March 17, 1897). Wife died 2 years ago, 9 of 10 children living, Zalmon of Hector, NY, Archibald of Montour Falls, NY, Ira N. of Montour, NY and Mrs. Ella H. **Labar** of Odessa, NY

Van Gordon Mrs. Hancy 81 in Weston, NY March 11, 1879. Born January 20, 1816 in Wayne, NY nee Hancy **Rice**. Married 1835 A. I. Van Gordon who died November 1883, 5 children 3 living, Mary of Weston, Phineas R. of Hornellsville, NY and Edward of Horseheads, NY. I sister Mrs. Fanny **Goodyear** of Northville, NY

Jaquish Johnson M. 63 in Hector, NY March 19, 1897. Born Hector. 2 daus by 1st wife, Mrs. David **Manning** of Iowa and Mrs. J. T. **Manning** of Hector. 2nd wife Louisa **Elliot** of Burdett, NY survives and 3 children, Alvah S., Mrs. Clarence **Ely** and James all of Hector

Cross Fannie widow of John, who died 2 years ago, in Reading, NY March 31, 1897. Born April 20, 1823 in Tompkins Co. nee **Bossard**. Married March 24, 1847, 6 children survive, Mrs. Eugene K. **Smith**, Mrs. Frank **Smith**, Mrs. John **Erway** of Kansas, Miles B. of Lookhaven, Pa., Mrs. William E. **Phinney** and Mrs. W. P. **Baker** also 1 brother Anson near Ithaca, NY

Bronson Calista Elizabeth widow of Sylvester in Dix, NY April 2, 1897, dau of Benjamin **Collins** of Tompkins Co. 3 children Nellie wife of Clarence **Millspaugh**, Mary E. at home and Frank. 1 brother Barnett C. Collins of Watkins, NY, 2 sisters, Mrs. John **Rhodes** of Moreland, NY and Mrs. Alonzo **Maine** of Orange, NY

Tennent Eugene abt 40 suicide in Burdett, NY April 1, 1897

Coon Julia 70 widow of Adam in Watkins, NY April 1, 1897. 2 children Frank of Watkins and Mrs. Libbie **Brown** of Dundee, NY

Rice Jane 80 at son's Burton Rice in Altay, NY April 1, 1897

Brouwere V. T. 79 of Hornby, NY April 2, 1897

Mc Connell Mathew 80 in Bennettsburg, NY April 8, 1897

Gofny Elizabeth wife of R. H. in Bennettsburg, NY April 11, 1897

Williams Mehitabel 84 widow of Samuel in Weston, NY April 13, 1897. 4 daus, Mrs. Almeda **Babcock** of Weston, Mrs. Putnam **Demming** of Dundee, NY, Mrs. Joseph **Meeks** of Barrington, NY and Mrs. Andrew **Lawrence** of Tyrone, NY

Palmer Susannah 68 wife of David C. in Reading, NY April 19, 1897. Born April 1, 1829 in Dix, NY dau of William and Eunice **Sickles**. Married July 29, 1846. 3 daus dec., Maryette an infant, Aphelia age 10 and Emma wife of Byron E. **Reniff** died September 1895. 1 son Nelson living

Buck Edith Culver April 19, 1897

Aldrich William formerly of Burdett, NY in Corning, NY April 22, 1897

Finger Sally E. 65 widow of Phillip in Monterey, NY April 18, 1897

Blunt George 87y 3m 15d in Watkins, NY June 2, 1897. Born England

Benjamin Flora wife of Howard in Pine Grove, NY June 5, 1897. 4 children, Mary wife of Milton **Van Duser**, Bert, Sadie and Fred at home

Kennedy Isaac in Watkins, NY June 7, 1897. Born Ithaca, NY 1832, 1 of 10 children. 1 sister Susan survives

Van Loon John 76 in Smith Valley, NY June 9, 1897. Born September 5, 1821 in Dryden, NY. Married (1) Lydia **Thomas** who died 1876, 3 children Mrs. Herman

DEATH NOTICES

Secord of Smith Valley, Mrs. Dan **Todd** of Cayuta, NY and Millard of Mi. Married (2) March 2, 1877 Mrs. Mary **Angle**. Served 107th Reg. Co. H. NY Inf.

Shelton Ralph 61 in Odessa, NY June 6, 1897. Leaves 1 son D. E.

Rogers Daniel in Beaver Dams, NY June 8, 1897. Born 1822 in Ulster Co. Surviving wife and 1 son Daniel of Hornby, NY, 1 dau Mrs. Martha **Dodge** of Corning, NY

Hanmer Peter 86 in Pine Grove, NY June 10, 1897

Cole Mary in 89th year widow of Charles in Beaver Dams, NY June 17, 1897, one of 1st settlers of Beaver Dams. Charles and brother Ira married sisters from Putnam Co. 5 children, H. T. of Corning, NY, Joseph of Dundee, NY, Mrs. L. D. **Obert** of Mi., Mrs. Frank **Coon** and Mrs. Charles **Master** of Iowa

Swick Elmer C. 49 in Steamburg, NY June 16, 1897

Miller Mrs. Andrew in N. Hector, NY June 16, 1897. Leaves 2 sons Warren and Thomas

Brooks John June 15, 1897. Leaves wife and dau

Drake John R. 78y 10m in Reading, NY June 18, 1897

Coolbaugh William 82 in Watkins, NY June 24, 1897. Born Barrington, NY eldest son Benjamin and Amelia (**Loomis**). Lived near Bath, NY, moved 10 years ago to dau. Family, Daniel of Woodland, Mi., Mrs. Irene **Raines** of Whitmor Lake, Mi., both deceased, Isabelle wife of Charles **Wheat** of Hornby, NY and M. A. of Altay, NY. Leaves wife and dau, Laura wife of A. F. **Corwin** of Wedgewood, NY and stepson Gen. L. G. **Rutherford** of Grand Rapids, Mi.

Clawson Nellie 72 wife of I. N. June 26, 1897 at San Francisco in train accident with 2 daus Clara and Daisy

Reed Elizabeth 57 wife of Edson W. in Watkins, NY June 27, 1897. Leaves husband 1 dau Mrs. E. J. **States**, 1 brother William B. **Snyder** of Odessa, NY, sister Thirza **Moot** of Trumbull Corners, NY

Casey John in Watkins, NY June 25, 1897. Born 1835 in Ireland. Leaves wife and 5 children, Mrs. Fred **Bomberage**, Daniel and Michael of Watkins, Mrs. **Mulcahy** of Geneva, NY and Margaret of Ithaca, NY

Moore Loren V. 19 in Beaver Dams, NY June 23, 1897

Drake J. R. in Reading, NY June 18, 1897

Baker Edward 35 in Monterey, NY July 3, 1897

Erway Martha Cogswell 20 in Peach Orchard, NY June 30, 1897

Kendall Mrs. Lyman in Catherine, NY June 30, 1897

Carpenter Mrs. A. B. July 4, 1897, buried Mehoopany, NY

Nares Mary 26 wife of Tunis D. Jr. in Corning, NY July 5, 1897, nee Mary **Quigley** of Dansville, NY. Married 3 months

Sipple Henry 64 suicide in Bath Soldiers Home June 30, 1897

Howe Rev. Franklin S. in Burdett, NY July 13, 1897. Born Vermont

Mattison Levi 90 in Altay, NY July 11, 1897

Dowling Michael 69 in Monterey, NY July 8, 1897

Burr Bradley 88 in Hector, NY July 11, 1897. Born 1809 in Fairfield, Conn. Married 1836 Lydia **Chase**, 2 children E. P. and Mrs. Amelia **Warren**

Mathews Clara wife of George in Burdett, NY July 17, 1897

Washburn W. B. 82 in Wayne, NY July 17, 1897. 7 children, J. M. of Keuka, NY, W. D., J., and Edward A. of Wayne, NY, Mrs. D. **Ellis** and Mrs. C. **Moody** of Dundee, NY and Mrs. J. H. **Walsh** of Keuka

Beebe William T. in 80th year at Townsend, NY July 26, 1897. Born Reading, NY son of Richard. Married Elizabeth **Mayo** of Hector, NY, 2 children Thomas W. and Sarah E. of Dix, NY. Buried Beaver Dams, NY

Weller Mary Ann in Beaver Dams, NY July 27, 1897. Born April 9, 1819 in Reading, NY. Leaves husband and 3 children Mrs. Dr. **Smith**, Leroy and H.

Hogencamp Mrs. Truman 24 in Dix, NY August 7, 1897

Donovan Dennis 21 of Townsend, NY in Elmira, NY August 16, 1897

Van Sice Charles Franklin in Montour Falls, NY August 14, 1897. Born December 18, 1836 in Genesee Co. Enlisted with 9 brothers in Civil War, 2 died. Leaves wife and 6 children, Frank, Addie, Lewis and Jessie at home, Mrs. Ransom **Mc Dougal** of Odessa, NY and Mrs. A. H. **Taylor** of Smith Valley, NY

Goodrich Samuel 83 in Watkins, NY August 29, 1897. Born Pittsfield, Mass. 1 of 9 children, 1 living Mrs. L. G. **Winton** of Penn Yan, NY. Married Mary E. **de St. Croix** at Havana, NY who died July 24, 1869. No living children. 6th lineal descendant of William Bradford

Chapman Edna 6 dau of W. W. in Tyrone, NY August 24, 1897. Leaves parents and 2 sisters Mabel and Minnie

Secord Herman 51 in Hector, NY August 20, 1897. Born 1846 in Hector son of Charles. Leaves wife and 3 children, Elmer and Ellsworth twins age 7, Frank age 10, Mother and sisters Mrs. J. B. **Phoenix** of Dundee, NY, Mrs. John **Agard** of Mecklenburgh, NY and Mrs. Charles **Washburn** of Alpine, NY. Wife was dau of John **Van Loon**

Keeler George W. 33 in Montour Falls, NY September 8, 1897

Hibbard George F. 75 in Watkins, NY September 6, 1897

Baird John 35 son of James in Orange, NY August 26, 1897

Everts Mrs H. 72 in N. Hector, NY September 1, 1897. Leaves husband and 8 children Mrs. Anna **Fenton**, Mrs. Rachel **Bond**, Mrs. Sarah **Burr**, George, Frank, Eugene, Irvine and Judson

Hennessey John 32 son of Patrick buried Watkins, NY September 11, 1897. 3 brothers James, Frank and Jerry of Watkins, 3 sisters, Nellie of Watkins, Mrs. **Curran** and Mrs. **Caverly** of Elmira, NY

Merrills Phillip 72 in Monterey, NY September 7, 1897

Ellis J. Martin 72 in Perry City, NY September 15, 1897

Rice Mrs. Dennis of Weston, NY at Lake Waneta September 17, 1897

Smith Libbie wife of Eugene K. nee **Cross** September 29, 1897

Earnest Hattie wife of George D. in Wayne, NY September 19, 1897. Born June 25, 1865 dau of Dr. Jacob **Runner** of Hornellsville, NY. Married March 15, 1885. 1 brother Olin H. Runner of N. Urbana, NY, 2 half sisters Mrs. Mary **Sanford** and Rena

Stevens Charles R. in Orange, NY October 9, 1897. Born July 1, 1849 in Orange son of Edward and Eliza. Married August 27, 1873 Celestia **Phelps**, 2 children Minnie died age 2y 6m and Orrin now age 15

Oldfield Elizabeth dau of William M. in Townsend, NY October 11, 1897

Goltry Paul 77 in Pine Grove, NY October 12, 1897. 2 sons Isaac and Harrison

Gould Carrie 14 dau of Lafayette in Beaver Dams, NY October 9, 1897. Buried Willard

Ruddick George D. formerly of Odessa, NY suicide in Kansas City September 5, 1897. Married twice, both wives deserted. Son of Mrs. George **Terry** by first husband William Ruddick. Leaves 3 children

Troxell Rev. H. B. in Tyrone, NY November 15, 1897. Leaves wife and 2 sons,

Dow at home and Leroy of Ovid, NY

Woodward Willard 79 in Beaver Dams, NY November 8, 1897. Leaves wife, son Charles of Rock Stream, NY and dau Mrs. Richard **Rogers** of Beaver Dams, NY, step-son George **Proper** of Painted Post, NY

Mc Clure John 55 in Montour Falls, NY November 18, 1897. Leaves wife and 3 children Mrs. L. M. **Gillett** of Elmira, NY, Fred and Max

Sharpe William L. 77 in Rock Stream, NY November 17, 1897. 2 brothers Ambrose and Clark of Rock Stream

Hitchcock George 85 in Watkins, NY November 26, 1897. Born 1812 in Fishkill, NY. Leaves 2nd wife of the Ely family, 1 dau by 1st marriage Mrs. Samuel C. **Keeler**

Simmons Mary 68 relict of Charles in Reading, NY November 22, 1897. Leaves 1 dau Mrs. Byron **O'Daniels** and 1 sister Martha **Wilcox**

Marshall Thomas 69 in Reading, NY November 24, 1897. Born Ireland

Harrison Millie 75 widow of William who died 1867, in Monterey, NY November 26, 1897, nee **Chamberlain**. Married 56 years ago, 8 children 3 living, Mrs. Mina **Jones** of Brockport, NY, Mrs. Delphine **Swarthout** of Monterey, NY and Charles of Elmira, NY

Hitchcock Lydia Margaret widow of George V. in Watkins, NY February 22, 1898, dau of Augustus and Olive (**Scoville**) Ely from Conn. Brothers and sisters, William B., Philo S. of NY, Olive Maria wife of Rev. C. C. **Carr** of Horseheads, NY, Polly Ann wife of J. M. **Hager** of Brooklyn, NY, Chloe S. wife of David **Hillerman** of Watkins, Mary wife of Henry S. of **Hudson** NY, and Harriet who died 4 years ago. Married November 26, 1852, husband died on 40th anniversary, 1 son William died age 17. 2 children of husband by 1st marriage

Reed Edson W. 58 in Watkins, ny February 21, 1898. Born Tompkins Co. Wife Elizabeth died 8m ago. 1 child living Mrs. E. J. **States** of Watkins. Brothers and sisters, James of Hartford, Conn., Edwin M. of M'kees Rock, Pa., Samuel H. of Elmira, NY and Orange S. of Mandan, N. Dakota.

Willover Mrs. Harvey suicide in Weston, NY February 18, 1898

Nagle Mrs. John in Montour Falls, NY February 18, 1898. Leaves Husband and 5 daus, Ella, Nora, Lizzie, Margaret and Belle and 1 son John

Bradley Julia A. widow of Edwin in Montour, NY February 25, 1898. Born 1813 dau of Lemuel **Shelton**, pioneer of Catherine, NY from Conn. in 1806. Leaves 1 brother James of Reading, NY, 2 sons, A. J. of Montour and Prof. L. H. of Watkins, NY

DEATH NOTICES

Pike Sewall in Montour Falls, NY February 28, 1898. Born Veteran, NY. Leaves wife, 1 son Hiram of Rochester, NY, 2 daus Mrs. J. T. **Mc Keg** and Sarah of Montour Falls. Brothers and sisters, H. E. Pike, Mrs. Mathew **Case**, Mrs. Noah **Squires**, Mrs. **Tompson**, Mrs. George W. **Ganung** of Watkins and Mrs. Albert **Beckwith** of Wedgewood, NY

Scott Mrs. in Reynoldsville, NY February 26, 1898. Leaves husband and 3 young children, youngest 2 weeks

Head Leroy in Odessa, NY February 24, 1898

Dickerson Sarah in 75th year widow of John in Peach Orchard, NY funeral February 15, 1898

Corbett Chester L. in E. Reading, NY March 3, 1898. Born 1851 2nd of 9 children to Otis R. Eldest Walter died. Buried Cleveland cem.

Goundry John in Watkins, NY March 3, 1898. Born July 28, 1843 in Barningham, Yorkshire, England. Father died January 18, 1864 in Monterey, NY. Moved to Reading, NY, Mother died February 4, 1872. Married November 28, 1866 Mary M. **Owen**, 3 children, 1 son died infant, Glen of Watkins and Cora wife of Charles N. **Blanchard** of Binghamton, NY. 2 brothers Joseph and Thomas and 1 sister Jane wife of Henry **Cowell**

Bennett John 18 hunting accident in Hector, NY March 3, 1898

Raymond Miss Therza 79y 10m in White's Hollow, NY March 14, 1898

Havens Hannah 83 widow of Charles in Watkins, NY March 15, 1898. Married over 50 years ago in Yates Co. Surviving children, Mrs. G. V. **Hazard**, Mrs. Susan J. **Walker** and Mrs. George W. **Mc Duffy** of Watkins, Mrs. Elizabeth **Smith** of Hornby, NY and twin brothers, Franklin and Francis of NY. Husband died 8 years ago

Tompson Allen age 68 unmarried in Watkins, NY March 13, 1898 at sister's Mrs. Eunice **Lattin**. Served Civil War 45th Pa. Inf.

Overton Thelma in Reading, NY March 10, 1898. Born July 4, 1897

Doane Morris age 30 in Monterey, NY March 8, 1898. Leaves wife and 4 children oldest 8y and youngest 15m.

Adamy Nancy 85 widow of Peter in Watkins, NY March 16, 1898

Rutherford Clarence in Grove Springs, NY March 13, 1898. Born June 19, 1847 in Bath, NY, 2 sisters living, Mrs. James **Bennett** and Mrs Viola **Robbins** and 1 stepbrother S. A. **Breck** all of Bath. Married August 7, 1867 Elizabeth **Corregan** of Bath. Children, Sarah wife of Edward **Griffin**, William A., Maud wife of Harry **Athaws**, John and Stella. Buried Mc Dowell cem.

Phelps Mrs. H. G. 82 in Montour Falls, NY March 22, 1898

Loop Buel 72 in Montour Falls, NY March 22, 1898

Diven Miss Eleanor in 91st year dau of Captain John and Eleaor Diven March 27, 1898. Came from Pa. about 1800. Brothers and sisters, Gen. A. S. of Elmira, NY, Charlotte who died 1894 and Mrs. Elizabeth **Washburn** who died 1872

Fitzgerald Nathan in Mecklenburgh, NY March 27, 1898. Born July 8, 1816 son of James and Elinor in Hopewell, NY. Married June 15, 1853 Susan **Rudy** who died several years ago. 3 children, 1 died 1864, E. E. of Mecklenburgh and Mrs. Ida M. **Horton** of Hector, NY

Baker Hiram 71 in Monterey, NY (date of Newspaper March 30, 1898). 3 children, David, Clarissa **Davenport** wife of Joseph of Watkins, NY and Charles

Overton Ezra brother of late Isaac of Reading, NY in Berlin, Wis. March 20, 1898, last of his generation

Wixon Randall at sister's Mrs. **Reniff** in Lockwood, NY, buried April 1, 1898. Born February 7, 1825 in Tyrone, NY youngest son of Solomon and Betsey who had 2 sons and 8 daus, 4 daus living. Married 1853 Cynthia **Giles** of Orange, NY, 5 children 2 sons living, Levi G. of Watkins, NY and F. E. of Canandaigua, NY. Dau died 8 years ago

Buck Edward 22 son of Charles in Reading Center, NY March 28, 1898. Married 2 years ago Miss **Culver** who died 1 year ago

Vail Samuel in 75th year at Watkins, NY March 28, 1898. Born Orange Co. 1 child Mrs. Sarah E. **Van Sickle**, 2 grand daus Mrs. H. C. **Jeffers** of Rochester, NY and Harriet of Reading, NY. 5 brothers Lewis of Buffalo, NY, Charles of Utica, NY, Dr. M. H. C. of Vailsburg, NJ, John M., and George of Montour, NY. Buried Middletown, NY

Murray Thomas E. 56 in Tyrone, NY April 2, 1898. Born October 31, 1842 in Starkey, NY. Married October 6, 1866 Beulah A **Potter** of Pine Grove, NY. 1 brother William H. of Monterey, NY

Culinane Dr. John A. 32 son of Michael of Reading, NY in Buffalo, NY March 31, 1898. Born Watkins, NY. 1 brother Dr. Charles of Buffalo, NY. Buried St. Mary's cem. in Watkins

Wasson Mrs. David in Tyrone, NY funeral April 3, 1898. Born 1814 in Co. Tyrone, Ireland dau of Andrew **Ellison**. Married 1854. Leaves husband and 1 dau Mrs. Andrew **Love** of Dix, NY. 3 brothers John and Andrew of Reading, NY and Thomas of Hornby, NY, sister Mrs. Ann **Faucett**. 2 brothers Samuel and James deceased

Wilson Lida A. 24 in Watkins, NY April 12, 1898 buried Pine Valley, NY

DEATH NOTICES

Barber Louisa 90 at son-in-law's Wesley **Ammock** in Perry City, NY recently (date of newspaper April 13, 1898)

Wortman Cora 1y dau of William P. in Reading, NY April 6, 1898

Barrett Osman in Reading, NY April 14, 1898. Born March 26, 1835 in Wayne, NY son of Marcus and Harilah (**Cole**) Barrett. 2 brothers Warren of Pleasant Valley, NY and Newman of Hector, NY, 3 sisters Mrs. Frank **Longwell** of Bradford, NY, Mrs. Frank **Mead** of Reading and Mrs. Emily F. **Cole** of Bath, NY. Married January 29, 1863 Susan Mc **Intyre**, 4 children Wellington R., Mrs. Hiel D. **Cary**, twin sister died infant and Mrs. Fred R. **Smith**

De Voy Mrs. Ann Lee 72 widow of John at dau Mrs. May **Mehan** in Tyrone, NY April 14, 1898. Born May 1, 1826 in Co. Wicklow, Ireland 1 of 11 children all deceased. Married May 15, 1858. Husband died 11 years ago

Brown Adeline R. formerly of Burdett, NY at son-in-law's C. F. **Reynolds** in Elmira, NY April 10, 1898. Born January 14, 1821 in Richmond, Va. and married 1837 O. D. Brown of NY. 7 children, 2 died infancy, George O. Md. of Baltimore, Md., J. P. H., Mrs. C. F. **Reynolds**, Mrs. J. Reeve **Martin** and Mrs. Orson **Brown** of Elmira, NY. Buried Burdett

Havens Clara B. 27 in Townsend, NY April 16, 1898. Leaves parents and 1 sister Mrs. George **Pangborn**

Jayne Mrs. Timothy in Hector, NY April 22, 1898. Buried Dundee, NY

Pinch William H. in Watkins, NY April 28, 1898. Born 1837 in Geneva, NY. Served in Civil War 126th NY Inf. Leaves wife and 1 dau Mrs. Grace **Brown** of Watkins. 3 sisters Miss Frank of Geneva, NY, Mrs. Spencer **Tompkins** of Buffalo, NY and Mrs. Albert **Kellogg** of Rochester, NY, half brother William G. **Wade** of Elmira, NY

Gaines Mrs. Catherine Dove colored 48 in Watkins, NY April 30, 1898. Born Cayuta, NY dau of late Peter **Lewis** of Alpine, NY. 4 children Mrs. Cora **Parsley** of Dix, NY, William, Charles and Clara **Dove** of Watkins

Mathews Betsey widow of Jeremiah in Logan, NY April 25, 1898. Leaves 2 daus Mrs. Aletta **Dewey** of Hector, NY and Mrs. Libbie **Erway**

Demunn Henry L. 46 in Watkins, NY May 6, 1898. Born Reading, NY and married Emily **Hoare** dau of Richard. Leaves widow, 1 brother Frank of Pa. and sister Mrs. **Mitchell** of Tyrone, NY

Feagles Mrs. Elizabeth 74 in Watkins, NY May 5, 1898. Buried Benton Center, NY

Woolever Carrie in Orange, NY June 1, 1898. Born December 25, 1873 dau of Samuel. Leaves parents and sister Mrs. Dennie **Palmer**

Miller George W. 53 formerly of Dix, NY in Corning, NY June 8, 1898. son of late Mathias of Dix. Leaves wife, 2 dau and 1 son

Wakely Mrs. George in Townsend, NY June 5, 1898, dau of Squire **Lybolt** and sister of Nelson. Leaves husband and 3 children James, George and Anna

Miller Ambrose of Hector, NY in Watkins, NY June 13, 1898. Leaves widow and children by 1st marriage, Amos of Montour Falls, NY, Mrs. Delila **Garrison** of Watkins, Mrs. Fannie **West** and Mathias of Dix, NY, Mrs. Jennie **Charles** of Odessa, NY and David of Hornby, NY, also 7 children by 2nd marriage (not named)

Little David at Willard Asylum June 9, 1898. Buried Watkins, NY

Van Liew Willie at Lodi Center, NY June 9, 1898. Buried N. Hector, NY

Cole Samuel in Reading, NY June 15, 1898. Born August 3, 1817 near NJ line. Married 1841 Sarah E. **Fenno**. Leaves wife, 2 sons J. M. of Reading and Charles of Watkins, NY

Mc Clure Miss Lucy in Altay, NY June 29, 1898. Born January 2, 1822 in Onieda Co. Leaves Mother and 2 brothers Warren of Cinncinati, Ohio and David G. of Cameron, NY

Maloney Thomas Francis 3y 26d son of Daniel in Watkins, NY July 26, 1898

Phelps Fred 30 by lightning in Gang Mills, NY July 19, 1898

Lott Samuel in Reading, NY August 9, 1898. Born April 11, 1813 in NJ. Came to Seneca Co. age 12. Married June 8, 1836 Elizabeth **Sutton** who was 3m younger and died December 16, 1890. 6 children Elizabeth died infant, Mrs. Kate **Sanford**, Mrs. J. T. **Finlan**, Henry and John of Reading, Mrs. W. N. **Hurley** of Watkins, NY

Hunter Dr. Abram L. 37 in Watkins, NY August 15, 1898. Born Peach Orchard, NY and married 13 years ago Minnie E. **Johnson** of Hector, NY. No children

Wright Robert in Chicago Ill. August 11, 1898, funeral at sister's Mrs. S. B. **Sackett**. Buried Union cem.

Lambert Benjamin funeral at Burdett, NY August 11, 1898

Wait Daniel in Watkins, NY September 9, 1898

Robbins Sarah Chapman age 85 widow of Archibald in Watkins, NY September 7, 1898. Born Saratoga Co. Leaves 7 children E. C. and Clarence of Watkins, Benjamin and Frank of Corning, NY, Mrs. W. L. **Norton** of Watkins, Mrs. Hiram **Seymour** of Canton, Ohio, Mrs. Lyman **Robinson** of Newark, NJ

Stewart Alexander in 80th year at Dix, NY September 10, 1898. Born Co. Tyrone, Ireland and immigrated age 15. Married almost 50 years, 14 children 7 sons and 7

daus, 1 dau died. Living, John J. of Reading, NY, Andrew and William of Dix, Thomas and David of Orange, NY, Robert in Binghamton, NY, Mrs. Charles **Sharp** of Campbell, NY, Mrs. Wallace **Wasson** of Dix, Mrs. Adelbert **Spaulding**, Mrs. Fitz **Knowles** in Binghamton, NY and Lizzie at home

Le Munyon William 70 in Wayne, NY October 8, 1898. Leaves widow and 2 daus Jennie and Icy. Buried Monterey, NY

Colegrove Mary 6y dau of Walter and Florence in Watkins, NY October 11, 1898

Wakeman John M. in Watkins, NY November 14, 1898. Born February 17, 1830 in Seneca Co. Married January 12, 1870 Anna S. **Goldsmith**. Leaves wife and 3 brothers Hiram of Mi., Almon S. of Smith Valley, NY, Thomas of Ill., 2 sisters and 2 brothers dec.

Smith Cynthia 66 widow of David H. of Watkins, NY at dau Mrs. Carl **Griswold** in Rochester, NY November 10, 1898. Husband died February 15, 1898, 2 other children living, Mrs. **Munson** of Medina and William W. of Watkins. Dau of late George W. **Phillips**

Powers Richard 37 in Rock Stream, NY November 13, 1898

Couch Joel M. age 79 in Catherine November 9, 1898

Townsend Abigail G. 71 wife of Horace in N. Hector, NY November 11, 1898. 3 sons Mortimer and George of NY and James of Hector

White Lazette 85 widow of Melancton in Watkins, NY November 20, 1898. Leaves 3 sons Myron and Ira of Dix, NY, Thomas of Washington state, and 1 dau Mrs. De Clerck **Smith** of Reading, NY, brother Milton **Raymond** of Reading and 2 sisters Mrs. James **Shelton** of Reading and Mrs. Ann **Duncan** out west

Carr Rev. Charles C. in Horseheads, NY November 18, 1898. Born March 22, 1812 in Romulus, NY. Married (1) 1841 Elinor **Folwell** of Romulus who died 1863. Married (2) Miss **Ely** dau of Augustus of Hector, NY

Silsbee Amanda Carr 78 wife of A. T. in Watkins, NY November 17, 1898 at sister's Mrs. A. C. **Kingsbury**

Huey Mrs. Lucinda 72 in Monterey, NY November 18, 1898

Van Vechten Emeline in 71st year formerly of Watkins, NY in Flint, Mi. November 27, 1898. Husband J. J. died 5 years ago. 2 sisters Mrs. Burr **Mitchell** and Mrs. William V. **Smith** of Watkins. Buried Mitchell cem.

Gray Alonzo W. 75 in Watkins, NY December 9, 1898

Swartwood Benjamin L. 44 of Cayuta, NY in Lodi, NY December 12, 1898. Leaves wife and dau Ann, father Charles R., brothers Charles B. and Lev W.

Sebring Nelson 83 funeral in Tyrone, NY December 11, 1898

Dickerman Eveline 70 wife of Jesse in Monterey, NY December 10, 1898

Coon Phebe 77 wife of Eli in Monterey, NY December 5, 1898. Children, Silas W. of Monterey, Gilbert of Kansas, Frank of Corning, NY, Mrs. Arvilla **Sample** of Orange, NY, Mrs. Maria **Chamberlain** of Monterey, NY and Mrs. Sarah **Rockwell** of Beaver Dams, NY

Smith Abram 70y 2m 10d in Reading, NY December 20, 1898. 2 brothers Clayton and Charles deceased, 3 sisters living

Kennedy Elizabeth 22 dau of James in Watkins, NY December 19, 1898

Dennis Francelia 55 in Watkins, NY December 21, 1898. Leaves husband and 2 sons Charles E. and Fred W.

Wilkes James D. 61 in Watkins, NY December 27, 1898

Paulding Thomas Paine in 93rd year at Tyrone, NY December 15, 1898. Born 1806 in Auburn, NY. Married (1) February 5, 1838 Emily **Chandler** who died September 17, 1840. Married (2) October 9, 1843 Emeline Powers **Havens** dec. 3 children

Clauharty Mrs. O. M. of Montour Falls, NY in NY City March 12, 1899

Putnam Eliza J. in Beaver Dams, NY March 10, 1899

Miller Martha Eddy 44y 7m 12d wife of Mattie in Dix, NY February 13, 1899. Born June 30, 1854 and married 1879. 2 children May and Frank

De Land A. I. 30 dau of John **Ferguson** of Catherine, NY in Odessa, NY March 13, 1899

Cooper Peter 86 at son-in-law's Burritt **Pearce** in Catherine, NY March 10, 1899

Hungerford Charles S. 61 in Monterey, NY March 23, 1899. Leaves wife and son John of Monterey and 1 dau Mrs. Fred **Coats** of Bennettsburg, NY

Sutfin Marion 53 in Breesport, NY March 27, 1899. 1 brother Byron of Weston, NY, 2 sisters Mrs. Charles **Ide** and Mrs. Benjamin **Hedges** of Bradford, NY

Gilbert David 91 in Reading, NY March 29, 1899

Sullivan Robert at Key West April 2, 1899. Wife former Rachel **Sproul** of Tyrone, NY

Kelly Mary nee **Fort** in 93rd year at Orange, NY April 14, 1899

Thompson Mrs. N. M. in Burdett, NY April 13, 1899

DEATH NOTICES

Woodford Betsey in 96th year widow of Alson in Bennettsburg, NY buried April 17, 1899

Ely Philo 81 in Hector, NY April 13, 1899. Born Hector on farm where he died. Married Esther **Osborn** of Hector

Fanton Hull 66 in Rochester State Hospital May 15, 1899. Born 1833 in Montour, NY son of Thomas L. Fanton who came from Conn. Served Civil War 107th Reg. NY Vol. Leaves wife and 1 dau

Meeks Ivah dau of Chauncey in Montour Falls, NY May 15, 1899

Burling Rebecca 82 in Watkins, NY May 9, 1899. Husband Robert died 1 year ago. 4 daus Mrs. Owen **Wilbur**, Mrs. Byron **Fountain**, Mrs. Birdsall **Carpenter** and Joanna

Mathews Mrs. Ezekiel 74 in Logan, NY May 9, 1899. Leaves husband 1 son Elmer and 3 daus Marion at home, Mrs. S. J. **Seybolt** of Logan and Mrs. Courtwright **Mathews** of Burdett, NY

Hoagland Mrs. Richard in Mecklenburgh, NY May 12, 1899

Rogers Mrs. John funeral near Burdett, NY May 15, 1899

Evans Solomon B. 67 in Mecklenburgh, NY May 21, 1899

Strait Marvin V. in Auburn Prison May 18, 1899. Buried Beaver Dams, NY

Knapp Mrs. in Wedgewood, NY May 19, 1899, buried Montour Falls, NY

Castner Isaac in Altay, NY May 20, 1899, buried Tyrone, NY

Beardsley Almira in 74th year widow of James in Watkins, NY June 2, 1899, husband and dau were killed in train wreck at Battle Creek, Mi. during World's Fair. 1 son Stephen and dau Mrs. Charles **Brown** of Odessa, NY

Worden William 59 in Orange, NY June 13, 1899. Leaves wife and 5 children Adelbert, James, William, Calista and Marietta

Andrews Alfred 69 in Townsend, NY June 13, 1899. Leaves wife and 2 sons Charles of Townsend and John of Monterey, NY

Mc Quillen Sarah 77 funeral in Burdett, NY June 12, 1899

Newton James 77 in Montour Falls, NY June 7, 1899

Stevens Don 13 son of George formerly of Beaver Dams, NY in Elmira Heights, NY June 7, 1899. Buried Beaver Dams

Proper Charles in N. Hector, NY June 19, 1899. Leaves wife and son Ellsworth age 8

Miller Johnson A. 77 in Watkins, NY June 14, 1899

Winslow Garrett F. 1y 10m 6d in Watkins, NY June 15, 1899

Warden William H. 77 in Monterey, NY June 17, 1899. Married (1) Lucinda **Underwood** of Hornby, NY who died January 1864. 7 children 5 living Levi, Orson, Helen, Edwin and Samuel. Married (2) Frances **Davison**, who survives

Tuttle Daniel S. in 31st year of Watkins, NY eldest son of Adrian in Reading, NY August 11, 1899. Married 4 years to Wilhemina **Newman** dau of late William. Leaves wife, parents, 1 brother Adrian Jr. and sister Adeline

Woodward Mrs. John in Sugar Hill, NY August 15, 1899

Drake John Hobert in Watkins, NY September 12, 1899. Born 1848 son of James A. Wife sister of A. F. **Chapman**. Leaves 1 son

Berry Mrs. Charles 48 in Watkins, NY September 8, 1899

Brooks Walter infant son of James in N. Hector, NY September 9, 1899

Hanny James in Watkins, NY September 26, 1899. Born 1825 in Ireland

Van Duzer Nancy Hughey widow of Milton in Watkins, NY September 16, 1899. Born May 3, 1809 in Ireland and married 1831. Leaves 3 children, 1 died young, James M. and Mrs. David **Waugh** of Manchester, Iowa. Husband died 1845

Ellison John Sr. in 88th year at Reading, NY September 19, 1899. Born May 9, 1812 in Ireland, immigrated age 11. 5 brothers, 2 sisters only 2 living, Andrew of Reading and Thomas of Hornby, NY. Leaves wife, 3 sons John Jr., Seymour and James of Reading and dau Alice wife of James F. **Wasson** of Dix, NY

Baskins Mrs. William S. 49 nee **Minnehan** of Tyrone, NY in Elmira, NY September 22, 1899. Leaves husband, 2 sons Edward and Thomas and dau Katherine, 4 sisters Mrs. O. P. **Shotts**, Minnie, Margaret and Ella of Corning, NY, brother John of Waterloo, NY

Drummond Waverly 19 in Altay, NY September 21, 1899

Smith Earl V. in Mecklenburgh, NY September 25, 1899

Leonard Sally A. 69 in Pine Valley, NY October 14, 1899. 2 sons Luther of Watkins, NY and Henry of Pine Valley

Willover Harvey F. in 60th year suicide in Savona, NY October 17, 1899, formerly of Weston, NY. Veteran of Civil War 189th NY Vol. Wife committed suicide 1 or

2 years ago

Howell Fayette 40 in Hector, NY October 13,1899

Longwell William S. formerly of Mechlinburgh, NY in Watkins, NY October 19, 1899. Leaves wife and 3 children

Noon Jennie 60 wife of Michael in Watkins, NY October 20, 1899

Cole Charles M. in Beaver Dams, NY October 20, 1899. Leaves Mother Adeline, 3 sisters Mrs. William **Harwood**, Mrs. Walter F. **Wasson** of Beaver Dams and Grace of Elmira, NY

Mallory William A. 21 son of A. Judson in Peach Orchard, NY October 22, 1899

Ellison Rachel 85 relict of John in Reading, NY September 19, 1899. Leaves 3 sons John Jr., Seymour and James of Reading and dau Alice M. wife of James F. **Wasson** of Dix, NY

Owens Benjamin in Dundee, NY October 28, 1899. Born 1822 in Putnam Co. son of Isreal 1 of 9 children, 5 living Mrs. Phoebe **Doty** in 89th year of Montour Falls, NY, Henry age 84 of Watkins, NY, Mrs. James **Vance** age 79 of Thurston, NY, Hester **Gustin** of Wisconsin and Sylvester of Arizona. Thomas died 1890 in Wedgewood, NY, William of Orange Co. died about 7 years ago and Mary several years. Married Samantha **Rumsey** dau of Elnathan who came from Delaware Co. Leaves wife and 4 children Mrs. George **Reilly** of Corning, NY, Mrs. J. G. **Hatfield** of Dundee, Mrs. W. W. **Owens** of Painted Post, NY, T. R. of Wedgewood. Dau Mrs. Edward **Huey** dec.

Baker Moses in Burdett, NY November 19, 1899

Stewart Mary J. 22 wife of William and dau of James **Jack** of Townsend, NY in Dix, NY January 10, 1900. Leaves son age 10m.

Dudgeon Rebecca in Odessa, NY Decemer 31, 1899 formerly of Watkins, NY. Leaves 4 children William of Odessa, Robert of Logan, NY, Andrew of Antrim, Pa. and Mrs. Daniel **Hall** of Burdett, NY. Husband died 5 years ago

Corbett George A. in 38th year at Reading, NY January 21, 1900. Born July 10, 1862 son of Otis R. and Adelia B. Brothers and sisters, John, Mary T., Sophia C., William and J. J. of Topeka, Kansas

Shears Mrs. in Catherine, NY January 18, 1900

Moran Joanna 32 wife of William J. and dau of John **Foley** in Watkins, NY January 28, 1900. Leaves 2 daus age 4 and 2

Stout Henrietta 34 wife of Frank in Watkins, NY January 24, 1900

Miller William B. 67y 6m in Watkins, NY January 24, 1900, son of Horace formerly of Mecklenburgh, NY. Leaves wife and dau Minnie M.

Houck William 22 son of Seymour drowned Lake Waneta January 24, 1900

Thompson Thomas 86 in Watkins, NY February 6, 1900

Wait Mrs. Daniel 70 in Dix, NY February 5, 1900. 5 children Montgomery, Mrs. John **Rarrick**, Mrs. John **Lloyd** of Watkins, NY, Charles of Linden, Pa. and William of Brooklyn, NY

Henderson James 86 in Pine Grove, NY February 2, 1900

Rogers John in Hector, NY February 3, 1900. Leaves 3 children Mrs. Zubea **Whalen**, Mrs. Chauncey **White** of Hector and Newell of Perry City, NY

Predmore George in N. Hector, NY February 3, 1900

Hoare James in 90th year in Watkins, NY February 8, 1900. Born January 1810 in England, immigrated 1858. 6 children Richard, John, Mitchell, Mrs. George G. **Freer**, Mrs. George H. **Ellis** and Mrs. George G. **Hill**

Cass Mrs. Frances Foot 54 in Watkins, NY February 12,1900. Was wife of Samuel who lives out west. Son Ira F. of NY and dau Lena of Watkins

Hall Rebecca 59 in Watkins, NY February 13, 1900. Sister Mrs. Emma **Shultz** and brother Uriah Hall of Millport, NY

Farrington Mrs. Isaac funeral in Mecklenburgh, NY February 11, 1900

Wixon Charles in Mecklenburgh, NY February 11, 1900

Corbett Charles M. of Reading, NY April 24, 1900. Born September 28, 1836 son of Chester and Sally. Brothers and sisters Otis R. and J. W. of Reading and Mrs. J. W. **Warner** of Watkins, NY. Married Mary A. **Brizzee** who died August 21, 1884. Leaves dau Ella M. wife of G. W. **Averill** of Rochester, NY. Son Edward E. died July 21, 1891 in 27th year

Rolfe Emory B. 68 in Hornby, NY April 28, 1900. Leaves wife and 3 children, names Mrs. Cora B. **Mead** of Burdett, NY

Mosher Charlotte S. widow of George D. in Watkins, NY May 1, 1900. Born August 17, 1840 in Suffolk Co. dau of David and Lydia **Stull**. Leaves 4 children Grant and Jennie of Watkins, Edna wife of Harry M. **Smith** of Reading, NY and Frank of Penn Yan, NY, step dau Mrs. B. W. **Norris** Jr. of Reading, NY

Knight Eleanor Tucker 98 in Tyrone, NY April 12, 1900. Born January 10, 1802. Husband Henry died 28 years ago. 4 sons Dr. Cyrus B. of Alma, Mi., Daniel, Thomas and James of Oregon

DEATH NOTICES 177

Rossiter John in Perry City, NY April 15, 1900. 2 daus Maggie of Perry City and Lizzie of Iowa

Paulding Hope 2y 10m dau of William in Altay, NY May 24, 1900

Seymour Maud 23 in Reynoldsville, NY and baby 1w at grandmother's Mrs. **Crippen**. (date of newspaper June 6, 1900)

Chesley Jehial of Bennettsburg, NY in Quebec June 5, 1900. Born 1861 near Geneva, NY

Kennedy Susan 62 in Watkins, NY July 27, 1900. Born Watkins dau of Isaac and Polly. Buried Union cem. in Hector, NY

Holden Christianna widow of Fox in Watkins, NY August 1, 1900. Born Merridian, Conn. dau of Hiram **Twiss**. Married (1) Fred **Robbins**, 3 children Mrs. F. T. **Bowles** of Elmira, NY, Mrs. D. W. **Mead** of Watkins and Charles of Aldrich, Ala.

Robinson Leslie 10m son of Henry G. in Watkins, NY July 20, 1900

Savacool George fell from barn roof in Cayuta, NY July 27, 1900

Keep Charles M. 52 in Bennettsburg, NY July 29, 1900

Andrews Homer E. 28 son of Joel E. of Watkins, NY in Dundee, NY August 4, 1900 at sister's Mrs. Ed L. **Evans**, also leaves father, step-mother, 2 brothers Edgar L. of Candor, NY and J. S. of Philadelphia, Pa.

Mc Kenzie Charles 37 of Lodi, NY in Watkins, NY August 4, 1900

Morris Isaac E. 5m in Burdett, NY August 6, 1900

Stanton Wilbur S. 60 of Washington D. C. August 30, 1900. Parents in Watkins, NY, wife is sister of J. H. **Drake** of Watkins. Leaves wife and dau Mrs. Charles W. **Rippey** of Washington D. C.

Kellogg Silas C. in Steamburg, NY August 31, 1900. Born 1814 in Otsego Co.

Lewis Mary C. 94 in Watkins, NY September 24, 1900. 4 children John of Corning, NY, Martin of Pa., Mary and Caroline of Watkins

Claughharty Col. Charles W. 73 unmarried in Montour Falls, NY September 25, 1900. Born Catherine, NY eldest son of Alexander. In Civil War Co. A 141st Reg. NY Vol. Brother Alexander of Adrian, Mi. and widowed sister Mrs. Sarah **Goulding** of Montour Falls

Alwood Ed over 90 in Reynoldsville, NY September 27, 1900

Smith Olin of Bennettsburg, NY in Mi. last week (date of newspaper November 7,

1900)

Green Mrs. Sarah S. 48 at Mother's Mrs. Mary **Bishop** in Watkins, NY October 31, 1900. Leaves son William in Watkins

Bump Franklin in 80th year at Catlin, NY November 9, 1900, also Edith Bump age 13 November 10, 1900 at Hector, NY. Buried Moreland cem.

Sanford Maria 88 in Watkins, NY November 8, 1900 at dau Mrs. Lucy S. **Crippen**. Buried Montour cem.

Denson Pearl H. 13y 6m at Mother's Mrs. Jacob **Williams** in Burdett, NY November 9, 1900. Born Yates Co., came to Burdett with Mother who was then Mrs. Halwick Denson

La Rue Sarah Finton wife of George at Foot's Hill, NY November 5, 1900. Born Burdett, NY dau of C. C. **Finton**. Twin sister Mrs. Charles **La Rue**, brother Howard and younger sister. Older sister Delia dec.

Cowell Mary wife of Fred at Crosby, NY November 19, 1900, only dau of late Delos **Williamson** of Mead's Crossing, NY

Mc Kiggen John in Mecklenburgh, NY November 15, 1900

Bennett Lucinda A. 50 widow of Thomas in Watkins, NY November 18, 1900

Rosebrook Mrs. William dau of Ephriam **Brock** of Spencer, NY. in Cayuta, NY December 1, 1900. Leaves husband and child age 8m

Linderman John at Irish Hill, NY December 7, 1900

Kendall Jerry at son's Ira in Townsend, NY December 18, 1900. Buried Millport, NY

Kelly Ida May 32 wife of Fred and dau of Charles **Rarrick** in Catlin, NY December 15, 1900. Buried Crisjohn cem. in Monterey, NY

Farrington Elizabeth 72 in Searsburg, NY December 9, 1900

SURNAME INDEX

Abbey 21, 36, 37
Abbott 1, 60
Abby 109
Aber 18, 85, 108, 148
Abrams 116, 153
Ackley 33, 48
Adams 3, 13
Adamy 3, 105, 167
Adem 83
Adriance 41, 76, 108, 142
Agard 101, 138, 165
Agins 17
Ahart 115
Albertson 7
Alden 96
Aldrich 32, 111, 162
Alexander 12, 83
Allbright 10, 147
Allen 5, 39, 47, 48, 53, 63, 78, 86, 95, 101, 103, 121, 124, 127, 139
Allwood 62
Alwood 177
Ameigh 10, 26
Ames 52, 133
Ammock 169
Amsden 14
Anable 6
Andrews 13, 20, 21, 23, 50, 107, 128, 131, 133, 137, 140, 142, 173, 177
Andrus 4
Angel 32
Angle 34, 163
Anthony 125
Archer 24, 64, 144
Armstrong 23, 28, 120
Arnold 17, 30, 76, 135
Arnot 81, 136
Aruwine 124
Ash 29
Ashley 60
Athaws 167
Atkinson 98
Atwater 6, 146
Auble 64-66
Ault 45
Austin 15, 29, 67
Averill 153, 176
Ayers 69, 85, 94
Aylworth 3
Ayres 90, 110, 136, 138, 154
Babbit 105
Babcock 1, 80, 162
Backer 14, 37
Backman 72
Badgely 13, 123
Badgley 105
Bailey 8, 12, 18, 35, 38, 41, 53, 56, 59, 72, 85, 90-92, 99, 137, 141
Baily 9
Bainbridge 35
Baird 165
Baker 14, 15, 36, 39, 48, 64, 90, 97, 101, 114, 120, 140, 147, 162, 163, 168, 175
Baldwin 8, 12, 19, 25, 49, 62, 68, 76, 85, 91, 92, 93, 98, 106, 116, 121, 158

Ball 58
Ballard 131
Ballou 150
Bandfield 32
Bange 119, 126
Bank 27
Banker 12, 27, 51, 97
Barber 12, 27, 44, 99, 169
Barclay 3
Barker 137
Barkman 100, 108
Barnes 13, 28, 37, 40, 48, 72, 101, 103, 110, 143
Barnum 124
Barrett 60, 61, 66, 110, 139, 169
Barrows 26, 72, 113, 131, 138
Barry 14
Bartholomew 125, 159
Bartlett 57, 99
Barto 45, 81, 95
Bartou 9, 123
Baskin 39, 40, 58, 99, 139
Baskins 174
Bassett 45, 86, 90, 109, 117, 132, 142, 159
Bates 3, 8, 31, 42, 43
Bateson 150
Batey 21
Batterson 21
Batty 42, 100
Baxter 3, 70, 71
Beach 41, 80, 87, 91, 102, 104
Beahan 136
Beam 143
Beard 7
Beardslee 35
Beardsley 2, 3, 7, 8, 14, 27, 44, 57, 61, 65, 74, 95, 117, 125, 140, 145, 157, 173
Beattie 126
Beck 46
Becker 84
Beckwith 24, 52, 84, 150, 159, 167
Beckworth 13
Bedient 34
Bedner 46
Beebe 61, 69, 72, 73, 164
Beecher 49, 83, 104, 149
Beers 44, 86, 101, 150, 155
Beery 50
Bell 18, 55, 120, 125, 131
Bement 6, 10, 18, 43, 53, 85
Benham 9, 10, 116, 130, 137, 141
Benjamin 3, 65, 138, 162
Bennett 4, 8, 17, 19, 24, 25, 45, 59, 72, 78, 83, 90, 95, 103, 106, 108, 109, 124, 137, 167, 178
Benson 7, 40, 42, 61, 133
Berring 35
Berry 17, 22, 33, 61, 66, 77, 80, 117, 145, 148, 152, 154, 174
Berthoff 65
Best 115
Betteridge 16, 122
Beyea 21, 132
Bigelow 24, 37, 96
Bigger 4
Bird 17, 59

Birdsall 91
Birge 111
Bishop 18, 20, 59, 178
Black 49
Blackwood 20
Blaine 55, 109
Blaisdall 127
Blanchard 43, 167
Blauvelt 44
Bliss 46, 75
Blodgett 24
Bloomer 98, 126, 150
Bloor 106
Blount 10
Blunt 162
Boardman 28, 80
Bodle 18, 40, 51, 76, 88, 114, 129, 143
Bogart 94, 134
Bogert 98
Bolhmer 108
Bolt 17, 105, 120, 157
Bomberage 61, 163
Bond 10, 17, 165
Bong 158
Booram 45, 46, 48, 126
Booth 87, 151
Boothroyd 9
Bossard 41, 162
Bost 25
Bostwick 157
Bovier 159
Bower 127, 146
Bowers 16, 43, 44, 51, 65
Bowlby 2, 7, 132
Bowles 177
Boyce 98, 130
Boyer 84
Boynton 148
Bozzard 20
Bradley 4, 43, 144, 166
Bradner 41, 58, 146
Brady 55, 59
Brainard 9
Bramble 50, 55, 62, 85, 152
Branson 53
Breck 167
Breese 115
Bremer 21
Brewer 34, 70
Brien 78, 110
Briggs 16, 34, 99
Brigham 26
Brightman 47
Brimmer 35
Brink 84
Briscoe 35
Bristol 86
Brizzee 153, 176
Broakman 116
Broas 30, 154
Brock 178
Broderick 11, 31
Brodrick 33, 39, 73
Brokaw 29, 37, 88, 89, 124
Brong 43
Bronson 5, 8, 35, 93, 107, 160, 162
Brooks 24, 53, 57, 60, 91, 104, 148, 163, 174

SURNAME INDEX

Brother 141
Brouwere 162
Brown 1, 9, 14, 16, 28, 31, 35, 38, 41, 47, 58, 59, 63, 65, 74, 77, 81, 83, 85, 91, 94, 96, 100, 109, 133, 137, 141, 142, 155, 162, 169, 173
Brunson 79
Brush 24, 27, 40, 57
Bryant 5, 6, 73, 85, 115
Buchanan 13
Buck 19, 20, 23, 47, 75, 124, 147, 162, 168
Buckley 94
Budd 50, 58, 63, 108, 158
Buggis 16
Bull 126, 138
Bump 59, 160, 178
Bunn 12, 139
Burch 90, 151
Burchfield 42, 52
Burd 25, 145
Burge 79, 145
Burgess 96, 112, 123, 127, 161
Burke 28, 107
Burlew 44, 90
Burling 173
Burnet 49
Burr 100, 141, 164, 165
Burrell 27
Burris 97
Burritt 21, 98, 102, 113, 132
Burt 47, 98
Bush 8, 11, 44, 64
Bushnell 133
Bussey 71
Butler 38, 51, 82
Butters 63
Button 160
Byram 118, 152
Byron 18
Cady 10, 138
Cahill 55
Cain 5
Caldwell 19, 48, 125, 152
Calkins 79, 81
Call 101, 122
Calvert 148, 150, 153
Campbell 2, 6, 11, 19, 38, 46, 55, 73, 80, 101, 106, 110, 119, 121, 125, 131, 155, 159
Canfield 3, 37, 54, 64
Cantine 34
Capell 116
Carbear 29
Card 79, 137
Carley 62, 160
Carlisle 41
Carlson 65
Carly 86
Carman 59, 112, 143, 145, 157
Carmer 9
Carmichael 44, 77
Carpenter 5, 19, 20, 32, 49, 50, 53, 114, 125, 126, 128, 144, 159, 160, 164, 173
Carr 41, 43, 67, 131, 166, 171
Carrigan 53
Carroll 26, 28

Carson 41, 103
Cary 169
Casbeer 47
Case 14, 31, 78, 114, 119, 147, 153, 158, 159, 167
Casey 61, 163
Cass 38, 72, 126, 176
Cassidy 53
Castner 55, 65, 173
Catlin 2, 6, 13, 14, 24, 27, 55, 72, 80, 82, 119, 125, 134, 137, 156
Caton 90, 92
Caughlin 141
Caverly 165
Caywood 31, 40
Chamberlain 35, 74, 166, 172
Chambers 94, 101, 121
Chandler 27, 113, 158, 172
Chapin 72
Chapman 6, 12, 19, 23, 26, 36, 38, 44, 47, 54, 82, 84, 86, 96, 100, 111, 116, 117, 120, 122, 138, 141, 153, 158, 164, 174
Chappel 144
Charles 15, 27, 67, 142, 170
Chase 44, 67, 107, 131, 159, 164
Cheney 105
Chesley 177
Chester 16, 157
Christopher 87
Chrysler 29
Chubb 123
Chubbock 114
Churchill 42, 54
Clapp 87
Clapper 134
Clark 22, 36, 37, 42, 48, 49, 51, 55, 63, 70, 92, 93, 115, 121, 126, 136, 139
Clarke 116
Clarkson 92
Claughharty 177
Clauharty 9, 150, 172
Clawson 12, 18, 59, 70, 106, 107, 142, 152, 158, 163
Clayton 57
Cleveland 1, 86, 130
Clizbe 115
Clock 45, 157
Close 35, 50, 54
Clute 95
Coats 15, 39, 40, 54, 85, 172
Cobb 51
Coddington 138
Coe 6, 8, 35, 62
Coger 158
Cogswell 1, 57
Cole 1, 5, 31, 48, 49, 95, 124, 132, 146, 157, 163, 169, 170, 175
Colegrove 11, 171
Coleman 52, 57, 131, 154
Collins 8, 55, 67, 120, 150, 156, 157, 162
Collum 100
Comb 37
Compton 2, 14, 23, 116, 118, 129,

Comstock 12, 20, 38, 61, 89, 97, 103
Conderman 78
Congdon 23
Conklin 34, 88, 89, 94, 110, 117, 126, 132
Conkling 90
Conley 34
Conover 30, 83, 127
Conroy 53, 57
Considine 143
Converse 106
Cook 21, 24, 41, 61, 77, 93, 109, 121, 146, 157
Cookes 39
Coolbaugh 28, 88, 163
Cooley 98, 134, 158
Coon 4, 12, 22, 37, 49, 51, 88, 91, 96, 101, 108, 112, 134, 161, 162, 163, 172
Cooper 4, 5, 9, 36, 39, 100, 135, 143, 172
Corbett 38, 84, 122, 153, 167, 175, 176
Corbin 18
Corey 58
Cormack 4
Cornelius 123
Cornell 91, 136
Cornish 51
Cornwell 77
Corregan 167
Corwin 29, 54, 55, 74, 163
Coryell 14
Costes 1
Cotey 135
Cotton 157
Couch 5, 88, 102, 171
Coughlin 53, 56
Couse 10
Covell 98, 99
Covert 61, 81, 85, 140, 160
Coville 86
Cowell 167, 178
Cowen 39
Cowing 84, 100
Cox 120
Coy 36
Coykendall 46, 99, 123
Coyle 124, 128
Craft 35
Craig 88
Cramer 64
Crampton 155
Crandall 76, 93, 132, 136
Crane 8, 33
Cranmer 55, 132
Crans 26
Cratsley 59, 151
Craver 93, 116
Crawford 7, 20, 46, 52, 58, 70, 82, 108, 135
Creeth 44
Creighton 112
Cressman 120
Crevelling 50, 132
Crickmore 71
Crippen 83, 177, 178
Crisfield 25, 29

SURNAME INDEX

Cronk 4, 5, 15, 31, 62
Cronkite 67
Crookston 30
Crosby 137
Cross 42, 162, 165
Crouch 75, 103
Crout 9
Crowell 9
Crum 3, 36, 44, 125
Cuffman 3
Culinane 168
Cullen 56, 63
Culver 4, 5, 10, 90, 98, 109, 120, 128, 129, 168
Cunningham 129
Cure 157
Curran 165
Curry 14, 89, 128, 132, 142
Curtis 30, 71
Cushion 37
Daggett 58
Dailey 160
Dalrimple 29
Danihu 71
Dann 120
Darling 1, 11, 44, 54
Darren 60
Dart 12, 67
Darwin 152
Dates 109
Daugherty 31
Davenport 37, 54, 56, 67, 85, 93, 130, 168
David 38
Davidson 3, 41, 67
Davis 39, 57, 73, 77, 88, 108, 139, 149, 156
Davison 86, 174
Davy 161
Day 9, 21, 150
De Camp 59
De Land 172
De Long 19
De Mont 85
De Munn 123
De St. Croix 164
De Voy 169
De Witt 26, 104
Dean 17, 29, 37, 42, 98, 106, 107, 114, 134, 157
Deavenworth 9
Decker 1, 15, 38, 42, 57, 61, 65, 100, 123
Degraw 47
Delameter 11
Deming 34, 44, 51, 97, 114
Demming 162
Demorest 110
Demund 123
Demunn 169
Denning 78, 86
Dennis 20, 172
Densen 48
Denson 178
Denton 143
Dewey 52, 155, 169
Dewitt 43
Dexter 42
Deyo 118
Dibble 70

Dickens 34, 52, 64, 117
Dickenson 10, 15, 139
Dickerman 172
Dickerson 104, 144, 167
Dickeson 89
Dikeman 41
Dill 4
Dilliston 118, 150
Dimon 151
Dingman 24
Disbrow 94
Diven 40, 64, 77, 79, 155, 168
Dixon 113
Doane 57, 81, 102, 167
Dodd 22
Dodge 163
Dodson 7, 89, 91, 93
Dohs 25
Dolan 92, 138
Dolph 10
Donohue 97
Donovan 161, 164
Doolittle 16, 25, 56, 132
Dorsey 71
Doty 3, 54, 102, 107, 121, 175
Douglas 8
Dove 169
Dowling 164
Downer 81
Downes 59, 129, 133
Downing 86, 100, 116
Drake 18, 19, 21, 28, 44, 46, 47, 104, 109, 112, 121, 129, 132, 134, 139, 144, 147, 153, 163, 174, 177
Drum 139
Drummond 30, 174
Dubois 12
Dudgeon 175
Dumar 3
Dumond 131
Duncan 171
Dunham 32, 40, 43, 53, 58, 151
Dunlap 12
Dunn 6, 62, 73, 98
Dunning 154
Durfey 116
Durkee 5, 71, 141
Durland 44, 92, 112, 142
Duryea 42, 89, 144
Dusenberry 53
Dutcher 14
Dutton 64
Duvall 11, 41, 66
Dyer 80
Eaker 10
Earing 61
Earnest 165
Easterbrook 19
Ector 60
Eddy 32, 47, 75, 105, 140
Edgecomb 43
Edgerton 44, 160
Edgett 93
Edmister 57
Edsall 58
Edson 46
Edwards 22, 34, 42, 159
Egbert 97
Eggleston 63, 159

Eldred 42, 82
Eldrich 92
Eldridge 12
Eli 48, 62
Elias 25, 60, 123
Elliot 61, 114, 152, 161
Elliott 155
Ellis 10, 15, 18, 25, 30, 31, 43, 45, 57, 98, 105, 120, 128, 133, 147, 152, 159, 164, 165, 176
Ellison 32, 37, 39, 46, 48, 65, 82, 103, 108, 112, 147, 153, 168, 174, 175
Ellsworth 46, 60, 78, 79, 111, 128, 134
Elwell 29, 143
Elwood 37
Ely 27, 30, 41, 58, 84, 107, 112, 130, 142, 161, 166, 171, 173
English 5
Ennis 9, 32
Enos 93
Ensley 148
Ervay 24
Erway 2, 42, 53, 135, 162, 164, 169
Erwin 27
Esley 22
Estabrook 96
Estell 119
Estelle 81
Esterbrook 45
Euternarks 132
Evans 77, 98, 100, 149, 173, 177
Eveland 93
Evelette 103
Everts 14, 22, 44, 45, 57, 90, 99, 105, 107, 112, 117, 119, 148, 150-152, 165
Ewing 78
Fairchilds 55
Fanton 13, 70, 84, 173
Farrington 39, 88, 146, 176, 178
Faucett 56, 168
Fausett 22, 78
Favill 98
Faville 157
Feagles 85, 133, 169
Featherly 23, 52, 114
Feenaughty 92
Fenno 61, 64, 138, 155, 170
Fenton 78, 116, 165
Fenwick 22
Ferenbaugh 143
Ferguson 13, 172
Fero 14, 66, 82, 121, 158
Ferris 13, 17, 55, 82
Fields 135
Fillmore 111, 136
Finch 70
Finger 34, 162
Finlan 11, 170
Finton 178
Fish 10, 21, 116, 143
Fisher 140, 146
Fitzgerald 6, 15, 168
Fitzpatrick 14, 146, 151, 152
Fitzsimmons 60, 123
Flanagan 135

181

SURNAME INDEX

Fleet 108
Fleming 73, 102
Fletcher 5, 29, 111, 158
Fogarty 36
Foley 153, 175
Folsom 42
Folwell 171
Foot 62, 104
Foote 35
Forbes 51
Force 9, 139
Fordham 52, 65, 66, 155
Forrester 75, 152
Forshee 36, 86
Fort 172
Fosdick 113
Foster 19, 63, 67, 137, 150
Fountain 35, 173
Fox 3, 135, 158
Frank 4, 21, 83
Franklin 6, 112, 122, 131, 152
Fraser 72, 86
Freeman 35, 121
Freer 20, 91, 101, 103, 119, 123, 126, 151, 176
French 19, 29, 35
Frost 2, 13, 15, 16, 31, 38, 70, 76, 79, 82, 87, 100, 115, 127, 129
Fulford 20
Fulkerson 129
Fuller 20, 42, 43
Gabriel 17, 46, 93, 122, 131
Gage 80
Gaines 169
Gano 2, 4, 26, 30, 156
Ganung 52, 72, 116, 159, 167
Gardiner 29, 106, 127
Gardner 26, 40, 82, 124
Garrison 170
Gates 43, 51, 75, 83, 131
Gay 138
Gaylord 7, 52, 100, 108
Gee 25
Georgia 143
German 25, 34, 72, 117
Gerow 109
Gibbons 96
Gibbs 26, 33, 56, 71, 117
Gifford 76, 99
Gilbert 37, 45, 57, 66, 122, 126, 128, 129, 144, 147, 160, 172
Giles 38, 48, 139, 146, 168
Gillespie 26
Gillett 116, 166
Gillette 38
Gillis 14
Gilmore 58, 104
Gleason 2, 52, 68, 127
Goble 26
Godard 134
Goff 70
Gofny 162
Golden 39, 98, 129
Goldsmith 25, 48, 81, 91, 110, 114, 148, 171
Goltry 11, 44, 61, 134, 138, 165
Goodier 38
Goodrich 66, 71, 129, 164

Goodyear 16, 161
Gorton 17, 130
Gottrey 156
Gould 14, 42, 43, 57, 62, 128, 165
Goulding 177
Goundry 51, 123, 167
Grady 92, 99, 139
Graham 28, 82, 104, 123, 129, 131, 134
Granger 10, 64
Grant 33, 40, 43, 53, 54, 63, 64, 87, 114
Grassam 83
Gray 16, 32, 94, 95, 126, 129, 171
Greeman 125
Green 14, 18, 31, 33, 79, 100, 115, 131, 141, 178
Greenley 157
Greeno 74
Gregory 11, 49, 73, 125, 134, 137, 161
Griffin 12, 167
Griffith 4, 10, 29, 39, 79
Grimes 26, 41, 63
Griswold 39, 98, 106, 114, 130, 171
Grover 122
Groves 100
Guernsey 140
Guinnip 13, 91, 118
Gulick 43, 63, 88, 94, 117, 131
Gullick 12
Gunderman 19, 30
Gurnett 155
Gustin 175
Guthrie 115
Haas 134
Hackett 17, 87
Hadly 113
Hager 50, 56, 74, 75, 77, 80, 82, 89, 108, 112, 116, 124, 127, 136, 158, 166
Hagerman 88
Haggerty 94, 143
Haight 4, 24, 75, 81, 112
Hair 126
Hall 1, 2, 8, 16, 19, 20, 22, 26, 55, 56, 66, 87, 102, 161, 175, 176
Halleck 106
Hallett 34, 71, 156
Halliday 115
Hallock 82, 110
Halpin 54
Halsey 21, 30, 128, 132, 142
Hamblin 70
Hamill 36, 59
Hamilton 1, 4, 6, 23, 57, 61, 71, 125, 131, 141
Hammond 5, 78
Hanes 8
Hanmer 27, 37, 105, 109, 124, 137, 163
Hannon 22
Hanny 174
Hapeman 147
Hardenburg 40

Haring 63, 76, 87, 100, 120, 125, 140
Harmon 79, 90
Harpending 86, 87, 126
Harrington 8, 37, 43, 52, 97, 99, 150
Harris 16, 23, 24, 54, 62, 73, 94
Harrison 17, 166
Harsh 16
Harvey 18, 29, 34, 38, 54, 102, 128, 136, 154
Harwood 175
Hasen 58
Haskell 94
Hastings 72, 73, 102
Hatch 21
Hatfield 89, 115, 120, 136, 175
Hathaway 144, 154
Hatt 33
Hause 79, 101, 118, 122
Hausner 98
Havens 55, 79, 128, 143, 167, 169, 172
Haviland 10
Hawes 128, 156
Hawkins 7
Haxton 115, 116
Hayes 9, 15, 19
Hazard 60, 103, 128, 167
Hazelitt 30
Hazelton 90
Hazen 3
Hazleton 27
Hazlett 102
Hazlitt 157
Head 167
Headley 160
Heald 56, 57, 77
Heath 118
Hebermith 105
Hedges 172
Heggie 156
Heist 57, 79, 138
Hemans 155
Hemingway 116
Hendershot 30
Henderson 4, 9, 21, 25, 31, 63, 115, 129, 176
Hendrick 59
Hendricks 45, 67, 89, 99
Hendrickson 101, 160
Hennessey 147, 165
Henry 5, 13, 55, 62, 78
Henyon 2, 53
Hern 154
Herrick 6, 136
Hetherington 33
Hevener 128
Hewett 77
Hewitt 125
Hibbard 23, 69, 71, 143, 165
Hibler 150
Hicks 28, 37, 47, 79, 118, 141, 149, 153
Higgins 2, 17, 121
Hildreth 110
Hill 8, 15, 32, 107, 116, 117, 119, 123, 146, 176
Hillard 78

SURNAME INDEX

Himrod 84, 152
Hinckley 30
Hinman 82, 126, 133, 137
Hitchcock 74, 166
Hoag 24, 89
Hoagland 153, 173
Hoare 80, 87, 96, 122, 169, 176
Hobbee 19
Hobson 33
Hodgekins 107
Hodges 14
Hoes 119
Hoffman 73, 152
Hogencamp 164
Holden 21, 32, 82, 114, 116, 156, 177
Holford 53
Hollett 133, 145
Holley 63
Hollingshead 100
Hollingsworth 23, 54
Hollister 105, 114
Holmes 3, 12, 111, 140
Holton 3, 72
Honeywell 138, 155
Hoover 46
Hope 39
Hopkins 26, 38, 67, 99, 108, 152
Hopson 49
Horn 32, 50, 126
Horne 151
Horning 144, 146
Horton 32, 48, 52, 56, 65, 91, 102, 103, 110, 125, 135, 168
Houck 58, 150, 176
Houghtaling 1, 10, 79
House 57
Houston 12
Hovencamp 129, 145
Hover 150
Hovey 50, 56, 123, 137, 159, 160
Howard 5, 20, 29, 32, 42, 81, 106, 132, 137, 160
Howe 164
Howell 10, 36, 37, 44, 48, 52, 53, 79, 98, 101, 139, 145, 148, 175
Hoxie 8
Hoyt 42, 104, 160
Hubbell 6, 30, 126
Hudson 39, 115, 166
Huey 21, 28, 48, 65, 86, 117, 120, 121, 126, 143, 145, 149, 156, 160, 171, 175
Huff 64
Huggins 20, 72
Hughey 22, 28, 31, 37, 52, 83, 96, 132, 159
Hughson 15
Hulett 12, 60, 69, 111
Hultz 24
Humiston 34, 112
Humphries 159
Hungerford 95, 119, 126, 172
Hunt 8, 24, 46, 75, 136, 160
Hunter 15, 22, 47, 49, 82, 99, 116, 140, 170
Huntley 32, 90, 113
Hunyan 76
Hurd 1, 48, 49, 61, 74, 75, 82,
90, 95, 103, 110, 112, 117, 122, 125, 129, 131, 144
Hurley 47, 49, 67, 74, 132, 144, 147, 170
Hurman 23
Huson 126, 143, 159
Huston 4, 62, 72, 118
Hutchings 124
Hutchins 11, 21, 153
Hutchinson 161
Hyatt 69, 71
Hynes 158
Hyslop 3, 4
Ide 172
Ingalls 39, 139
Ingersoll 2, 101, 103, 157
Inscho 66
Insco 37, 151, 154
Ireland 106
Ireton 2
Irish 156
Irvin 7
Irvine 145
Jack 13, 37, 125, 159, 175
Jackson 3, 6, 7, 10, 41, 69, 70, 84, 90, 91, 107, 132, 142
Jacobs 100
Jacobson 34, 83
Jacoby 1
James 20, 52
Jamison 114, 127, 145
Jansen 29
Jaquish 34, 40, 161
Jayne 28, 169
Jeffers 16, 49, 57, 132, 150, 168
Jefferson 14, 38
Jenks 122
Jessop 99, 103
Jessup 2, 43, 61
Jewell 148
Jobbit 5
Johnson 3, 8, 9, 18-20, 30, 38, 51, 61, 94, 119, 123, 125, 130, 140, 141, 143, 170
Johnston 13, 54
Johson 29
Joiner 19
Jones 9, 11, 13, 23, 46, 61, 63, 65, 85, 100, 128, 135, 166
Jordan 39
Judd 71
Kays 113
Kaywood 63
Keefer 108
Keeler 100, 165, 166
Keep 142, 177
Kees 129
Keeton 121
Kellie 57
Kellogg 22, 36, 44, 48, 54, 78, 86, 169, 177
Kelly 38, 41, 48, 58, 59, 145, 172, 178
Kels 29, 47, 107, 111
Kelsey 32
Kempton 40, 106
Kendall 21, 25, 29, 45, 63, 80, 126, 139, 164, 178
Kennedy 64, 97, 162, 172, 177
Kent 46, 51, 61
Kenyon 39, 144
Kester 39
Ketcham 25
Keyser 94, 148
Kidder 143
Kies 39, 79, 152, 154, 156
Kilborn 18
Killman 96
Kimball 108
Kimber 15
Kimble 27, 119, 139, 140, 149, 158
King 11, 12, 30, 35, 63, 75, 128, 143
Kingsbury 7, 171
Kingsley 55, 111
Kingwell 72
Kinnan 84
Kinner 64
Kinney 101
Kirkendall 79, 140, 142
Kirtland 62
Kishpaugh 21
Kleckler 52
Kline 9
Knapp 2, 5, 15, 64, 85, 103, 123, 126, 146, 173
Kniffen 47
Knight 23, 66, 176
Knowles 171
Knox 122
Koch 67
Koon 45
Kress 10, 22, 34, 36, 87, 101, 111
La Coste 109
La Fever 3, 24, 36, 55, 75, 87, 128, 129, 132, 133, 147, 158
La Rue 178
Labar 44, 67, 98, 161
Ladow 19, 34, 145
Lafor 19
Lalor 156
Laman 7
Lambert 40, 116, 151, 170
Lamkin 6
Lamoreaux 14, 45, 48, 50, 58, 64
Lamphier 31
Lane 10, 130
Lang 102
Langdon 23
Langridge 151
Lanning 14, 15, 40
Lanphere 19
Lanternman 150
Lapham 84
Laraby 48, 123
Latier 135
Lattin 116, 167
Lawrence 70, 80, 101, 106, 120, 123, 162
Lawton 20, 34
Lazear 26
Le Munyon 171
Leake 118
Leary 81
Leavitt 148
Lee 8, 73, 119, 130, 141
Leek 3
Leffler 28, 41, 61, 137
Leland 6

SURNAME INDEX

Leonard 4-6, 28, 62, 69, 85, 154, 174
Leslie 35
Letts 41, 157
Levine 132
Lewis 18, 24, 25, 29, 33, 39, 50, 82, 87, 102, 104, 107, 118, 125, 127, 141, 153, 154, 156, 169, 177
Lillis 53
Lindenberry 149
Linderman 178
Lindsey 67
Liseum 155
Littell 55, 63, 95, 104, 107, 141
Little 170
Livermore 127
Livingston 105
Lloyd 176
Locke 17
Lockwood 16, 28, 40, 96, 105, 121, 161
Loder 75
Logan 130
Loncoy 129, 150
Loney 38
Long 23, 51, 151
Longcore 27
Longwell 43, 62, 85, 99, 150, 169, 175
Look 4, 71
Loomis 40, 77, 163
Loop 168
Lord 74, 129
Losey 12, 62
Lott 11, 18, 52, 58, 89, 113, 147, 151, 156, 170
Love 13, 21, 38, 50, 54, 60, 65, 66, 77, 83, 123-125, 159, 168
Loveless 113, 160
Lovell 71, 116, 151
Loveridge 127
Low 10, 35
Lowrey 85
Luce 104
Lundy 57
Lybolt 141, 170
Lynch 120, 157
Lyon 7, 9, 94, 112, 146
Mack 81, 91
Mackenzie 69
Mackey 159
Macreery 58
Magee 32, 34, 79, 80, 87, 161
Mahoney 141
Maine 58, 162
Mallerson 59, 159
Mallet 8
Mallory 26, 27, 47, 69, 175
Malona 44
Maloney 52, 67, 125, 170
Manchester 149
Mandeville 1
Mann 51, 60
Manning 34, 62, 115, 161
Mapes 3, 32, 46, 73, 96, 97, 109, 113, 143, 161
Margeson 13
Mariner 26

Markell 42
Marriot 125
Marrow 34
Marsh 135
Marshall 27, 29, 44, 49, 77, 114, 118, 125, 130, 166
Martin 119, 146, 155, 169
Marvin 75
Mason 73
Massiker 72
Master 163
Masters 33
Mathews 6, 16, 30, 33, 47, 50, 51, 54, 64, 65, 90, 99, 107, 111, 112, 114, 118, 121, 122, 136, 138, 141, 143, 147, 158, 164, 169, 173
Mattison 116, 164
Maugham 23
Maxwell 8, 69, 81, 108
Maynard 9
Mayo 164
Mc Cain 48
Mc Cannon 144
Mc Carthy 59, 60, 76, 80
Mc Caul 131
Mc Caw 26
Mc Connor 109
Mc Clure 2, 63, 81, 96, 166, 170
Mc Connell 2, 156, 162
Mc Coy 52, 146
Mc Creary 142
Mc Dermott 132
Mc Donald 3, 6, 107, 110, 138, 158
Mc Donnell 161
Mc Dougal 164
Mc Dowell 108, 140
Mc Duffee 132
Mc Duffy 167
Mc Elheney 86, 116
Mc Elwee 140
Mc Elwell 24
Mc Henry 125
Mc Intyre 14, 33, 60, 101, 122, 139, 169
Mc Keg 167
Mc Kenzie 177
Mc Kiggen 148, 178
Mc kinley 66
Mc Kinney 17, 135
Mc Lachlin 62
Mc Lafferty 54, 110
Mc Lalland 96
Mc Lean 96
Mc Manus 111
Mc Millan 85
Mc Nair 26
Mc Neil 86, 122
Mc Nemer 23, 159
Mc Quillan 78
Mc Quillen 173
Mc Stay 10
Mc Swain 18, 98
Mc Vamara 10
Mc Whorter 97
Mc Wiliams 150
McCaul 131
Mead 5, 48, 54, 124, 146, 157,

Meddick 154
Meeker 45, 131, 139, 143
Meeks 130, 162, 173
Mehan 169
Mekeel 29, 93, 96
Menzie 49
Merchant 67, 72
Merrick 133
Merrifield 137
Merrill 60, 69
Merrills 37, 165
Merritt 113
Messenger 35
Mettler 94, 134
Mewkill 68
Mickel 17
Mickle 144
Miles 15, 67, 149
Millage 81
Millard 41
Miller 5, 10, 23, 24, 32, 33, 35, 42, 49, 50, 51, 55, 61, 66, 67, 69, 71, 80, 89, 97, 99, 101, 109, 115, 119-121, 123, 128, 132, 142, 148, 149, 157, 163, 170, 172, 174, 176
Milliman 128, 149
Mills 39, 72, 75, 89, 120
Millspaugh 76, 162
Milspaugh 33, 54
Minard 71
Minier 76, 91
Minnehan 174
Minturn 113
Mitchell 6, 10, 21, 100, 133, 141, 144, 160, 169, 171
Monroe 18, 117
Montgomery 32
Moody 164
Moonan 14, 146, 152
Moore 7, 17, 40, 46, 47, 49, 53, 77, 119, 147, 150, 152, 163
Moot 135, 163
Moran 123, 153, 175
Morehead 85
Morehouse 2, 137
Moreland 97
Morgan 4, 7, 11, 44, 45, 136, 141, 152
Morris 43, 56, 68, 103, 117, 144, 146, 177
Morrison 9
Morrow 37
Morse 25, 103
Mosher 11, 55, 90, 100, 113, 153, 176
Mosier 84, 103
Moss 50
Mottram 47
Moulton 120
Muckey 38
Mulcahy 163
Mulford 2, 44
Muller 101
Mulligan 66
Munger 7, 89
Munson 3, 50, 171
Murdock 29, 75, 117, 135
Murphy 18, 25, 36, 139, 148, 160

SURNAME INDEX

Myers 41
Myres 106
Nagle 67, 166
Nares 103, 164
Nash 3
Neate 25
Nelson 42, 60
Nevins 6
Newall 154
Newcomb 22, 105, 108, 119, 146
Newfield 28
Newman 26, 50, 136, 145, 147, 174
Newton 78, 173
Nicholai 39
Nichols 1, 11, 19, 22, 34, 52, 67, 79, 81, 112, 138, 142, 147, 148
Nickerson 12, 119
Niven 65
Nivison 67
Noble 71, 73, 74
Nobles 63, 127, 135
Noon 175
Norman 42, 97, 133, 136
Norris 16, 48, 63, 142, 148, 153, 176
North 4, 17, 35
Northrop 87
Norton 93, 125, 134, 137, 150, 170
Noyes 36, 116
Nugent 86
Nutt 127
Nutting 139
Nye 2, 44, 58, 103, 110, 154
O'Connell 155
O'Daniels 112, 115, 129, 166
O'Neil 47
Obert 163
Ogden 11, 23, 51, 100, 130
Oldfield 94, 165
Olin 41
Oliver 87
Olmstead 20, 39, 73, 79
Oltz 20
Orcutt 104
Orr 46, 66
Osborn 53, 56, 64, 116, 144, 156, 157, 173
Osborne 25
Osgood 50, 86
Osmun 86, 123
Osterhout 5, 100
Ostrander 111
Otto 17
Ovenshire 36
Overhiser 24, 63, 95, 127
Overhizer 95
Overshire 28
Overton 34, 45, 167, 168
Ovitt 19
Owen 8, 15, 22, 27, 56, 60, 72, 100, 120, 167
Owens 3, 7, 21, 26, 60, 73, 175
Page 80, 84, 97, 144, 146
Paige 116
Paine 98
Palmer 6, 36, 62, 65, 83, 94, 98, 109, 112, 134, 156, 159, 162, 169
Pangborn 19, 66, 121, 169
Pangbourn 15
Parish 25, 149
Parker 15, 65, 68, 89, 154, 158
Parks 80, 81
Parsels 55
Parshall 27
Parsley 169
Parson 150
Partridge 78
Patchen 124
Patten 85, 96
Patterson 29
Pattison 97, 106
Paulding 172, 177
Payne 14, 76, 92, 125, 137, 143
Pearce 172
Pearsall 160
Pease 17, 31, 126, 131, 149
Peck 10, 31, 50, 56, 57, 66, 74, 104, 113, 118, 136, 153, 159
Pellett 68, 161
Pennington 141
Penny 66
Perham 76
Perkins 136
Perry 17, 46, 60, 62, 105, 123, 134, 135, 137
Personius 5, 41, 65
Peterson 120
Pettingill 24
Phelps 3, 4, 27, 48, 69, 110, 122, 145, 165, 168, 170
Phillip 46
Phillips 39, 59, 95, 117, 140, 171
Philp 62
Phinney 24, 47, 84, 91, 131, 147, 159, 162
Phoenix 165
Pickering 113
Pierce 4, 22, 39, 65
Pierson 38, 77, 138
Pike 40, 59, 159, 167
Pinch 97, 102, 169
Pine 71
Pitcher 27
Platt 26, 82, 123, 137
Plume 105
Plumstead 23, 27
Pollis 149
Pope 13, 46, 62, 99, 124, 134, 147
Poppino 149
Porter 26, 30, 89, 132
Post 12
Pott 139
Potter 31, 96, 168
Potts 145
Powell 130
Powers 52, 133, 151, 171
Poyner 16
Pratt 75, 94
Prebasco 123
Predmore 66, 176
Prentiss 36, 134, 139, 155
Preston 54
Price 16, 17, 33, 49, 56, 66, 68, 75, 134, 139, 147, 150
Priest 82
Prince 16, 70
Probasco 51, 134
Proper 25, 166, 174
Prosser 124
Protts 13
Pruden 51
Pullen 138
Purdy 27, 37, 40, 56, 58, 81, 126
Purple 10
Putnam 37, 106, 136, 172
Pyle 136
Quance 67
Queal 26
Quick 59, 97, 104
Quigley 9, 164
Quigly 71
Quin 57
Quinby 83
Quirk 140
Race 55, 148
Raines 163
Rallings 45
Ralston 62
Randall 16, 47, 138, 142, 157, 158
Ransom 2, 69
Rapalee 155
Raplee 27, 128
Rapplee 106
Rappleye 30
Rappleyee 27
Rarrick 46, 59, 98, 176, 178
Rawling 50
Rawson 29
Raymond 44, 80, 155, 167, 171
Raynor 47
Read 53
Reed 10, 64, 77, 116, 135, 163, 166
Reid 23
Reilly 175
Reisinger 13
Remer 148
Reniff 162, 168
Reno 99
Ressing 47
Reynolds 20, 30, 49, 63, 97, 110, 116, 124, 126, 131, 134, 138, 169
Rhinehart 32
Rhodes 13, 137, 141, 156, 162
Rial 111
Rice 48, 109, 125, 143, 161, 162, 165
Rich 28, 47, 124, 144, 147
Richards 54, 133
Richardson 20, 161
Rightmire 121
Ring 51
Ringer 41, 115
Rippey 177
Risdon 9
Rising 33
Roat 62
Robbins 22, 31, 42, 80, 167, 170, 177
Roberts 15, 40, 50, 92, 93, 111, 115, 117, 119, 122, 124, 126, 136, 139, 147, 149, 157
Robertson 27, 38, 46
Robinson 1, 16, 22, 33, 38, 50,

SURNAME INDEX

55, 111, 112, 118, 130, 137, 141, 148, 155, 170, 177
Roblyer 105
Robson 13, 39, 43, 138
Robyen 8
Robylier 6
Rockwell 4, 107, 172
Roe 3, 46, 53
Rogers 5, 30, 50, 63, 94, 103, 113, 141, 159, 161, 163, 166, 173, 176
Roleson 36, 45
Rolfe 33, 54, 62, 176
Rolison 144
Roloson 5, 65
Rood 39, 54
Roof 125
Rooney 117, 124
Roor 28
Roosa 16
Roscoe 90
Rose 93, 132
Rosebrook 178
Ross 6, 8, 13, 81, 122, 127
Rossiter 177
Roushey 134
Routlege 160
Rowland 50
Rowlee 102
Rowley 150
Royce 42, 74, 84, 100, 119
Ruddick 165
Rudy 55, 159, 168
Rumsey 7, 9, 13, 15, 16, 25, 59, 102, 175
Rundle 96
Runner 165
Rusco 56, 101, 142
Ruscoe 117
Russell 16, 49, 54, 76, 127, 135, 161
Rutherford 36, 163, 167
Rutledge 84
Ryall 117
Ryan 51, 53, 115
Ryerson 132
Ryon 8
Sackett 28, 29, 48, 83, 119, 146, 150, 170
Sage 23, 81
Sample 28, 172
Sanford 19, 72, 89, 156, 165, 170, 178
Sargeant 154, 156
Savacool 177
Savory 32, 124
Sawyer 32
Saxton 45
Saylor 39, 49, 75, 110, 112, 113, 131
Sayre 26, 89, 126, 145
Schuyler 48, 117, 151
Scobey 76, 118
Scofield 20, 98
Scott 15, 18, 58, 64, 100, 128, 129, 150, 167
Scoville 155, 166
Scudder 87

Seals 51
Seaman 13, 22, 26, 52, 133, 147, 150
Seamans 134
Searles 61, 114
Sears 12, 57, 127
Sebring 14, 17, 31, 33, 42, 46, 53, 65, 77, 86, 94, 139, 160, 172
Secor 49, 93, 95, 96
Secord 118, 163, 165
Seelye 5
Sellen 16, 121, 126
Sellick 7
Seneare 75
Seybolt 173
Seymour 30, 60, 160, 170, 177
Shadrick 45
Shafer 40, 98
Shannahan 63
Shannon 27, 34, 103, 123, 138
Shapper 11
Sharp 2, 30, 34, 56, 65, 97, 135, 171
Sharpe 65, 166
Shattuck 18, 149
Shay 105, 112
Shea 49
Sheardown 2, 83, 118, 133
Shearer 100, 105, 116
Shears 175
Sheldon 47, 147
Shelton 5, 7, 15, 45, 85, 92, 107, 121, 132, 140, 149, 163, 166, 171
Shepard 120
Sherer 138
Sherman 19, 32, 39, 41, 53, 54, 70, 94, 106, 156
Sherwood 8, 32, 44, 70
Shewman 20, 65, 144
Shillette 156
Shipman 124
Shoemaker 42
Shotts 174
Shriner 54, 77
Shulman 52
Shultz 176
Sickles 162
Sidney 31
Sidway 137
Silsbee 40, 155, 171
Silvernale 22
Simmons 8, 22, 29, 64, 141, 143, 160, 166
Simonds 87
Simonson 23
Simpson 2, 22, 32, 43
Sipple 164
Sirine 146
Sivern 134
Skellenger 13, 74, 88
Skiff 23, 30, 36, 75, 87
Skinner 11, 19, 81, 96, 108, 128
Skuse 19, 112
Slaght 18, 20, 24, 58, 82, 104, 140, 150
Slater 31, 36, 63
Slaughter 79
Slawson 14

Sloan 7, 15, 25, 85, 100
Slocum 5, 132
Slosson 83
Small 25
Smalley 101
Smeltzer 30
Smelzer 30, 131
Smith 2, 7, 13, 17, 21, 22, 23, 24, 26-29, 31, 34-36, 40, 42-44, 48, 50, 51, 59-61, 63-66, 69, 70, 71, 77, 79, 80, 82, 83, 88, 90, 92, 93, 96, 98, 100, 101, 102, 103, 106, 112, 113, 118, 119, 122, 123, 127, 130, 133, 137, 140-142, 145, 148, 149, 153, 157, 159, 160, 161, 162, 164, 165, 167, 169, 171, 172, 174, 176, 177
Snow 111
Snyder 36, 56, 135, 157, 159, 163
Somerton 119
Soper 56, 154, 157
Soule 32, 33
Spaulding 27, 35, 82, 110, 146, 148, 171
Spear 25
Spears 149
Speary 141
Speed 92
Spence 66, 95, 137
Spencer 52, 84, 118, 141, 147
Spicer 61
Spink 86, 88
Sprague 30
Spriggs 64
Sproul 14, 76, 77, 122, 147, 159, 172
Sprowl 111
Sprowls 123
Squire 9, 53
Squires 80, 99, 159, 167
St. John 129
Stacey 154
Stackhouse 20, 151
Stamp 35, 102, 122, 127, 136, 149
Stanley 96, 132, 151
Stannard 159
Stanton 30, 32, 56, 76, 128, 177
Staring 109
Stark 46
Starkey 21, 34, 110
Starks 58
Starkweather 107
States 50, 51, 163, 166
Steel 58
Steiner 67
Sterling 21, 35, 40, 150
Stevens 13, 19, 28, 44, 46, 65, 70, 76, 97, 110, 126, 144, 165, 173
Stevenson 68
Stewart 9, 23, 132, 170, 175
Stillwell 16, 96
Stilwell 28, 56, 67, 131, 136
Stocum 63
Stoddard 152
Stoll 61, 113, 131
Stone 4, 9, 65, 140
Storrs 62

## SURNAME INDEX

Stothoff 44, 67, 95, 106
Stoughton 31, 61, 126
Stout 69, 110, 175
Strader 36, 53, 58, 94, 139
Strait 173
Straitor 2
Strang 55
Stratton 58
Strong 7
Strowbridge 45
Stuart 51
Stull 87, 176
Sturdevant 2, 31, 32, 141
Sullivan 25, 46, 59, 160, 172
Sunderlin 26, 68, 81, 95, 97, 126, 135, 144
Supplee 136, 154
Sutfin 172
Sutherland 24
Sutphen 118
Sutton 22, 23, 41, 47, 62, 113, 151, 159, 170
Swan 5, 158
Swarthout 15, 18, 24, 33, 34, 37, 56, 85, 92, 103, 117, 134, 144, 156, 157, 166
Swartwood 105, 108, 111, 171
Swezey 75, 109, 121, 144, 147
Swick 10, 20, 33, 45, 55, 96, 102, 132, 146, 158, 159, 163
Swift 21, 60, 121
Swim 122
Switzer 46
Symonds 11
Taber 16, 39, 104
Tabor 58, 126, 157
Taylor 26, 53, 57, 60, 94, 96, 106, 144, 164
Teats 71
Teeter 28, 128
Teetsel 65
Teller 126, 143
Templar 49
Tenbroek 11
Teneyck 17
Tennent 162
Tenny 60
Terrell 40
Terry 16, 165
Terryberry 17, 79
Terwilleger 49
Thayer 87, 111
Thomas 64, 79, 147, 154, 162
Thompson 11, 21, 23, 25, 29, 31, 33, 34, 37, 41, 47, 49, 53, 57, 59, 63, 76, 90, 104, 107, 121, 124, 127, 128, 130-132, 137, 138, 149, 172, 176
Thurston 28
Thynne 128
Tibbs 140
Tichenor 145
Tidd 7
Tifft 55
Tillotson 8
Tinker 88
Titchener 10
Titchner 49
Todd 27, 65, 163
Tolbert 14, 33

Tomar 75
Tompkins 17, 33, 43, 49, 52, 58, 93, 134, 169
Tompson 98, 104, 106, 119, 161, 167
Topping 113
Torey 12
Totman 62
Totten 29, 155
Tower 57, 122
Townsend 1, 22, 25, 36, 40, 50, 84, 107, 119, 125, 133, 138, 158, 161, 171
Tracy 1, 6, 18, 26, 30, 33, 57, 71-73, 80, 108, 116, 128, 141
Traverse 148
Travis 1, 25, 38, 41
Tregilious 4
Treman 41, 58, 87, 88, 91, 114, 145
Troxell 165
Tucker 46, 63, 141
Tuell 135
Tum 109, 119
Tunison 42
Turk 105
Turner 8, 33, 59, 103
Tuthill 4, 6, 53, 112
Tutman 52
Tuttle 7, 9, 35, 61, 81, 87, 88, 118, 130, 136, 174
Tweedie 42
Twiss 66, 177
Twist 96
Tyler 70, 107, 119, 132
Tyrell 40
Tyrrell 30, 154
Underhill 62
Underwood 75, 134, 174
Updike 30, 120, 138
Usher 66
Vail 121, 168
Van Allen 25, 38, 81, 103, 145
Van Amburg 22
Van Arnum 144
Van Cleef 133
Van Deusen 68
Van Deventer 140
Van Doren 12, 53
Van Dorn 95
Van Duser 147, 149, 162
Van Duzen 151
Van Duzer 66, 174
Van Dyke 49, 121
Van Etten 53, 83
Van Fleet 131
Van Gorder 11
Van Gordon 161
Van Horn 54, 127
Van Kuren 37
Van Liew 43, 98, 130, 132, 170
Van Loan 34
Van Lone 100
Van Loon 42, 52, 162, 165
Van Norman 114
Van Nortric 107
Van Sice 164
Van Sickle 57, 168
Van Valer 113
Van Vechten 6, 80, 97, 141, 171

Van Vleet 30, 31, 36, 43, 92, 102
Vance 175
Vanderhoof 33, 37, 152
Vanderpool 134
Vaneps 31
Vann 104
Varey 69
Vaughan 119
Vaughn 24, 52, 81, 83, 92, 117, 139, 143, 146, 149
Venn 143
Vernon 8
Vescelius 20
Vickery 84
Viele 15
Vine 104, 121
Vining 40
Voak 43, 95, 97, 120, 133, 137
Vorhees 45, 55, 114
Vosburg 78, 86, 94
Vosburgh 19, 38
Wade 20, 169
Wager 15, 18, 31, 43, 59, 102, 108, 120
Wagner 23, 112, 119, 133
Wait 52, 94, 148, 153, 170, 176
Wakefield 2
Wakely 3, 10, 102, 170
Wakeman 73, 88, 140, 152, 161, 171
Wakley 66
Waldron 137
Walker 47, 51, 88, 128, 149, 167
Wallace 50, 64
Wallen 64
Wallenbeck 18, 38, 105
Walling 40
Walsh 151, 164
Walter 9, 32, 77
Walters 136
Wanzer 1
Wanzo 123
Ward 4, 39, 145
Warden 174
Warner 1, 14, 136, 153, 176
Warren 112, 164
Washburn 28, 67, 77, 164, 165, 168
Washburne 112
Wasson 13, 16, 38, 57, 103, 125, 130, 132, 151, 168, 171, 174, 175
Waterman 87
Waters 21
Watkins 6, 7, 80, 88, 118
Watson 38, 41, 45, 104
Watworth 5
Waugh 6, 37, 49, 65, 66, 82, 128, 174
Wayland 50
Weaver 94, 133, 147
Webb 43, 52, 106, 116, 142
Webber 22, 32, 105, 148
Webley 1
Webster 51
Wedgewood 18, 54, 82, 115, 155, 158
Weed 124
Weeks 1, 16
Weidman 21, 64

Welding 74
Weller 11, 87, 98, 122, 159, 164
Wellover 121, 157
Wells 16, 23, 35, 57, 153
Welply 81
Welsh 12, 142
Wemple 144
Wentz 13, 14, 80, 145
Wescott 11
West 16, 18, 51, 56, 66, 106, 115, 144, 170
Westcott 97
Westfall 123
Westlake 35, 125
Whalen 59, 176
Wheat 163
Wheaton 33
Wheeler 1, 13, 20, 70, 78, 81, 91, 101, 114, 115, 130, 135
Whippy 7, 23, 31, 70, 106, 121, 140
Whitcomb 127
White 7, 14, 47, 62, 82, 102, 113, 114, 117, 136, 148, 149, 151, 152, 154, 171, 176
Whitehead 14
Whiteman 45
Whitfield 135
Whiting 52, 78
Whitmore 128
Whitney 93, 127, 128
Wickham 55, 59, 65, 67, 75, 118, 150, 153
Wideman 109
Wigg 134
Wiggins 36, 38
Wightman 41, 99
Wilbur 2, 24, 66, 173
Wilcox 6, 19, 48, 66, 83, 166
Wilkes 37, 145, 154, 172
Wilkin 99, 140
Willers 158
Williams 13, 15, 18, 26, 27, 33, 35, 45, 49, 53, 73, 77, 78, 83, 84, 88, 92, 105, 110, 122, 131, 138, 151, 153, 162, 178
Williamson 118, 178
Willis 60, 157
Willover 166, 174
Wilmot 12, 91, 111
Wilson 12, 18, 22, 24, 38, 91, 123, 168
Wing 149
Winslow 61, 174
Winter 144
Wintermute 93
Winters 143
Winterstein 84
Winton 2, 8, 69, 84, 164
Wisner 73
Withiam 45
Witter 21
Wixom 40, 44
Wixon 20, 168, 176
Wolcott 55, 91
Wolverton 73
Wood 3, 5, 7, 21, 28, 41, 47, 50, 54, 64, 67, 69, 71, 74, 84, 101, 105, 123, 125, 130, 160

Woodhouse 36
Woodhull 114
Woodruff 4, 11, 25, 80, 120
Woodward 11, 28, 36, 45, 62, 76, 78, 92, 99, 105, 106, 112, 117, 124, 143, 151, 153, 158, 166, 174
Woodworth 12, 113, 128
Woolever 169
Woolsey 90
Worden 131, 173
Worth 125, 137
Wortman 95, 96, 160, 169
Wright 6, 19, 28, 40, 48, 61, 170
Wygant 31, 133
Wynn 148
Yapple 143
Yarington 12
Yauger 46, 67
Yaw 153, 158
Yost 31
Young 17
Youngs 51, 94, 126
Zimmerman 156

www.ingramcontent.com/pod-product-compliance
Lightning Source LLC
Chambersburg PA
CBHW050802160426
43192CB00010B/1614